IDEAL DISCIPLES

IDEAL DISCIPLES

A COMMENTARY ON

Matthew's Beatitudes

DANIEL DALEY

BAYLOR UNIVERSITY PRESS

Cover design by *the*BookDesigners
Cover image: Fra Angelico (Guido di Pietro/Giovanni da Fiesole, c. 1387–1455), *The Sermon on the Mount*, 1442 (fresco), Museo di San Marco, Florence, Italy. Photo © Nicolò Orsi Battaglini/ Bridgeman Images.
Book design by Ely Encarnación

The Library of Congress has cataloged this book under ISBN 978-1-4813-1938-6.

Library of Congress Control Number: 2024931833

For my grandparents, Mike and Rosalie Dooley,
for modeling ideal discipleship

CONTENTS

PREFACE

This book is somewhat of a sequel to my previous one, *God's Will and Testament*, also published by Baylor University Press (2021). In that book I argue that Matthew's Jesus seeks to recalibrate both Jews and gentiles around his own brand of "ideal discipleship" and that ideal disciples receive an inheritance from God the Father in the form of a share in Jesus' kingdom. That book features a large section on Matthew's beatitudes but only provides a detailed analysis of one beatitude in particular (Matt 5:5). Since its publication I've been asked by several readers to write a more focused treatment of the beatitudes as a whole, reproducing my findings and applying them to the other beatitudes on the list. Then, in early 2023, I gave a lecture on the beatitudes at Calvin Theological Seminary (where I have since joined the faculty as a professor), and the idea of a commentary received further interest. This book is the result of those discussions.

In light of that there are two important points to make regarding the content. First the book is geared toward use in an academic environment, both for students and teachers. I have no doubt that pastors who are preaching through the beatitudes will find it helpful, and so I have geared certain parts of the book for pastors and other readers. For example, I have transliterated individual Greek and Hebrew words on their first occurrence (though this is not done for longer phrases or passages). However, although I hope the book is helpful to preachers and other interested readers (I have my own wife in mind here!), it is largely written for teachers and students.

Second it is important to point out that this book is a commentary and is therefore not preoccupied with what is "new." I make a case, in the introduction that follows, that the academic obsession with "unique contributions," while perfectly healthy in some respects, should not always be the goal of every publication. Often readers benefit greatly from a new distillation of old ideas. Rather than an entirely new argument, some readers are blessed by a unique presentation, one that matches with their own sensibilities in just the right manner (the one explanation that "clicks" for them) so that they reconsider familiar ideas in a new light. This "matching of sensibilities" has value, and connects writers to readers, and creates new avenues of understanding. This is generally the reason why commentaries, which often focus more on presentation than complete innovation, continue to contribute positively to the interpretive traditions of which we are a part. New generations of readers benefit from new generations of scholarly interpreters because the manner of explanation evolves, even when the arguments do not. An aspect of this process requires a new filtration of familiar ideas. This book was birthed out of a positive response to my own presentation of the beatitudes, both regarding the newer ideas it contains as well as my own distillation of old ideas.

Having said that, there are a few places where this book offers something "new." Primarily this is done through engagements with Second Temple compositions, such as 4QInstruction and 1 Enoch, that are not often placed in conversation with the beatitudes. The exegesis here relies heavily on seldom-discussed thematic parallels with specific antecedent Jewish traditions. Secondarily I make an argument that the "character" of the beatitudes is best described not through *one* of the possible options found in recent scholarship but in a nuanced combination of *three*. The details of this can be found in part 1. And finally, although much of the material here will be familiar to readers who have read widely on the beatitudes, I have organized the material in a way that I have not found in previous studies. My hope is that certain readers will benefit from encountering the material as I've arranged it.

Readers of my previous book will notice that some of the material here is brought over from that one, with permission from Baylor University Press. This is especially true of part 1. Most of the common material has been reworked, rewritten, and recontextualized, and a few of the common paragraphs are directly reproduced and left relatively unchanged. Most of the rest of the book, including most of the commentary in part 2, the introduction, and the conclusion, are newly written.

I want to express my considerable gratitude to Cade Jarrell and the entire team at Baylor University Press for their unique contributions to this book. I had to finish the writing during a busy time in life, when my family and I made an international move and I transitioned into a new teaching position. BUP was patient and supportive, graciously extending deadlines, and I'm grateful for our partnership.

Introduction

Recently I've been experiencing the sensation of the freefall down the rabbit hole of classical music fandom. One of the oddest experiences of this descent has been seeing how my proclivity toward completism has manifested itself in the way that I venture into this new creative territory; for example, it's not enough to own one accomplished version of Bach's *The Goldberg Variations*; I need to own several. This scene is becoming all too common: my wife and I "diving" in a record store,[1] where I find a version of a sonata or concerto I do not have but recorded by contemporary artists I recognize, and so I add it to my pile. My wife, seeing this, inevitably says (though, to her credit, always in an understanding tone), "You already own copies of that," and I respond enthusiastically, "But I don't own *this* version by *these* musicians. I need to hear how *they* interpret these pieces."

Sometimes a new interpretation offers a compelling new vision, a near complete and innovative reworking of the material to dramatic effect, where the listener can detect the original composer's likely intentions but is confronted with such invention that they must rethink their understanding of the music. A substantial example of this is Max Richter's near complete recomposition of Vivaldi's *The Four Seasons*,[2] which discarded about three-quarters of Vivaldi's original material. The result is a balancing act of conservation and renovation, which evokes enough familiarity for comparison but also enough freshness to place Vivaldi into a conversation with an entirely new epoch.[3] However, most new recordings of older compositions are not striving for reinvention; they are simply looking to

1 "Diving" refers to aimless browsing, flipping through vinyl in search of a surprise purchase. When we lived in Belgium, record stores had boxes called "divers," which were full of records that did not fit easily into the arranged category tabs.

2 Released in 2012 as *Recomposed by Max Richter: Vivaldi, The Four Seasons*.

3 The recomposition was so well received that Richter reworked his own recomposition in 2022, releasing *The New Four Seasons: Vivaldi Recomposed*. The result is smaller and more intimate than the 2012 version, which the album's website describes with aplomb as a "sonic starburst" that catapults the

be faithful to established tradition while also participating in that tradition with their own unique expression of rhythm and personal ethos. This too has value and often serves as an avenue to introduce established traditions to new listeners. Each generation needs its own interpreters, those who can translate that which has endured for those who hunger for it but need it distilled into a particular milieu. To every piece its listener.[4]

This serves as a helpful analogy for much interpretation of biblical texts and other ancient material. At every academic conference I attend, without fail, I enter into a discussion with someone who laments that too many of the offered papers are little more than exercises in rearranging the interpretive furniture. This observation is such a part of the current proverbial wisdom of our field (and other academic fields, I'm sure) that I think many attendees express it as a matter of course. Ironically the statement itself has become a part of the conference furniture.

There is some wisdom to the lamentation that the field of theology and biblical studies too often replicates previous studies and catalogs the same results—every field needs innovation and writers and researchers who are willing to take risks. However, I do not share a distaste for all forms of rehearsal. Dipping our feet into an ancient creek is still refreshing, and because the landscape is always in transition, each visit has the potential to be both familiar and revealing, orthodoxy exhilarated by a distinct experience of it. In the same way, as each new interpreter explains their own experience, perspective is gained both in the rehearsal of that experience and in the hearing—I might have been to this ancient creek several times, but understanding it through *this* person's encounter has the potential to be an entirely new event, especially if this person is a keen observer. It is in a fresh new telling that I might find it possible to revisit the old creek and see it in a new way, even if the new telling offers no new information and nothing more than a description of the landscape that resonates with (or challenges) my own manner of thinking.

There is another scene that is also all too common: I buy another book about Jesus' beatitudes in Matthew's Gospel, and despite having several, I cannot wait to open the next one. I've read many, but I've not read *this* book

---

listener "through the cosmos by this epiphanic soundworld." See maxrichter-fourseasons.com.

4 This serves for any genre of music. I've spent entire evenings searching the internet for covers of Bill Evans' piano works or Bonnie "Prince" Billy's "I See a Darkness," and each accomplished version helps me to experience the music in a new way.

by *this* writer, and I know I'll learn something new about the beatitudes as I engage with this interpreter's own experiences with them. Typically I'm not looking for new "data"; I'm looking to experience the beatitudes through the unique sensibilities of the interpreter. Matthew's beatitudes might be the topic of more reflection, discussion, teaching, and writing than any other passage in the Bible, but because it is often seen as a summation of the heart of Jesus, it is a richly textured, layered, and penetrating passport into Christ-oriented dispositions that requires consideration by its readers and constant reappraisal by careful interpreters. The passage speaks not only to Jesus' goal for its first hearers, and Matthew's goals for its first readers, but also into the lives of readers throughout the centuries and into the present day. It's difficult for all readers, from the most evidence-minded scholar to the most personally invested devotee of Jesus, to read the beatitudes and not consider one's situatedness to Jesus' vision for his disciples described therein. These evocative lines evoke curiosity and almost demand thoughtful deliberation, and fervent engagement often leads to a profound personal inventory where one wonders if they see themselves in Jesus' descriptions. This leads to a personal engagement with the text, even as one attempts to uncover the historical circumstances of the text as objectively as possible. This tussle between reflection and objectivity breathes life into our interpretations and constantly draws me toward new examinations offered by careful readers whose own stories allow them to digest Jesus' teachings in unique ways. As versatile writer Frederick Buechner writes, "At its heart most theology, like most fiction, is essentially autobiography." Theologians are all "working out their systems in their own ways and in their own language." To their credit, writes Buechner, the best of them are able to mediate between their ideas and their experiences, but these things cannot be separated entirely.[5] Although many would disagree, I do not think complete separation between ideas and experiences is desirable.

The debate regarding objectivity is an old one, and a now classic volume edited by Robert Morgan, and featuring essays by Morgan, William Wrede, and Adolf Schlatter, lays out well enough the stakes of personal expression

5 Frederick Buechner, *The Alphabet of Grace* (San Francisco: HarperCollins, 1989), 3–4. Buechner includes himself in a class of poets and artful dodgers who are unable to mediate between their ideas and experiences. This does not make Buechner more objective but the opposite—he believes that his experiences dominate his understanding of everything.

in scholarship.[6] The essays are primarily concerned with historical-critical versus theological analysis and interpretation, and the issue of objectivity is central to each essay. In Wrede's view the scholar must do the work of a historian, possessing a disinterested concern for knowledge and divesting oneself from all presuppositions and personal commitments toward the task of historical investigation. Conversely, Schlatter argues that the removal of presupposition and self-interest is a form of self-annihilation and is therefore both impossible and undesirable. A careful observer might notice that both Wrede's and Schlatter's arguments are largely dictated by their own personal commitments, thereby demonstrating Schlatter's point. Wrede is of course correct that personal bias has the potential to strip one of their abilities to follow the evidence, and Schlatter concedes this point. But it is not possible for any scholar or theologian to be completely objective, so navigating the tension between evidence and interest is the best chance we have of shedding light on ancient texts and ideas. To Schlatter's point, we do best not to annihilate the self or subdue our self-interest as an avoidable nuisance but to embrace it and allow for our interpretations to extend from our experiences. We must learn to be honest about the historical data but also with the fact that God has made us to be who we are as we approach the text.[7]

[6] Robert Morgan, *The Nature of New Testament Theology: The Contribution of William Wrede and Adolf Schlatter* (Eugene, Ore.: Wipf & Stock, 1973).

[7] An insightful discussion on these issues is found in Dale C. Allison Jr., *The Historical Christ and the Theological Jesus* (Grand Rapids: Eerdmans, 2009), 19–20. Allison describes the ways that personal agendas often shape scholars' conclusions regarding the historical Jesus. Noting the tension, he argues that interpreters have an ability to navigate evidence and personal interest. Allison writes, "We necessarily see with our own eyes, and whenever we enter a text we cannot leave ourselves behind: the first person singular we always have with us. . . . While we inevitably read ourselves into the texts, we can at the same time come to conclusions that neither arise solely from our expectations nor simply confirm our wishes." Allison argues that scholars have the ability to move beyond their own motives and follow evidence toward warranted conclusions. However, when predispositions do manifest themselves, the views of various scholars in the guild come together to form a "communal dialectic" that allows interpreters to enlarge themselves by entertaining new ideas and therefore sharpening their own. Allison goes on to argue that our prejudices can actually "help as well as hinder." For example, because Jesus was a religious person who described an unseen world, other religious persons are in some ways better equipped to understand him than those who strive for disinterested objectivity.

It is through the navigation between data and experience that we find value in new contributions to old traditions. The role of the scholar is not only to present that which is "new" but also to recontextualize ideas for new audiences. It is often in an interpreter's own manner of wrestling with an ancient text and communicating the results that certain new readers are able to receive insights about the text most effectually. To return to the previous metaphor, sometimes rearranging the furniture is all it takes to let new light into an old space. Adding personal expression to erudite exegesis helps each individual study of an ancient text appeal to particular readers who need to explore that ancient text in just such a fashion. To every book its reader.

None of this is to suggest that interpretation is trivial or surrendered to ultimate subjectivity. As television character Stuart Bloom once quipped, "It's a *little* wrong to say a tomato is a vegetable; it's *very* wrong to say it's a suspension bridge."[8] There are many valid ways to understand ancient texts and ideas, but there are also boundaries surrounding reasonableness. Once we agree that certain interpretations go beyond those boundaries, the job of the researcher is to chip away at the evidence and argue for what they regard as the most reasonable among the valid options.[9] It is within these boundaries that the personal background, life experiences, and preferences of the researcher enter into the interpretive matrix and comingle with the evidence to produce perspective, and it is this perspective that speaks to certain readers in ways that other studies might not.

In a provocative book on the interpretation of Matthew's Gospel, Ulrich Luz argues that all interpretations bear the mark of the historical and social circumstances of the interpreter. As Luz writes, "Interpretations change because situations and interpreters change." The understanding of a text is different for people who live in different situations, be they temporal, geographic, or cultural. I've experienced this firsthand, having

8 As played by Kevin Sussman in season 2, episode 20 of the *Big Bang Theory* titled "The Hofstadter Isotope."

9 Including the possibility that there are several valid options that all contain aspects of the truth, even when certain options compete with one another and are perceived as incompatible. For example, on the Sermon on the Mount, see Daniel Patte, *Discipleship according to the Sermon on the Mount: Four Legitimate Readings, Four Plausible Views of Discipleship, and Their Relative Values* (Valley Forge, Pa.: Trinity Press International, 1996), who argues that exegetical results often depend on methods and their use and that there are a variety of legitimate ways to read the text.

studied the Bible in the United States, Scotland, Ireland, and Belgium and in discussing the Bible with readers from all over the world; even readers within similar traditions but from different parts of the world tend to show variation in the way that they receive texts and ideas. Luz points out that the interpretation of a text contains two elements: first, the stable element, which is the text itself; and second, a variable element, which is the interpreter within their given circumstances. For Luz this convergence of a stable and variable element "is not to be lamented but seen as necessary for understanding."[10] This is not merely because we engage with the text within our own religious and cultural experiences and are positively informed by those experiences but also because, when we are willing, we can be enriched by the insights of others who engage with the text differently from ourselves.

This state of affairs is obvious to anyone who has spent time investigating the reception history of a given text. When the beatitudes are read from a wide variety of vantage points, the interpretive options are overwhelming, but a reader who allows themselves to be energized by the insights of careful interpreters throughout history will inevitably draw closer to the text. Rebekah Eklund, who has to my mind written the best reception history on the beatitudes, makes this point well: engaging with other readers is like a guardrail that keeps the text from being held captive to our own whims, wounds, and joys. Becoming familiar with interpretive history helps us to examine our own assumptions and see things we otherwise might have missed.[11]

There isn't space here to enter into a comprehensive discussion on the reception history of the beatitudes and the myriad of interpretive options. This has been done well enough in other places,[12] and some of this will

[10] Ulrich Luz, *Matthew in History: Interpretation, Influence, and Effects* (Minneapolis: Fortress, 2007), 26. Similar is Dale C. Allison Jr., *Studies in Matthew: Interpretation Past and Present* (Grand Rapids: Baker Academic, 2005), 62, who writes, "Although we may be grateful that the plain sense of a text usually guarantees some stability of meaning across the centuries, we may be equally grateful that such stability does not prevent the ceaseless and creative reapplication of the Scriptures, from which we can bring forth treasures new as well as old."

[11] Rebekah Eklund, *The Beatitudes through the Ages* (Grand Rapids: Eerdmans, 2021), 8–9.

[12] A comprehensive analysis is offered by Eklund, *Beatitudes*. A shorter reception history of the beatitudes is offered by Ian Boxall, *Matthew through*

feature in the ongoing discussion where relevant. Instead this book is my own contribution to the robust tradition of the interpretation of the beatitudes, based on an earnest interest in the passage, several years of engagement with other insightful readers, and an ongoing desire to grow closer to the text—to its significance for myself and others and to Jesus who instructed his disciples in this way.

Some readers might open this book looking only for that which is "new." Others might open it hoping to find a guide that facilitates greater familiarity with Jesus' beatitudes, greater familiarity with Jesus' designs of *ideal discipleship*, and greater familiarity with Jesus. It is my hope that certain readers connect to this book as my own offering into the interpretation of Jesus' beatitudes in Matthew's Gospel and that they find some resonance with the organization of the material. Additionally this interaction between personal perspective and areas of interest is relevant not only to our modern context as readers and interpreters, but it was profoundly relevant to the ancient context as well. Before describing the nature of the beatitudes in part 1, it is important to clear the way by considering two important aspects of the production of the beatitudes: first, the role of the Gospel writers as interpreters of Jesus and, second, the role of Gospel readers as interpreters of both Jesus and the Gospels. Brief comments about both of these are helpful. Following these discussions I will briefly consider Jesus' own role as one who has authority to proclaim the beatitudes, and then conclude with a few important points regarding the sources for the beatitudes in Matthew's version of the passage.

Gospel Writers as Interpreters of Jesus' Beatitudes

Versions of Jesus' beatitudes appear in two Gospel accounts: Matthew and Luke.[13] Their respective beatitude lists are similar enough that they appear to be different versions of the same basic teachings. Individual beatitudes

---

the Centuries, WBBC (Hoboken: Wiley Blackwell, 2019), 110–19. Shorter, helpful treatments of the history of interpretation for the full Sermon on the Mount, including major trends and the place of the beatitudes within those trends are offered by Dale C. Allison, *The Sermon on the Mount: Inspiring the Moral Imagination* (New York: Crossroad, 1999), 1–26, and Jeffrey P. Greenman, Timothy Larsen, and Stephen R. Spencer, eds., *The Sermon on the Mount through the Centuries: From the Early Church to John Paul II* (Grand Rapids: Brazos, 2007).

13 Matt 5:3–12 and Luke 6:20–23.

are often called "makarisms,"[14] due to the Greek term μακάριος (*makarios*), which is the first word of each beatitude. All four of Luke's beatitudes appear in Matthew, but there are differences between them in both form and vocabulary. Both versions couple their makarisms with woes,[15] but Luke pairs the makarisms and woes together in their immediate context, while Matthew's list is longer, and the writer(s) separate(s) the makarisms and woes on opposite ends of the text (Matt 5 and 23, respectively).[16]

Precisely how these beatitude lists came down to us in different forms is a matter of some debate. It is often pointed out that preachers reuse their best material (this I know from experience), so it's possible that Jesus preached various versions of the beatitudes at different times to different audiences and that he adjusted the overall sense of the beatitudes, in terms of language and themes, depending on the audience's needs.[17] In this case versions of Jesus' beatitudes would have been passed down through written documents, first-person accounts, oral traditions, or some combination of these, and Matthew's and Luke's writers would simply have used the version that they knew, or if they knew more than one, they would have chosen the preexisting versions that best fit their narrative purposes.[18]

[14] There are two ways that this term is often spelled, either "makarism" or "macarism." Some scholars might insist on one spelling over the other, but both appear frequently in the secondary literature. For what it's worth, Wikipedia has separate dictionary entries with each spelling, defining the word the same way. It might be helpful to think of "macarism" as an English word referring to the attribution of happiness or blessedness and "makarism" as a closer transliteration of the Greek term *makarios*. Although I make use of the spelling "makarism" in this book, I have no preference for one spelling over the other.

[15] I use the term "makarisms" here in place of the term "blessings" due to difficulties when translating *μακάριος*, the first term in each beatitude. The meaning and translation of this term is discussed in part 1 below.

[16] That Matthew's makarisms and woes function as a unit is not recognized by all scholars, largely due to their considerable separation within the composition. However, when Matthew is read as a single narrative and the place of the makarisms within that narrative is appreciated, the relationship between the makarisms and woes becomes more important. This is discussed in detail in part 1 below.

[17] For a recent expression of this view, see Metropolitan Hilarion Alfeyev, *Jesus Christ, His Life and Teaching*, vol. 2: *The Sermon on the Mount* (Yonkers, N.Y.: St. Vladimir's Seminary Press, 2019), 8–13.

[18] Also possible is that Matthew's writer had Luke's Gospel on hand or that Luke's writer had Matthew's and that one of them used the other as one of their sources. Discussions regarding the tradition history of the makarisms and their differences in form and content have largely centered on questions

Another possibility is that the version found in each Gospel account was designed by the Gospel author to fit the overall narrative purposes of the text. This would be true whether Jesus preached only one version of the beatitudes or several.[19] This would also be true whether each evangelist had access to one version of Jesus' teaching or several. Regardless of the version(s) they knew, Matthew's and Luke's writers likely made changes to the original to fit the beatitudes into their overall narrative, both for compositional integrity regarding the rhythm and structure of the text and to contribute powerfully to the theological aims of the story. As Eklund writes, "I see Matthew and Luke as careful curators of their material, rather than as mere transcribers."[20] Each evangelist records the beatitudes in their own distinctive style, which matches and contributes to the distinctive styles and agendas of their full Gospel narratives. As Eklund states, "The evangelists have incorporated the beatitudes with care into the larger narratives of their gospels."[21]

I see no reason to choose between these two major options. Anyone who watches stand-up comedy knows that one only needs to see the same joke told three or four times before one is able to regurgitate that joke verbatim, often even with the ability to mimic cadences and facial expressions of the comedian. How much greater is our ability to recite idioms, sayings, or teachings that have a pronounced importance for us, especially if we've heard them or read them on several occasions. That Jesus taught variations of the beatitudes and repeated them frequently and that these teachings were valued enough to be memorized and passed on with care within the oral tradition is more than reasonable.

---

related to the Synoptic problem, the use of a sayings source, the development of oral tradition, and the redactional activity of the evangelists. The "Synoptic problem" is a complicated one, and it is beyond the scope of this book to enter into complex scenarios regarding the relationship between the Gospels and the nature of their sources. A helpful analysis is found in Michael F. Bird, *The Gospel of the Lord: How the Early Church Wrote the Story of Jesus* (Grand Rapids: Eerdmans, 2014), 125–213.

19 A version of this idea is suggested by John Calvin, *Sermons on the Beatitudes*, trans. Robert White (Edinburgh: First Banner of Truth, 2006), 17. Calvin argues that the Gospel writers each recorded a summary of Jesus' teachings and "were not concerned to record every word" but rather general instructions for the disciples collected out of various discourses. Calvin does not elaborate on the possible agendas of each Gospel writer that might have dictated word choice.

20 Eklund, *Beatitudes*, 16.

21 Eklund, *Beatitudes*, 15.

At the same time there is obvious evidence that each beatitude list has been carefully edited into the surrounding context of its respective Gospel account and that individual beatitudes have been chosen and worded in such a way that they serve the narrative goals of each Gospel writer. Each list plays an important role in the development of its respective Gospel narrative—linguistically, thematically, and theologically—so it's clear that the lists used by both Matthew's and Luke's writers were designed intentionally to fit their fuller stories. This does not mean that these beatitude lists are entirely or even primarily the products of the evangelists; the texts clearly portray the beatitudes as the teachings of Jesus, so the beatitudes are his.[22] However, all four Gospels were written by theologically minded storytellers who, like architects drawing blueprints, sought to assemble their materials in a creative and thoughtful way. Jesus' beatitudes likely circulated in many forms and were communicated in a wide variety of contexts so that there is no reason to believe that the nature of their message

[22] Of course, not all scholars would accept this claim so plainly. Take, for example, Jacques Dupont, *Les béatitudes*, vol. 2: *La bonne nouvelle* (Paris: Gabalda, 1969), 7, who argues that the four beatitudes shared by Matthew and Luke are authentically attributable to Jesus. Matthias Konradt, *The Gospel according to Matthew: A Commentary*, trans. M. Eugene Boring (Waco, Tex.: Baylor University Press, 2020), 66, argues that only three of the beatitudes can be demonstrated as authentically attributed to Jesus. The others are the products of the post-Easter community or Matthew's writer's creative engagement with antecedent traditions. This view is common among redaction critics. See also Korinna Zamfir, "Who Are (the) Blessed? Reflections on the Relecture of the Beatitudes in the New Testament and the Apocrypha," *SS* 5 (2007): 75–100, who argues that Jesus' original beatitudes were salvation oracles announcing the reign of God but that Matthew's writer turned them into a list of virtues to govern the Christian life and therefore moved them in a new direction from Jesus' own intentions. Although it is certain that the first evangelist creatively reworked the material to function within the goals of the Gospel, I am not so inclined to assume that they were not adapted from authentic Jesus traditions. For example, Jesus likely taught in Aramaic. As Jonathan T. Pennington, *Reading the Gospels Wisely: A Narrative and Theological Introduction* (Grand Rapids: Baker Academic, 2012), 63, argues, what we have in the Gospels is an accurate representation of Jesus' "voice" rather than his actual words. Craig S. Keener, *The Historical Jesus of the Gospels* (Grand Rapids: Eerdmans, 2009), 218, suggests that some of the verbal differences between Matthew's and Luke's beatitudes reflect different ways of translating Aramaic into Greek. If these lists were translated from an original Aramaic source, this strengthens the arguments that they go back to the earliest Jesus traditions, which raises the likelihood that they reflect the tenor of Jesus' teachings.

is disassociated with Jesus' own aims. As the Gospel writers shaped the beatitudes (both individually and as fuller lists) to fit their own narrative goals and to align with their own use of sources, the message of the beatitudes fits with what we know of Jesus' teachings.

Because these beatitudes are reflections of the teachings of Jesus, they are not in competition with one another, but their differences are considerable enough that the two lists cannot be easily harmonized and their contributions to their individual narratives cannot be minimized. As Eklund argues, having two lists means they exist in creative tension, but this tension is generative: "they're a gift that prompts exploration and deeper reflection."[23] Because of this, it is unwise to interpret the meaning and function of each list without consideration of their places within their respective wider narratives, and it's just as important to understand the narratives of each Gospel before comparing Matthew's and Luke's lists.[24]

Many interpreters argue that Luke's list declares a future hope toward the eschatological reversal of unfortunate circumstances, while Matthew's list is rooted in wisdom traditions and describes the ethics of the kingdom of God. For example, Luke 6:20 refers to the "poor," likely an economic condition. In this case the listener would long for a reversal of poverty and immediate kingdom-oriented blessings as relief of their circumstances. Conversely, Matt 5:3 refers to the "poor in spirit," possibly a religious and ethical disposition.[25] In this case Matthew's version of the same beatitude refers to a virtue to be embraced and pursued. If these interpreters are right, then Luke's beatitudes aim to provide hope and comfort to those who are struggling with life's great difficulties, while Matthew's version aims to describe the demeanor and manner of life of Jesus' followers. Luke's list is aimed at providing consolation to the forlorn, while Matthew's list aims to describe the religious dispositions of a new kingdom community centered on the teachings of the Jewish Messiah. Few scholars would deny that Matthew and Luke contain both ethical and eschatological dimensions, but the emphasis of each Gospel influences the way interpreters understand Matthew's and Luke's use of Jesus' beatitudes based on the particular profile and

23 Eklund, *Beatitudes*, 20.

24 Eklund, *Beatitudes*, 15, refers to the beatitudes as arrows pointing toward the future, relevant to the unfolding and ending of each Gospel story. When read in light of the resurrection, they serve as elements of God's gracious deliverance of Israel and a testament to God's power that he gives life to the dead.

25 See, for example, Georg Strecker, *The Sermon on the Mount: An Exegetical Commentary* (Edinburgh: T&T Clark, 1988), 30.

agenda of each narrative.[26] Providing a detailed analysis of Luke's intentions for Jesus' beatitudes goes beyond the scope of this study.[27] Although part 2 will compare Matthew's and Luke's lists when helpful for interpretation, this is a book about Matthew's version of Jesus' beatitudes and the ways that they serve the author's goals. To be clear, the assumption here is that Matthew's list corresponds to Jesus' own teaching, so I will use phrases such as "Matthew's list" and "Jesus' beatitudes" interchangeably. And in this regard there are two facets of analysis featured in this study that are two sides of the same coin. First, there is Jesus' purpose in proclaiming these beatitudes. Jesus had goals in mind when he taught these beatitudes, and an attempt is made here to describe what I think Jesus communicated through these statements. Second, there are the intentions of Matthew's author in writing and constructing these beatitudes in such a fashion that they contribute to the overall narrative of the life of Jesus found in Matthew's Gospel. Before proceeding to the analysis, it is helpful to say something about the role of Gospel readers as interpreters of the text.

Gospel Readers as Interpreters of Jesus' Beatitudes

A number of scholars have opted for sociocritical approaches in an attempt to reconstruct a Matthean community that may have either produced the text or been its intended audience. Lines are typically drawn ethnically, with two primary options for how the community was constituted. First, a number of scholars argue that the Matthean community was a blended one of Jews and gentiles that had completely parted ways with Judaism. The church and the synagogue were at odds, and the Matthean community arose out of God's rejection of Israel. These circumstances created a "new race" over and against both Jews and gentiles, and Matthew's Gospel functioned as an apology of Christianity against their

[26] For example, Allison, *Sermon*, 43–44, argues that Matthew's list focuses on reversals of misfortune but that it also contains implicit imperatives that exhort the reader/hearer toward ethical obligations. Concerning Luke's list, Darrell L. Bock, *A Theology of Luke and Acts* (Grand Rapids: Zondervan, 2012), 202, acknowledges the eschatological reversal motif in Luke's list but argues that they are placed within an overall ethical context in the surrounding narrative.

[27] Analysis of Luke's list from a source and redaction-critical perspective and its relationship to Matthew's list is found in Robert A. Guelich, "The Matthean Beatitudes: 'Entrance Requirements' or Eschatological Blessings?" *JBL* 95 (1976): 415–34. The social circumstances that might account for differences between Matthew's and Luke's list are described by Thomas Hoyt Jr., "The Poor/Rich Theme in the Beatitudes," *JRT* 37 (1980): 31–41.

Jewish opponents.[28] The parable of the wicked tenants (Matt 21:33–46) is a central passage for this position. In the parable, Jesus states that the kingdom of God will be taken away from the Jewish leaders rejected by God and given instead to those who will yield proper fruit (Matt 21:43). Proponents of this view typically regard the Jewish leaders as representatives and ciphers for the entire Jewish community whom God has rejected in favor of the new community of Jesus' followers. Jesus' criticisms of the Jewish leaders amount to criticisms of all Israel,[29] and the Matthean community rose up as an alternative both to Judaism and the surrounding gentile world. This is relevant to the purpose of Matthew's version of Jesus' beatitudes because Matthew's writer would have constructed the list with the purpose of instructing, comforting, and preparing the Matthean community for a future as a marginalized group. This is especially true of Matt 5:11–12 regarding persecution. Under this perspective, Jesus prepares the community as "the faithful minority which is again under attack."[30]

A second position agrees with proponents of the first view that Matthew's community was alienated both from its own local Jewish body and also from the gentile world and that the community might have been sectarian. The First Gospel served as a narrative about Jesus as the Messiah in order to affirm the identity of this sectarian community. However, although gentiles might have been incorporated into the community, its commitments were to Judaism; they were committed to a Jewish Messiah who embodied the Jewish context, and Matthew's Gospel is best interpreted as a Jewish document.[31] The community's Judaism was qualified by the coming of Christ, but their Jewish traditions made

28 A well-known proponent of this view is Graham Stanton, *A Gospel for a New People: Studies in Matthew* (Edinburgh: T&T Clark, 1992).

29 See Ulrich Luz, *Studies in Matthew* (Grand Rapids: Eerdmans, 2005), 12, who argues that Matthew's rejection of the Jewish leaders becomes a polemic against the whole of the Jewish people.

30 Stanton, *Gospel*, 150.

31 For advocates of this basic view, albeit with variations between them concerning the details, see J. Andrew Overman, *Matthew's Gospel and Formative Judaism: The Social World of the Matthean Community* (Minneapolis: Fortress, 1990); Anthony J. Saldarini, *Matthew's Christian-Jewish Community* (Chicago: University of Chicago Press, 1994); David C. Sim, *The Gospel of Matthew and Christian Judaism: The History and Social Setting of the Matthean Community* (Edinburgh: T&T Clark, 1998); and John Kampen, *Matthew within Sectarian Judaism* (New Haven: Yale University Press, 2019).

up the foundation and content of their faith. Rather than total distance between Matthew's community and their Jewish opponents, the two existed in a state of conflict despite maintaining ideological similarities. Those rejected by Jesus in the parable of the wicked tenants are the failed Jewish leaders alone; they do not represent the whole of Israel, and Jesus has not rejected the Jewish people or anything about his Jewish heritage. Some advocates of this view draw parallels between Matthew's community and the community (communities) behind certain sectarian documents found among the Dead Sea Scrolls, which renounced affinity with other Jewish communities but still considered itself thoroughly Jewish. According to this view Matthew's makarisms are replete with sectarian vocabulary and themes. For example, Matthew's focus on righteousness (Matt 5:6) designates particular expectations of a certain way of life that distinguishes righteous Jewish groups from all others, and to be "pure in heart" (Matt 5:8) emphasizes the need for purity that is at the center of all sectarian legislation found among the Dead Sea Scrolls.[32] Matthew's makarisms serve as boundary-marking mechanisms that distinguish Matthew's community from the failed Jewish leaders, and members of the community are blessed because they are loyal to Jesus and will therefore be persecuted for Jesus' sake (Matt 5:11–12), but this community has not made a break with their Jewish heritage or identity.

A third view serves as a via media between the other two. Although Matthew is a considerably Jewish text that emphasizes its continuity with Judaism throughout, there are also significant signs of theological innovation that are consistent with but adapted beyond antecedent Jewish traditions.[33] Matthew's Gospel reflects faithfulness to its Jewish past in collision

[32] See Kampen, *Matthew*, 74–85, for one account of the ways that each of Matthew's beatitudes fit into a sectarian milieu. Kampen argues that the makarisms "show evidence of vocabulary familiar to us from the sectarian texts from Qumran, in which they are employed in a significant manner for self-designation. These distinctive indicators of sectarian identity serve as boundary marking mechanisms pointing to the members of a particular group, in this case the followers of Jesus. In using these indicators, the author is employing a vocabulary already utilized by previous sectarian groups in Second Temple Jewish life" (77–78).

[33] An advocate of this view is Donald A. Hagner, "Matthew: Apostate, Reformer, Revolutionary?" *NTS* 49 (2003): 193–209. Hagner argues that Matthew's Gospel shares important features with Judaism, such as monotheism, covenant, election, and Torah but that the Matthew-within-Judaism proponents often neglect the newness of Matthew's Gospel and its differences with the Judaism of its time.

with the newness of Christ. While the Matthean community "continued in a uniquely Jewish mode of existence,"[34] it explored its Jewish commitments in dramatically new ways from its received customs. Rather than remaining situated entirely within its Jewish milieu or completely alienated from it, the Matthean community represented one step in the eventual parting of the ways between Jews and followers of Christ, and the aspects of old and new in the text reflect a community in transition.

The Jewish law is an important example that might illustrate the third view. Although Matthew's writer affirms the law (Matt 5:17–20), Jesus is presented as a teacher par excellence (Matt 23:8–10) who interprets the Torah in radical ways.[35] Matthias Konradt is insightful on Jesus' "fulfillment" of the law in Matt 5:17–20, arguing that for Matthew's writer, continuity between Jesus and the law is not a matter of basic agreement but rather the intent of God's will in the Torah is brought to light through Jesus' teaching. Konradt comments, "Thus Jesus does not do and teach the Torah like others before and alongside him, but on the basis of his direct, intimate familiarity with the will of the Father (11:27)." Konradt comments further that for Matthew's writer, "God's will is brought to bear by the one teacher (cf. 23:8, 10) in a way that is in principle in accord with the Torah, but in a new way—for Jesus fulfills the Torah and Prophets by revealing and living out the full meaning of what God offers in them."[36] Furthermore, Matthew's presentation of its Christology and Messianism would likely have been problematic for many Jewish readers/hearers. This is true in several respects, but primary among them might be Jesus' affirmation of the future suffering of his followers and the Messiah's violent crucifixion. Many Jews at the time were longing for a Messiah who would remove them from suffering, not enter deeper into it. Matthew's Gospel does not present a radical break with Judaism, but it does refashion its presentation as a fulfillment of Judaism through Messiah Jesus as a unique son of God in ways that most Jews would likely not have expected. According to this third view, the Matthean community would have viewed itself as loyal to Israel and its

34 Hagner, "Matthew," 197.

35 See Hagner, "Matthew," 202–3.

36 Konradt, *Gospel*, 74. See also Martin Pickup, "Matthew's and Mark's Pharisees," in *In Quest of the Historical Pharisees*, ed. Jacob Neusner and Bruce D. Chilton, 67–112 (Waco, Tex.: Baylor University Press, 2007): "The halachic disputes between Jesus and the Pharisees are not addressing whether the Torah is binding, but how the Torah is to be applied" (112).

heritage while also recognizing that Jesus had introduced an alteration to the ways that the community understood its Jewish identity. Such an alteration would require explanation, so it's possible that Matthew's Gospel was written to encourage a community in the midst of a crisis of identity and to help readers/hearers understand their own story.[37]

This third perspective does not require an outlook toward sectarianism but instead views Matthew's narrative as an inclusive one. There might have been a particular "Matthean community," and many of the features of the First Gospel might reveal details about their constitution and social circumstances, but the disputes between Jesus and the religious authorities reveal details about Jesus' ethical instructions and his calls to live according to the will of God for all people. In this case Matthew's beatitudes are not directed toward a secluded community or embedded with an exclusive agenda but are instead an open invitation to living out kingdom-oriented dispositions for anyone answering Jesus' calls for repentance.

Any attempt to discern the possible identity of a "Matthean community" by ethnic boundaries is made difficult by the text's ambivalence toward Jews and gentiles. The text paints both a positive and negative picture toward both groups. Matthew is more entrenched in Jewish tradition than any of the four Gospels, showing an obvious affinity for its Jewish heritage, and yet it portrays the Jewish leaders negatively.[38] In fact, as Anthony Le Donne demonstrates, the Jewish leaders in Matthew receive more venom than in any of the other Gospels and the Pharisees in particular "become lightning rods for criticism."[39] Similarly, Matthew portrays gentiles in a positive light and integrates them into important places in the narrative,[40] but gentile culture is depicted as an example to be avoided (cf. Matt 6:7, 32; 20:25–26). This discussion raises two questions worth addressing here: first, how does Matthew's Gospel depict Jesus' attitude

[37] On this, see Ulrich Luz, *Matthew 1–7*, Hermeneia (Minneapolis: Fortress, 2007), 54–55.

[38] On the conflict with Jewish leaders in Matthew, see Reinhart Hummel, *Die Auseinandersetzung zwischen Kirche und Judentum im Matthäusevangelium* (Munich: Kaiser, 1963), 12–14, and Matthias Konradt, *Israel, Church, and the Gentiles in the Gospel of Matthew*, trans. Kathleen Ess (Waco, Tex.: Baylor University Press, 2014), 101–66.

[39] Anthony Le Donne, "The Jewish Leaders," in *Jesus among Friends and Enemies: A Historical and Literary Introduction to Jesus in the Gospels*, ed. Chris Keith and Larry W. Hurtado (Grand Rapids: Baker Academic, 2011), 212.

[40] See Donald Senior, "Between Two Worlds: Gentiles and Jewish Christians in Matthew's Gospel," *CBQ* 61 (1999): 14–16.

toward his Jewish heritage, and second, who is the intended reader/hearer of Matthew's beatitudes?

First, Matthew clearly positions Jesus as a specifically Jewish Messiah and savior. The Gospel begins with a record of Jesus' Jewish genealogy in which he is called the Messiah, "the son of David, the son of Abraham" (Matt 1:1). At the conclusion of this record, Joseph is told by an angel that Jesus "will save his people from their sins" (Matt 1:21), which in the context refers to the Jews. It is impossible to imagine that Matthew's writer recorded these words with the intention, later in the narrative, to suggest that this mission failed and that God has now rejected the Jews in favor of another group. The reference to Abraham in Matt 1:1 calls the reader/hearer back to the Abrahamic promise and the responsibility of the Jews to be a light to the nations; the rest of the text sows the seeds of this hope for gentiles throughout the narrative, which then concludes with a post-Easter mission to the nations (Matt 28:18–20). Universal salvation is Jesus' ultimate goal, but this salvation is anchored in Israel. Salvation to the nations does not replace salvation to the Jews, but rather salvation for the Jews is the first step toward the salvation of the other nations. Jesus' conflict was with the failed Jewish leaders, not the Jewish people widely, and his offer of salvation to the nations is based not on a rejection of the Jews by God but as a fulfillment of the Scriptures and by Jesus' authority as the resurrected Messiah. In this way, I affirm the basic understanding presented by the third view described above: Jesus is presented as the Jewish Messiah who came not to reject Israel or replace it with another people but to fulfill the Israelite story and inaugurate its eschatological potential by blessing the nations. Rather than reject Israel, Jesus came to guarantee its future, but he does this by introducing a new salvation-historical situation. Jesus gathers both Jews and gentiles around him and offers them a vision of discipleship and a hope for the future.

Of course, this understanding needs to be established by an evaluation of the beatitudes. Dale Allison is right to caution that any interpretation that depicts Jesus' teaching as "altogether a bolt from the blue, as something fundamentally unprecedented," is mistaken.[41] Matthew's writer takes linguistic cues from both antecedent Jewish traditions and the Greek and Roman world, and the beatitudes can be situated squarely within Jewish wisdom and apocalyptic traditions. Still, an argument is made throughout this book that Jesus' beatitudes demonstrate a faithful but innovative engagement with antecedent Jewish traditions and a stirring, universal call to discipleship for

[41] Allison, *Sermon*, 7.

those willing to commit to Jesus' unique vision. Matthew is faithful to its Jewish heritage, and it also describes much that is new.

What about Matthew's first readers/hearers? Not all scholars are convinced that there was such a thing as a "Matthean community,"[42] and this insight has important ramifications on the way we understand the construction of Matthew's beatitudes. Many scholars posit that Matthew's beatitude list was constructed in part or in whole by the writer(s), not with an interest of fidelity to the pre-Easter timing of the narrative but for the purpose of satisfying the post-70 CE conditions of the so-called Matthean community.[43] In other words, it is often proposed that the situation of the Matthean community—their own expressions of faith and conflicts with their surrounding Jewish and gentile combatants—conditioned the particular features of the beatitudes so that what we find in Matthew can hardly even be a representation of the teachings of the historical Jesus. In this case Jesus' authority is appropriated to inspire readers/hearers with very particular localized needs so that it is difficult, if not impossible, to separate Jesus' vision with Matthew's pastoral concerns.[44] Such reconstructions might have us believe that like the crowds who marveled at Jesus' teachings (Matt 7:28–29), it is really the words of Matthew's writer(s) that have long impressed us so.

Many critics of the notion of a "Matthean community" have often noted that the reconstructions of such a community are often too speculative, and there are signs that the First Gospel was not written to a closed community with a specific, localized agenda.[45] A Matthean community is possible, but it's just as possible that Matthew was written as a circular text that was intended to be read by a wide variety of communities of Christ followers. Matthew and Luke both used Mark as a source, meaning Mark was in circulation at the time. It is likely that Matthew's and Luke's writers

42 See, for example, the essays in Richard Bauckham, ed., *The Gospels for All Christians: Rethinking the Gospel Audiences* (Edinburgh: T&T Clark, 1998).

43 A version of this approach is by John P. Meier, *The Vision of Matthew: Christ, Church, and Morality in the First Gospel* (Eugene, Ore.: Wipf & Stock, 1991). Meier argues that Matthew's writer was concerned with received tradition, but that rather than being written to depict Jesus' life and teachings within Jesus' own settings, the Gospel is an example of tradition that was reworked to fit the needs of the community within which it was produced.

44 See the discussion by Alfeyev, *Sermon*, 1–7.

45 See, for example, Matthew D. C. Larsen, *Gospels before the Book* (Oxford: Oxford University Press, 2018), 12–14, who argues that Mark and Matthew circulated without name attributions or titles because they were written to be circulated as contributions to a fluid literary tradition.

intended to supplement (or replace) Mark and therefore also engage a wider readership.[46] Many of Matthew's unique features can be accounted for without appeal to a reconstructed Matthean community. For example, Matthew's beatitudes do not explicitly appeal to a specific target audience (aside from those in attendance when Jesus preached the sermon) but instead draw on popular antecedent Jewish traditions such as the Latter Prophets and the Psalms, traditions that would have been known by Jews in many different communities.[47] While some of the features of Jesus' beatitudes that are unique to Matthew might have been designed by the writer and motivated by sociocultural considerations, it's just as possible that the material came down to Matthew's writer from various traditions about Jesus and the writer felt compelled to include them by artfully integrating them into the overall narrative. We simply don't have enough information about Matthew's writer(s) to speculate too deeply on any sociocultural agenda.

The goal here is not to completely dispel the possibility of a Matthean community. However, even if such a community existed, reconstructions are highly speculative. Although theorizing makes for interesting thought experiments and such experiments have value when trying to understand aspects of the text, the nature of such a community is elusive enough that it cannot be decisive for interpretation, and positing its existence can corrupt interpretation if the writer of Matthew had larger goals in mind. So the question then becomes, if we cannot rely on a reconstructed Matthean community to describe Matthew's first Gospel readers, then to whom exactly were the beatitudes written?

The Expected Audience of Matthew's Beatitudes

In Matt 4:18–22, Jesus calls his first disciples. At the start of the Sermon on the Mount (Matt 5:1), it is with these disciples that Jesus sits and teaches them, beginning with the beatitudes (Matt 5:3–12). The end of

46 Richard Bauckham, "For Whom Were the Gospels Written?" in *The Gospels for All Christians: Rethinking the Gospel Audiences*, ed. Richard Bauckham (Edinburgh: T&T Clark, 1998), 11–13.

47 Other features are discussed by Nathan Eubank, *Wages of Cross-Bearing and Debt of Sin: The Economy of Heaven in Matthew's Gospel*, BZNW (Berlin: De Gruyter, 2013), 22, such as the fact that Matthew uses nearly all of Mark, indicating that Matthew's writer(s) did not intend his narrative to be limited to an insular community, the fact that the whole Gospel ends with a mission to gentiles, and the speedy and widespread dissemination and acceptance in the early church, indicating that it was likely distributed to a wide readership quickly after its composition.

the sermon also explicitly tells us that the neutral but interested crowds were present and that they were astonished at his teaching (Matt 7:28). I posit that for Matthew's writer and for Jesus, the intended recipients of the beatitudes are the same now as they were among the sermon's initial hearers: the beatitudes serve as instruction for Jesus' disciples and anyone who might answer Jesus' call to come and "follow me" (cf. Matt 4:19, 16:24, 19:21). This does not mean that the language and ideas found in the beatitudes are generic in nature or easily digestible to a general crowd. As Eklund notes, they are peppered with language from particular traditions that must be understood in order to comprehend the true significance of Jesus' instructions. These lines are "drawn from the well of Judaism and shaped by a specific person (Jesus of Nazareth) and by the people who came to believe that God had raised this crucified person from the dead and exulted him to God's right hand."[48] The crowds as interested listeners are invited along, but the beatitudes are not window dressing; they are the substance of followership and an introduction to the nature of those who are committed to observing the lifestyle subsequently described by the rest of the sermon (Matt 5–7). The crowds are invited to learn and evaluate, but the beatitudes function as instruction for Jesus' *ideal disciples*.

It is also argued throughout this book that Jesus' teachings and expectations for his ideal disciples are contrasted with the behavior of many of the Jewish leaders. Throughout the Matthean narrative, the Jewish leaders serve as a foil for Jesus and his followers, constantly questioning Jesus' actions and motives and eventually instigating the events that led to his death. It is argued throughout this book that the beatitudes serve as dispositions for those who seek God and his will and that these beatitudes are directly contrasted with the woes of Matt 23, where the Jewish leaders fail to demonstrate the character of God and to lead the people into God's kingdom (Matt 23 explicitly refers to the scribes and Pharisees, but Matthew portrays other groups as opponents of Jesus, such as the chief priests). The contrast between the kingdom-oriented dispositions described by the beatitudes and the hypocritical dispositions attributed to the Jewish leaders become in Matthew's Gospel a structural and narrative device that aids in better understanding the ramifications for failing to properly lead God's people into greater righteousness.

48 Eklund, *Beatitudes*, 24.

Jesus' Conflict with the Jewish Leaders

It is important here to address an area of growing discontent among some scholars regarding the portrayal in the Gospels of many of the Jewish leaders, especially the Pharisees. There is a long-standing tendency, especially among preachers and faith communities, to perceive the Pharisees as legalistic, hypocritical bad guys, and this sentiment is so pervasive that the term "pharisaical" has become synonymous with these deplorable behaviors when they are found among community leaders and members. This one-sided caricature of the Pharisees has been increasingly challenged in the academic environment for at least two primary reasons.

First, in Jewish tradition, the Pharisees are the good guys. They are remembered as respected teachers of the Second Temple period, who cared about God's people and careful readings of the Torah and who helped to preserve Jewish tradition in the aftermath of the destruction of the temple in 70 CE. One-sided caricatures fail to consider what Jewish authors have written about their own traditions and fail to appreciate the tremendous good done by many Pharisees among the Jewish people during the period in which they were active.

Second, negative stereotypes of the Pharisees have been used by those outside of Judaism to instigate, facilitate, and exacerbate anti-Semitic discourse for centuries.[49] By and large, the Pharisees had commendable goals but are only remembered by many as greedy, self-righteous moralists whose jealousy and hunger for power contributed to the death of God's Son, humanity's savior. Unbalanced caricatures of the Pharisees are often passed onto Jewish people widely and used to develop derogatory stereotypes, which lead to prejudice, conflict, and even violence.

As the argument goes, one-sided (and even inaccurate) depictions of the Pharisees have contributed to supersessionist readings of the New Testament that view Israel as a failed project, with the church elevated as the replacement for the Jews as a failed people group. These supersessionist readings have led many scholars on a mission to correct inaccurate understandings of the Pharisees and rescue their reputation; to demonstrate that, rather than failures, they are models who demonstrate Judaism's values. This endeavor has led many scholars to frame the conflict depicted in the Gospels as a failure not of the Pharisees but the reverse, as a failure

[49] See the framing of the issues in the preface to Joseph Sievers and Amy-Jill Levine, eds., *The Pharisees* (Grand Rapids: Eerdmans, 2021).

of either the Gospel writers or of Jesus himself. The Gospel writers either exacerbated or invented the conflict and have it wrong. Rather than placing the blame for anti-Semitic readings on later interpreters, some scholars place the blame on the Gospel writers for fueling these inevitable readings through slanderous portraits. The Gospel writers were motivated not by an interest in history but by their own bias based on the conditions of their own communities, and they wrongly depicted the Pharisees to fuel their own narrative needs.[50]

Because I argue throughout this book that Jesus had a deeply contentious relationship with many Jewish leaders and that the leaders he criticized served as a contrast to his kingdom values, it is important to address a few issues related to the conflict and the reception of that conflict in current scholarly discussion. First, as I argue above, supersessionist readings of Matthew offer, in my view, an inaccurate assessment of the data within the Gospel. Although Jesus extends to the nations an invitation into the kingdom (Matt 28:18–20), his saving mission begins with Israel (Matt 1:21), and there is no indication throughout the narrative that Jesus abandons his fellow Jews or his mission to reach them. An argument has been made by some scholars that Matt 21:43 indicates that the kingdom has been taken away from all Israel and given to another people (usually either the nations or the church), but I have argued in detail elsewhere that I do not think this is the right reading of that passage.[51] Instead Jesus' conflict is with the Jewish leaders in particular, rather than Israel as a whole, and the Jewish leaders are replaced with other leaders, namely Jesus' own disciples (cf. Matt 19:28). This change in leadership is not done as a judgment against Israel but in favor of it. In Jesus' compassion for Israel and in his role as their messiah, he condemns the leaders for their poor leadership and trains those who will lead people into a flourishing life based on God's values.

50 For a recent example of this approach, see Adela Yarbro Collins, "Polemic against the Pharisees in Matthew 23," in *The Pharisees*, ed. Joseph Sievers and Amy-Jill Levine (Grand Rapids: Eerdmans, 2021), 168–69, who argues that rather than going back to Jesus, the woes in Matt 23 were likely invented by Matthew's writer, and she impugns Matthew for his depiction of the Pharisees. In the event that the woes do go back to Jesus, then Collins argues that this would be an example that not even he is "always living up to a high standard."

51 See my *God's Will and Testament: Inheritance in the Gospel of Matthew and Jewish Tradition* (Waco, Tex.: Baylor University Press, 2021), 321–37.

Second, it has been argued that Jesus' conflicts with the Pharisees were halachic in nature, meaning Jesus was not condemning Judaism, but he was disagreeing with the Pharisees over the way that it should be practiced. Jesus and the Pharisees argued particularly over issues such as Sabbath observance, purity regulations, the kind of company one could keep, and their understanding of righteousness so that the conflict was not between two unrelated groups but was largely an interpretive conflict between two Jewish groups.[52] This argument is often made to understand the Pharisees' perspective and demonstrate their good intentions. Although I agree that approaches to Torah are the central issue, I do not think the matter is merely an interpretive one, nor do I think it minimizes the complicity of the Pharisees in the conflict. The nature of the disagreement between Jesus and the Pharisees broadly concerned the nature and timing of the kingdom, and as I argue in part 2 of this book, it also concerned the complete misunderstanding among the Jewish leaders regarding God's heart and will. The Pharisees challenged Jesus over halachic disagreements, but Jesus accused them of neglecting mercy and allowing injustice to prevail. The conflict was not only about the interpretation of Torah but also the moral treatment of God's people.

This second point leads to the third. Jesus' woes against the scribes and Pharisees in Matt 23 do not place Jesus in conflict with Judaism but instead place him squarely within its traditions. Jesus' judgments are prophetic in nature and recall the rich history of Israelite prophets who condemned Israel's own leaders for dereliction of responsibility. In Matt 9:13, Jesus condemns the Pharisees for neglecting mercy and does so by quoting Hosea, a prophet who also called out Israel's leaders for their focus on less consequential issues of law and for their failure to emphasize those matters that were closer to God's heart.[53] If we're willing to concede that certain leaders in Israel's distant past were capable of failure and were in need of correction, it seems odd that there is a recent resistance to the possibility that at least some of the Pharisees could have been in need of the same such correction. Jesus argues that ancient Israel was often guilty of rejecting its prophets, a claim supported by the textual evidence (e.g., 1 Kgs 18:4, 13; 2 Chron 25:16; Hos 9:7; Neh 9:26; Jer 26:20–23). That Jesus fits within this tradition and was himself rejected as a prophet among at

52 See, for example, Kent L. Yinger, *The Pharisees: Their History, Character, and New Testament Portrait* (Eugene, Ore.: Cascade, 2022), 75–79.

53 This passage is discussed in part 2 under Matt 5:7.

least some of the Jews and their leaders is not inconsistent with Israel's story. Based on their halachic disputes, it makes sense that the Pharisees would question Jesus and even outright reject his approach, but this doesn't guarantee they weren't wrong, nor does this mean that Jesus was wrong in pronouncing judgment against them. As I discuss below, the Gospel writers suggest that Jesus had the authority to make his pronouncements, and this authority is based on his role within the Jewish story. Any suggestion that at least some of the Pharisees were in error does not require supersessionist readings, nor does it require that we view all Pharisees or Jewish leaders as those in error, nor does it require countersuggestions that the Gospel writers invented the stories or got them wrong.

Fourth, in an effort to rescue the Pharisees' reputation, some scholars have suggested that Matthew's depiction of the conflict between Jesus and the Pharisees was either heightened by the Gospel writers or that portions of the conflict were invented in whole by the Gospel writers to satisfy their narrative and theological agendas. Within this view, the Gospel writers do not portray the Pharisees with historical accuracy but instead present a biased portrait. This is problematic for at least four reasons.

(1) The Gospel writers are not the only ones to depict the Pharisees in a negative light. Josephus was critical of them,[54] and although they are not mentioned by name in the Dead Sea Scrolls, they are likely depicted in those texts,[55] where they are also viewed negatively.[56] Some scholars argue that there is polemical bias in each of these sources, but the fact that negative perceptions of the Pharisees arise from such

[54] See Steve Mason, *Flavius Josephus on the Pharisees: A Compositional-Critical Study* (Boston: Brill Academic, 2001).

[55] It would be difficult to determine exactly where the Pharisees were in view. Compositions such as 4QMMT, the Hodayot, and the Damascus Document are critical of Jews who lead Israel astray with incorrect interpretations of Torah, and strong arguments have been made that the Pharisees are included in these depictions. See James C. Vanderkam, "The Pharisees and the Dead Sea Scrolls," in *In Quest of the Historical Pharisees*, ed. Jacob Neusner and Bruce D. Chilton (Waco, Tex.: Baylor University Press, 2007), 225–36.

[56] This is not to say that the criticisms of the Pharisees are the same in each of these sources. They are not. A reductionist and all too simple but not altogether inaccurate summary might suggest that the Pharisees viewed Jesus as too loose in his observance of Torah and that the Qumran community viewed the Pharisees the same way. The depictions of the Pharisees in Josephus and the New Testament do bear some important similarities. On this, see Jens Schröter, "How Close Were Jesus and the Pharisees?" in *The Pharisees*, ed. Joseph Sievers and Amy-Jill Levine (Grand Rapids: Eerdmans, 2021), 225–28, 231.

varied sources should at least open to us the possibility that some of these criticisms are valid.

(2) The evidence suggests that the conflicts between Jesus and the Pharisees entered the tradition from its earliest points and therefore do not merely reflect later conflicts from a post–70 CE perspective. Pharisaic opposition appears in Mark (e.g., Mark 2:16, 18, 24), and Jesus criticizes the Pharisees in parallel passages in the double tradition (Matt 23:23–28; Luke 11:39–44). The conflict is also reported by Paul (Phil 3:5–6). Several early sources validate the nature of the conflict.[57]

(3) Jesus' altercations with the Pharisees cohere with other historical conflicts within Judaism and develop the way we might expect based on the nature of the disputes. All of the traditions report the nature of the disagreements the same way and center on things such as Jesus' authority to forgive or to heal on the Sabbath or to teach distinctive ideas, such as the love of enemies. These "in-house" Jewish controversies fit the larger pattern of the ongoing debates between Jewish groups of that period, and Jesus' rhetoric fits polemical conventions of the time, so that (a) there is nothing anti-Semitic about the conflicts, and (b) there is nothing about them that suggests they do not fit within the frame of Jesus' own ministry context.[58]

(4) Although it's true that the Gospels are theological narratives from a post–70 CE perspective, they are vital sources of information about Jesus, his followers, and his opponents, and they reflect genuine fidelity to their sources and to the evidence we have regarding the development of Jesus traditions.[59] Jesus' conflicts with the Jewish leaders, including the Pharisees, clearly left an impression on the source record and on those who transmitted the oral traditions from the time of Jesus to that of the Gospel writers. Although there are important differences in the ways that the individual Gospels depict the details of those conflicts[60] and in the ways that they

57 See Keener, *Historical*, 224–26. Keener also argues that for those who hold to the existence of a Q source, evidence suggests that the Q tradition featured important passages regarding the conflict.

58 Keener, *Historical*, 231.

59 See, for example, Keener, *Historical*, 163–348. On Jesus' conflicts with the Pharisees, see specifically pp. 223–37. See also Schröter, "How Close," 222.

60 For an account of the differences between the Gospels in their depiction of the Jewish leaders, see Anthony J. Saldarini, *Pharisees, Scribes and Sadducees in Palestinian Society* (Grand Rapids: Eerdmans, 2001), 144–98.

> categorize the leaders,[61] the overall impression of the conflicts provided by the Gospel writers is a consistent one. To suggest that the Gospel writers simply "got it wrong" would require more evidence against their depiction than has yet been provided.

This fourth point does not eliminate recognition of redactional activity on the part of the Gospel writers. As stated here, the depictions of the Pharisees from one account to the next are peppered with redactional activity, such as scribes appearing in a Markan version of a story and then being replaced by Pharisees in Matthew's version of the same story (e.g., Mark 12:28; Matt 22:34). Regarding Matthew in particular, it is certainly the case that the writer(s) intensified Pharisaic opposition to Jesus. However, this is not the same as suggesting that the post–70 CE situation of the Gospel writers dictated their understanding of the conflict between Jesus and the Jewish leaders to the point that their depiction is inaccurate. Their portrayals might have been "influenced by their post-70 experiences," but they are "historically related to a pre-70 profile."[62] As Craig Keener argues, the most likely scenario is that Matthew's writer(s) adapted stories in which it was possible or likely that Pharisees were involved.[63]

So what shall we say about anti-Semitism and the role that our interpretations of the Pharisees plays in anti-Semitic views of both the New Testament and of Jewish communities throughout history and today? Let me say unequivocally that I share this concern. Anti-Semitism has no place in our view of the Bible and no role in our modern-day society. Furthermore, as stated above, I disagree with supersessionist readings of

[61] It has been recognized that Matthew presents the various groups among the Jewish leadership as one amalgamated group rather than treating them as separate groups with separate views and agendas. This has been argued by, among others, David E. Garland, *The Intention of Matthew 23* (Leiden: Brill, 1979), 43–46, who argues that Matthew uses the various groups of Jewish leaders homogeneously as a collective literary convention. For Matthew, what each group believes and how they function is less important than his portrait of many Jewish leaders as equally complicit in failing to live righteously and to provide justice and mercy to the lost sheep of Israel. It is important not to overstate this, as Matthew's writer(s) clearly shows signs that he knows the differences. For example, he is aware of the differences between the Pharisees and Sadducees regarding their views of the resurrection of the dead (cf. Matt 22:23–40). On the whole, Matthew tends to flatten out these differences more than either Mark or Luke.

[62] Schröter, "How Close," 224.

[63] Keener, *Historical*, 224.

Matthew, not only because of the terrible effects such readings have had in contributing to anti-Semitic perspectives, but also because, as a scholar, I think such readings make poor use of the evidence. I've also been convinced by the recent wave of scholarship that our one-sided caricatures of the Pharisees are reductive, inaccurate, and unfair and that the ways these caricatures have contributed to poor stereotypes of Jewish people in general has been destructive. As Keener writes, we can certainly all agree that the Pharisees did not go around trying to kill or arrest anyone with whom they disagreed,[64] and the nature of their disagreements with Jesus should force us to understand precisely why they felt what they did about his behavior. We have very little information about the historical Pharisees, but the evidence we do have suggests that on the whole, the Pharisees were a group of interpreters who sought to provide careful readings of Torah and lead their fellow Jews into close observance.

However, I do not think it is either anti-Semitic or supersessionist to view Jesus' conflicts with the Pharisees of his time as both real and vital to his ministry. Nor do I think it is supersessionist to accept that the depiction of these conflicts in Matthew's Gospel reflects reality. Clearly there was a disagreement between Jesus and several groups among the Jewish leadership over purity rules, food laws, and Sabbath observance. Jesus actually agreed with what was taught by the Pharisees (Matt 23:2–3) but disputed whether those with whom he had conflict were living up to their own teachings. More than anything else, the conflict centered on Jesus' identity and his authority to heal or pluck heads of grain on the Sabbath, to dine with sinners, and to show mercy toward those in need at times the Pharisees thought inappropriate. The Pharisees interpreted Torah according to the "tradition of the elders" (cf. Matt 15:2), while Jesus interpreted Torah on his own authority.[65] These circumstances clearly created the conditions for conflict, and insofar as the Jewish leaders failed to live up to the standards of Messiah Jesus regarding God's heart for the lost sheep of the house of Israel (Matt 10:6), they became the counterexample for ideal discipleship and objects of Jesus' prophetic pronouncements. It is both possible and reasonable to maintain that historically the Pharisees had a positive impact on Jewish life and that within Jesus' time and ministry, many of the Pharisees he encountered did not live up to God's standards for mercy and justice. Therefore, it is both possible and reasonable that even if the Pharisees were historically good for Israel, Jesus was right about his criticisms, at least regarding the specific

64 Keener, *Historical*, 224.
65 See Schröter, "How Close," 238.

Pharisees with whom he had conflict. All of this should be viewed within the milieu of Jewish culture—that Jesus criticized the Jewish leaders of his time, Pharisees included, for the good of Israel rather than in judgment of it.

It also important to point out (and this is the success of recent scholarly attempts to reclaim the Pharisees within Jewish tradition) that there were likely a few thousand Pharisees throughout the region at the time of Jesus, and his disputes were particularly with those ones who challenged him and questioned his ministry. There are also positive portrayals in the Gospel accounts (e.g., John 3:1–2), the Pharisees were popular with the people for good reason, and in the end, it was not the Pharisees who were Jesus' most significant opponents but rather the chief priests and the elders (Matt 21:23; 26:3, 47; 27:1, 3, 12, 20). Indeed, after Jesus' woes against the scribes and Pharisees in Matt 23 and at the climax of the narrative, the Pharisees largely disappear from the story. It is the chief priests and elders who have political involvement in Jesus' death.[66]

The arguments in this book are concerned with the depiction of the Jewish leaders within the Matthean narrative and for the purpose of interpreting Jesus' design for ideal discipleship. Therefore, I will not concentrate on historical-critical arguments regarding the Pharisees. However, I think it is important to clarify that although I stand resolutely against supersessionist readings of the New Testament and against anti-Semitism, I assume that Jesus' conflicts with the Pharisees were historical and not a product of the Gospel writers based on their own social circumstances. Modern depictions of the Pharisees might be unbalanced and unfair, but Jesus clearly had conflicts with many of them, and these conflicts are important to Jesus' own statements regarding ideal discipleship. In my view, how one feels about the nature of the disagreements between them will largely depend on one's view of Jesus' authority to declare his negative pronouncements.

The Reception of Jesus among the Crowds

If the beatitudes feel counterintuitive and countercultural, that's because they are,[67] and this is illustrated by Matt 11:28–30, a passage with several

[66] See Saldarini, *Pharisees*, 161. See also Craig L. Blomberg, *Jesus the Purifier: John's Gospel and the Fourth Quest for the Historical Jesus* (Grand Rapids: Baker Academic, 2023), 83, who argues that "one can no longer convincingly claim that the Pharisees were Jesus' major antagonists, at least not in Jerusalem at the time of the crucifixion, even if one thinks that Jesus did have a few major spats with them, especially in Galilee."

[67] Cornelius a Lapide, *The Great Commentary*, trans. Thomas W. Mossman (London: John Hodges, 1890), 1:180–81, who argues that the beatitudes are a

important parallels to the beatitudes.[68] In the context, Jesus reproaches those cities that rejected his words and deeds (Matt 11:20–24). While speaking with the crowds (Matt 11:7), Jesus invites them to "come to me, all you that are weary and are carrying heavy burdens, and I will give you rest. Take my yoke upon you, and learn from me; for I am gentle and humble in heart, and you will find rest for your souls. For my yoke is easy, and my burden is light." This invitation is also a part of the reproach. The Pharisees are guilty of imposing heavy burdens on the people (cf. Matt 23:4), but Jesus invites the crowds into a new form of discipleship characterized by gentleness and humility, and this leads to rest for the souls of those who follow him. That this rest refers to discipleship is illustrated by the fact that Matthew's writer appears to take linguistic cues from Jer 6:16 in which God declares, "Stand at the crossroads and look, and ask for the ancient paths, where the good way lies; and walk in it, and find rest for your souls." In discussing this connection, Konradt comments that rest "appears as the consequence of walking the old paths of the people of God with their God. For Matthew, this is now the way of discipleship to which Jesus here calls the people."[69] In the Jeremiah passage, the hearers respond, "We will not walk in it." According to Jesus' reproach many of his hearers are making the same mistake. The crowds are familiar with the teaching of the scribes and Pharisees, teachings that are embedded into their cultural experience and therefore resonate with their cultural intuition, and this has led people in some cities to reject Jesus' demonstrations of power. However, Jesus calls the crowds to see past their cultural intuition in order to walk a new path, a path that consequently relates to a very old one. The crowds must look past the paths set by their current leaders, which lead them astray. Such paths cause them to miss out on the clear indications that Jesus is the sent one of God and that Jesus is the one who can truly connect them to the ways of God found in their oldest traditions, ways that will lead them to proper rest.

The beatitudes, and the rest of the Sermon on the Mount, leave the crowds astounded because they've never heard anything like it—they've never encountered a teacher with such authority (Matt 7:29). But in the same way that Jesus describes himself as gentle (Matt 11:29, 21:5), he calls

---

"paradox of the world" due to the way they upend cultural expectations. See also Allison, *Sermon*, 43, "the beatitudes were intended to startle." They present things opposed to our expectations. "To take them seriously is to call into question our ordinary values."

68 This is explored in more detail in part 2 below.

69 Konradt, *Gospel*, 184.

his disciples to be gentle (Matt 5:5)[70]—the beatitudes are a counterintuitive and countercultural introduction to Christlikeness and ideal discipleship. Although observing the instructions of the beatitudes and the rest of the Sermon on the Mount are far from easy, Jesus refers to his own yoke of teaching and discipleship as light because he compares his way with the corrupt and oppressive ways of the scribes and Pharisees. This contrast is presented prolifically throughout the text but is explicitly connected to the beatitudes by the contrast between makarisms and woes—in this case the woes are used in Matt 23 to condemn the Pharisees at length. Much of the entire First Gospel can be viewed as a record of contrasting modes of discipleship—between the ways of Jesus and the ways of the Pharisees—and it is through this contrast that Jesus can confidently refer to his own path as easy and his burden as light.

Parts 1 and 2 of this book explore in detail the contrast between ideal disciples and the failed path of the Pharisees, but it is helpful here to discuss two aspects about Jesus as the one on whom ideal discipleship is based. First, we must address Jesus' authority to declare the nature of ideal discipleship, and second, we must understand Jesus as the exemplar of his own instructions.

Jesus as the Authority for His Beatitudes

Understanding the identity of Jesus as the proclaimer of the beatitudes is an important aspect of interpreting them. This includes both his authority to proclaim them as a counterintuitive and countercultural form of discipleship and his role as an exemplar who lives out the beatitudes in his own life and ministry. Matthew's Gospel account begins with the declaration that Jesus is the long-awaited Jewish Messiah, the son of David, the son of Abraham. It is through Abraham that the nations of the earth will be blessed (cf. Gen 12:3, 18:18, 22:18), and as the son of Abraham, Jesus is presented by Matthew as the solution to the universal need for salvation.[71] In Jewish tradition it is God who redeems his people from their iniquities (cf. Ps 130:8), but Matthew clearly extends this authority to Jesus (cf. Matt

[70] Usually translated in Matt 5:5 as "meek," meek and gentle are translated from the same Greek word: πραΰς. This connection is described in greater detail in part 2 below.

[71] Jesus as a "Jewish" savior with relevance to the wider world is recognized by gentiles in the narrative, such as the magi honoring Jesus as "king of the Jews" (Matt 2:2) and a Canaanite woman appealing to him as "Lord, son of David" (Matt 15:22).

1:21, 9:2, 26:28). As the son of David, Jesus is the meek king (Matt 21:5) who becomes the heir of David's own divine sonship (2 Sam 7:14), though Matthew extends this notion through the Spirit's direct involvement in Jesus' conception (Matt 1:20) and God's affirmation of Jesus at his baptism (Matt 3:17). Jesus is the Son of God in a unique way (cf. Matt 16:16–17),[72] which is the core aspect of Matthew's Christology,[73] and as God's unique son, Jesus has the authority to declare God's ways in contradistinction to those who have gone astray from God's will.[74] A strong argument has also been made by many scholars that Jesus is depicted by Matthew as a new Moses; the chapters leading up to the beatitudes feature several Moses typologies and the setting of the Sermon on the Mount is likely intended as a recall to Moses' association with Mount Sinai as the giver of the law.[75]

As the Messiah, the son of David, the son of Abraham, and the unique son of God, Jesus is now the one with the authority to instruct God's people concerning God's will, and in the structure of Matthew's Gospel, the beatitudes are his first salvo in his opening discourse. In the beatitudes Jesus does not promise imminent rewards to his followers. Instead he describes an eschatological inheritance for the children of God. So if the disciples are in a present state of mourning and persecution but the rewards are eschatological in nature, then why should anyone listen to him? Why would the disciples not find a teacher that promised present relief? As Dale Allison argues, Jesus' disciples must trust in the authority

72 See Stephen Westerholm, *Understanding Matthew: The Early Christian Worldview of the First Gospel* (Grand Rapids: Baker Academic, 2006), 113–17, who illustrates the unique nature of Jesus' sonship of God through Jesus' use of the phrase "my Father."

73 Konradt, *Gospel*, 35, states that "throughout Matthew, Jesus as Son of God is *the* central Christological category" (emphasis original).

74 See Michael F. Bird, *Jesus Is the Christ: The Messianic Testimony of the Gospels* (Downers Grove, Ill.: Intervarsity Press, 2012), 58, "Matthew's Jesus stands as the embodiment of Israel's Davidic hope, while presenting him also as the leader of the messianic community of the new age." For a recent analysis of Jesus as Messiah and Son of God in New Testament texts including Matthew, see Stanley E. Porter and Bryan R. Dyer, *Origins of New Testament Christology: An Introduction to the Traditions and Titles Applied to Jesus* (Grand Rapids: Baker Academic, 2023), 65–89, 135–56.

75 See Robert H. Gundry, *Matthew: A Commentary on His Handbook for a Mixed Church under Persecution* (Grand Rapids: Eerdmans, 1994), 66, and Dale C. Allison Jr., *The New Moses: A Matthean Typology* (Eugene, Ore.: Wipf & Stock, 1993), 137–89.

of Jesus and proceed in the confidence that he has the ability, as one who speaks for God, to deliver on his promises.[76] It is through Jesus that God is with his people, and Matthew declares this both at the beginning of the Gospel (Matt 1:23) and the end, when Jesus declares his authority over heaven and earth and states that he will be with God's people to the end of the age (Matt 28:18–20).

Evidence for Jesus' claim to authority is provided by his character and his success as a moral exemplar of his teachings. To preach what Jesus preaches is another way of preaching Jesus himself because his teachings explain his own way of being in the world. Matthew's writer goes to great lengths to demonstrate that Jesus models what he commends to his people in the beatitudes. As Jonathan Pennington states, "The Beatitudes relate intimately with the entirety of Matthew, and the Beatitudes and Matthew as a whole illuminate one another in a mutually informing way."[77] Jesus is poor in spirit and humble (Matt 5:3, 5 compared with 11:28–29, 21:5), he mourns (5:4 compared with 23:37), he hungers and thirsts to live righteously according to the will of God (5:6 compared with 26:36–46, 27:19), he is merciful (5:7 compared with 12:1–14), he is pure in heart (5:8 compared with 4:1–11), he is a peacemaker (5:9 compared with 26:26–30), and he was persecuted for his righteousness by those who reviled him (5:10–11 compared with 26:57–68).

One of the most important examples of this Matthean pattern is the way that Jesus is consistently presented as one who models his teachings for those who would be his ideal disciples. What is true for the disciples must be true for the master first, and the First Gospel is artfully arranged so that Jesus' words and deeds are two ways of understanding the same

[76] Allison, *Sermon*, 19.

[77] Jonathan T. Pennington, *The Sermon on the Mount and Human Flourishing: A Theological Commentary* (Grand Rapids: Baker Academic, 2017), 149. This interrelation was not always appreciated by interpreters who viewed Matthew's writer more as an editor than an author. See, for example, Hans Dieter Betz, *Essays on the Sermon on the Mount*, trans. L. L. Welborn (1985; repr., Minneapolis: Fortress, 2009), 17–36, who argues that the beatitudes are best read as an independent unit. Konradt, *Gospel*, 1, expresses well the more recent recognition by Matthean scholars that Matthew is an artfully rendered whole with interweaving themes and ideas when he writes, "later sections are alluded to in advance, earlier themes are taken up again, patterns are repeated in such a way that they become common coin, while at the same time such repetitions are embedded in lines of development that drive the narrative forward and infuse it with dynamic power."

ideas about Jesus' identity and authority as the Jewish Messiah and unique son of God. The beatitudes aren't just Jesus' teachings; they are a summary of his own dispositional character that his disciples will encounter as examples of his words, and as the disciples follow Jesus, the beatitudes also become descriptions of their own dispositional character.[78] The beatitudes are implicit exhortations that invite Jesus' disciples into the fullness and flourishing of a Christ-patterned life.

Henri Nouwen, in his classic book on the prodigal son, describes how this Christ-patterned life found in the beatitudes is so counterintuitive and countercultural. Nouwen points out the significance of the position of the beatitudes in the narrative to Jesus' testing in the wilderness by the devil, who offers Jesus the world and its splendor (Matt 4:1–11). Jesus was able to rebuff these offers because he knew his worth was not confirmed by that which the world values but by his position as a child of God. If one is secure in their relationship with God already, then obtaining the world by nefarious means loses its appeal. Nouwen argues that the beatitudes are "a self-portrait of Jesus, the Beloved Son," and because they explicitly claim that they are a portrait of all of God's children (Matt 5:9), then living the beatitudes is a way of imitating Jesus. Imitating Jesus is a way of finding the narrow gate into God's kingdom rather than the kingdoms of the world.[79]

In many ways, this observation by Nouwen illustrates the primary perspective on the beatitudes taken in this commentary. The impetus for this book is not only to contribute to the long tradition of beatitude interpretation, but more succinctly it is a part of an ongoing project of mine to engage Matthew's Gospel with the theme of ideal discipleship, which I find to be a driving theme of the entire composition.[80] An argument is made throughout this book that Matthew illustrates discipleship by placing Jesus and his followers on one side of the discipleship divide and the failed

78 Eklund, *Beatitudes*, 37–38, argues that viewing the beatitudes as "a biography or portrait of Jesus" is one shared by the majority of interpreters down through the ages. Jesus fulfills and models them so that they become descriptions of who he is, and this functions as a teaching tool for the disciples who should expect to look like their master. The disciples also embody the beatitudes because they follow Jesus. In the words of Calvin, *Sermons*, 19, they embody the beatitudes by entering "the school of our Lord Jesus Christ."

79 Henri J. M. Nouwen, *The Return of the Prodigal Son: A Story of Homecoming* (London: Darton, Longman and Todd, 1992), 54.

80 This project began with my *God's Will and Testament.*

Jewish leaders on the other, with the crowds serving as a neutral party who are faced with a decision between these two paths.[81] Jesus, as the Jewish Messiah and unique son of God, presents the path toward alignment with God's will, but the countercultural nature of this presentation both intrigues the crowds and becomes a stumbling block. Jesus offers stinging critiques of the Jewish leaders, and the Pharisees often attempt to prevent the crowds from embracing Jesus' teachings and works (cf. Matt 12:22–24, 21:14–17). The beatitudes serve as an entry point for Jesus' path to discipleship to those who long for the kingdom of heaven (Matt 5:3, 10), which is explicitly contrasted with the scribes' and Pharisees' failed attempts to create the same path (Matt 23:13). Part 1 of this study describes the beatitudes as a unit, including their structure and overall meaning, while part 2 features exegesis of each individual beatitude according to the purpose of the beatitudes described in part 1. Before moving into part 1, a few brief comments are helpful regarding the sources that were available to and used by the writer(s) of Matthew's Gospel.

Matthew's Sources

Any useful and sophisticated discussion regarding Matthew's sources would be book length in itself. Such a discussion would require attention to Matthew's relationship to the other Gospels and the speculative existence of additional written sources of Jesus traditions, such as "Q" (the so-called Synoptic problem), as well as attention to the specifics of oral tradition, communal/social memory, and a specific sociocritical profile of Matthew's earliest readers. An analysis of these issues is not necessary for an investigation of the meaning of Matthew's beatitudes and does not feature in the following discussion. I assume, with the majority of Gospels interpreters, that Mark's Gospel was written earlier than Matthew, and Matthew's writer(s) used Mark as a source. This assumption is not

[81] See Craig S. Keener, *The Gospel of Matthew: A Socio-rhetorical Commentary* (Grand Rapids: Eerdmans, 2009), 48–49, who argues that Matthew writes to critique the failed Jewish leadership just as Israel's prophets critiqued the failed leadership in previous times. Matthew views the Jewish leaders as failed spokespersons and "illegitimate guardians of their heritage." See also Konradt, *Israel*, 126–48, who argues that the conflict between Jesus and the Jewish authorities puts pressure on the crowds to choose a side. The crowds show consistent interest in Jesus (cf. Matt 7:28, 9:33, 14:13–14, 15:10), but the Jewish leaders are depicted as failed shepherds (cf. Matt 9:36) and blind guides (Matt 15:14, 23:16–26).

controversial in Gospels scholarship and is backed by several studies and by most recent commentaries. Because Mark does not feature a formal list of makarisms to match Matthew's and Luke's, Mark will not play a part in the following analysis. Furthermore, it is all but certain that oral traditions played a role in Matthew's gathering of material, but the extent of the writer's reliance on such traditions is difficult to ascertain.[82]

The relationship between Matthew and Luke is far less clear, and no attempt is made here to clear up that relationship, even when Matthew's and Luke's makarisms are compared with each other. Instead the focus on Matthew's list is literary, narrative, linguistic, theological, and intertextual. In other words, this study focuses on questions that can be answered with greater precision, such as how do these beatitudes fit into Matthew's overall story, what factors affected Jesus' (and/or the writer's) word choices, what sort of life do these beatitudes describe, and what antecedent texts and other linguistic and theological traditions influenced the words, shape, and structure of Matthew's list? Concerning the relationship between Matthew and Luke, the majority of scholars argue that Matthew's list features greater levels of authorial and editorial development, and therefore Luke's list is likely drawn from earlier traditions.[83] This is possible, but as argued above, there is no reason to think that either Luke's or Matthew's lists are inconsistent with versions of the beatitudes taught by Jesus at various times and to particular audiences. Comparison between Matthew's and Luke's lists

[82] Brief treatments of Synoptic sources are provided by Craig A. Evans, "Sorting out the Synoptic Problem: Why an Old Approach Is Still Best," in *Reading the Gospels Today*, ed. Stanley E. Porter (Grand Rapids: Eerdmans, 2004), 1–26, and James D. G. Dunn, "How Did Matthew Go about Composing His Gospel?" in *Jesus, Matthew's Gospel and Early Christianity: Studies in Memory of Graham N. Stanton*, ed. Daniel M. Gurtner, Joel Willitts, and Richard A. Burridge, LNTS 435 (London: T&T Clark, 2011), 39–58. For a more detailed summary of the Synoptic problem, see Bird, *Gospel*, 125–213.

[83] According to Allison, *Sermon*, 27–28, this is the view of most interpreters. For example, because makarisms and woes often belong together as a pair, it is more likely that Matthew separated the makarisms from the woes for structural reasons than that Luke brought them together. Also it is more likely that Matthew added "in spirit" to the makarism about the poor for theological reasons than that Luke removed that phrase (compare Matt 5:3 with Luke 6:20). Conversely, for an argument regarding the possibility that Luke's beatitudes are secondary, see Mark Goodacre, *The Case against Q: Studies in Markan Priority and the Synoptic Problem* (Harrisburg, Pa.: Trinity Press International, 2002), 133–51

are featured only as a way to explicate Matthew's meaning since differences between them often highlight meaning by comparison of intentions.

Although the Synoptic problem and the potential for a "Matthean community" are not addressed here, this study does explore Matthew's broader Greek, Roman, and Jewish milieu. For example, Pennington has argued persuasively that Matthew's beatitudes reflect both the Jewish wisdom tradition and Greco-Roman virtue traditions, and Matthew's use of ethical terms reflects both Jewish sources and Greek and Roman ethical norms.[84] Roman life and culture likely had an influence on Matthew's author(s), but because Matthew is a text marinated in Jewish culture and its eschatological atmosphere, Jewish traditions take pride of place, and in some ways the Roman cultural reality appears to have pushed Matthew's writer(s) deeper into the Jewish Scriptures and the theological matrix of the biblical story.

Finally it is helpful to address Matthew's use of its Jewish sources. As Konradt argues, "Matthew's Jesus-story, from 1:1 through 28:20, is told with constant reference to the Scripture later known as the Old Testament. . . . The Matthean Jesus-story rings out within the echo chamber of Scripture, and gains in resonance and tone when heard in a context permeated by biblical reverberations."[85] Additionally I argue throughout this study that, although the canonical material in the Hebrew Bible (Old Testament) dominates Matthew's intertextual references and allusions, the writer also demonstrates some familiarity with noncanonical traditions, such as those recorded in Sirach, the Psalms of Solomon, 4QInstruction, and other Second Temple period compositions. If it is the case that Matthew's Gospel is saturated in the language, theology, and themes of various antecedent Jewish texts and traditions, important questions arise concerning the methods by which Matthew's writer(s) became familiar with them.

For example, an argument is made throughout this study (especially in part 2) that Isaiah and certain Psalms are engaged and quoted directly by Matthew's author. At times, the author interweaves these sources and creates composite quotations meant to draw the reader/hearer back to both sources simultaneously. Did Matthew's writer(s) have physical copies of

[84] Pennington, *Sermon*, 29–40. For a recent study situating Matthew within its Hellenistic context, see Robert S. Kinney, *Hellenistic Dimensions of the Gospel of Matthew* (Tübingen: Mohr Siebeck, 2016).

[85] Konradt, *Gospel*, 1–2.

both texts, Isaiah and the Psalms? Were the composite quotes already a part of some oral tradition, or were they developed as an aspect of a community's social memory? Like the circumstances surrounding the Synoptic problem, answers to these questions are difficult to come by. Even though these discussions are fruitful, they do not feature in the following analysis.[86] This book is a *narrative* study, meaning the primary mode of analysis is focused on the ways that the beatitudes fit within and are explained by the actual story told within the text. Often in studies on the beatitudes, the individual words and phrases are explained by nebulous connections to comparable ideas. Instead my argument throughout this book is that Jesus' beatitudes in Matthew are best explained by the context of Matthew itself. My focus is Matthew as a composition and the intertextual citations and allusions that comprise Jesus' (and the author's) moral and theological thought world. The goal is to explain what Matthew's beatitudes mean rather than the precise nature of the means by which Matthew's writer(s) came to know the antecedent material that influenced word choices and theology. This study refers to the "texts" of books such as Isaiah, the Psalms, Hosea, and more, while recognizing that Matthew's writer might have had several methods for obtaining the material other than physical documents.[87]

[86] Although see Richard B. Hays, *Echoes of Scripture in the Gospels* (Waco, Tex.: Baylor University Press, 2016), 186–87, who argues persuasively that Matthew's composite quotations were designed by Matthew's writer(s) based on the style, frequency, and application.

[87] Studies on Matthew's use of sources often refer to "intertextuality," a term applied to an understanding of one author's use of other *textual* sources. However, a more fluid understanding must include a text's impact on its larger interpretive environment and the way it is communicated and developed in various strands of tradition. Textual traditions move through culture as dialogue partners with other traditions, which affects meaning and usage in dynamic ways. Antecedent traditions used by Matthew's writer(s) can be subsumed under the rubric of intertextuality, even if the traditions made their way into the First Gospel by means other than written documents. For a brief discussion on this related Matthew's Gospel, see W. J. C. Weren, *Studies in Matthew's Gospel: Literary Design, Intertextuality, and Social Setting*, BIS 130 (Leiden: Brill, 2013), 89–106. Erin M. Heim, *Adoption in Galatians and Romans: Contemporary Metaphor Theories and the Pauline Huiothesia Metaphors*, BIS 153 (Leiden: Brill, 2017), 61–66, deals particularly with intertextuality in Paul's letters, but her comments are helpful in understanding the cultural realities of intertextuality regardless of which texts are in view.

Part I
Understanding the Matthean Beatitudes

Matthew 5:3–12, as a unit, is typically referred to as Matthew's "beatitudes." It has often been regarded as the centerpiece of Christian virtue and a sort of magna carta for citizens of the kingdom of God.[1] Gregory of Nyssa argued that participation in the beatitudes means nothing less than to have communion with God.[2] The term "beatitude" comes from the Latin *beatus*, which is a translation of μακάριος (*makarios*), the Greek word that begins each beatitude. Depending on the context, μακάριος can be rendered into English with terms such as "happy, blissful, fortunate, or flourishing."[3] Nearly every English Bible renders μακάριος in Matt 5 as "blessed," implying the divine favor of God, which is passively received by the subjects of the makarisms. A growing number of scholars are challenging the correlation between μακάριος and the concept of "blessing," arguing that although makarisms can anticipate divine favor and eschatological blessings, many beatitudes in Jewish literature refer to human flourishing and the fullness of an earthly life.

The multifunctionality of makarisms in Jewish literature is illustrated by two examples: Prov 3:13 describes a flourishing life based on present circumstances, while Tob 13:14 envisions the eschatological reversal of unfortunate present conditions.[4] The purposes of a makarism can be

[1] Ian Boxall, *Matthew through the Centuries*, WBBC (Hoboken: Wiley Blackwell, 2019), 111.

[2] St. Gregory of Nyssa, *The Lord's Prayer, the Beatitudes*, ACW 18 (New York: Paulist, 1954), 87.

[3] See Jonathan T. Pennington, *The Sermon on the Mount and Human Flourishing: A Theological Commentary* (Grand Rapids: Baker Academic, 2017), 42.

[4] See Dale C. Allison, *The Sermon on the Mount: Inspiring the Moral Imagination* (New York: Crossroad, 1999), 41–44.

varied and interpretations depend on their use in a given context.[5] The variety of traditions that feature makarisms raises questions regarding the character of those found in Matt 5. Most scholars argue that Matthew's list fits into either one tradition or the other: either blessings for the future or ethical descriptions for the life of Jesus' followers. However, there is a growing sense among recent interpreters that choosing between these options misunderstands the dynamic dimensions of Jesus' gospel strategy. Although Matthew's makarisms do have an eye toward eschatological blessings, they also describe ideal discipleship and the active pursuit of a flourishing life. Because of the multifaceted nature of Jesus' teaching, the simple passivity implied by "blessed" is misleading. Many scholars have offered other suggestions for a more helpful translation of μακάριος, such as "happy," "fortunate," "honorable," and "flourishing."[6] The translation of μακάριος is discussed later in part 1. Before proceeding to a discussion concerning the full character of Matthew's makarisms, it is important to understand the careful arrangement of the beatitudes in Matthew's overall narrative and the ways that their placement in the structure of the text points to their function as instruction for discipleship.

5 See W. D. Davies and D. C. Allison, *Matthew 1–7*, ICC (London: T&T Clark, 1988), 432–34, who categorize several makarisms found throughout Jewish biblical and nonbiblical texts based on their wisdom or eschatological contexts.

6 Rebekah Eklund, *The Beatitudes through the Ages* (Grand Rapids: Eerdmans, 2021), 33–35, discusses a number of options.

1

Jesus' Beatitudes in Matthew's Structure

That the beatitudes are an aspect of discipleship is indicated by their placement within Matthew's structure. At the end of the prologue introducing Jesus as the Jewish Messiah (Matt 1:1–4:17), Jesus proclaims the need for repentance because "the kingdom of heaven has come near" (4:17b). Jesus' ministry begins, his mission is laid bare, and he calls on others to repent of the ways that they had wandered from God's will. The next section of the text is bracketed by Jesus' calls for others to join him on his mission: first, he calls his first disciples (4:18–22), and at the end of the section he sends his disciples on their first missionary journey (9:36–11:1).[1] These brackets frame another set signaled by nearly identical verses:

> Matt 4:23—Jesus went throughout Galilee, teaching in their synagogues and proclaiming the good news of the kingdom and curing every disease and every sickness among the people.

[1] Where the section begins is a matter of some disagreement. Robert H. Gundry, *Matthew: A Commentary on His Handbook for a Mixed Church under Persecution* (Grand Rapids: Eerdmans, 1994), 10, begins a subsection at 4:17, arguing that the call to repentance and the beginning of Jesus' ministry is a major turning point in Jesus' life. Similar is Matthias Konradt, *The Gospel according to Matthew: A Commentary*, trans. M. Eugene Boring (Waco, Tex.: Baylor University Press, 2020), 3, who argues that 4:17–11:1 functions as a section calling the disciples to continue Jesus' mission. Craig A. Evans, *Matthew*, NCBC (Cambridge: Cambridge University Press, 2012), 10, begins the section at 4:12, with John's arrest and the beginning of Jesus' ministry, and begins the next section at 11:2, where John inquires about Jesus from prison after hearing about everything he was doing. All of these are defensible, and Gundry is right to caution that interpreters risk being more precise about Matthew's structure than the author ever intended. However, the call of the disciples in 4:18–22 and the declaration that Jesus had finished instructing them in 11:1 provides a unified agenda for the section and a clean transition into the next.

> Matt 9:35—Then Jesus went about all the cities and villages, teaching in their synagogues, and proclaiming the good news of the kingdom, and curing every disease and every sickness.

These two verses summarize the content of the entire section: Jesus teaches (5–7), and he heals (8:1–9:34). Immediately following the summary in 9:35, Jesus gathers his disciples and grants them the authority to continue this work (10:1), but first the disciples must properly be prepared through Jesus' teaching and the model he provides of compassion toward his people. Following the beatitudes, Jesus tells his disciples that they are the salt of the earth and a light to the world (5:13–16); they are to let their light shine before others "so that they may see your good works and give glory to your Father in heaven" (5:16). Matthew 5:13–16 is a transitional passage that takes the reader from the dispositional description of a disciple in 5:3–12 to Jesus' declarations of the laws and ethics of God's kingdom in 5:21–7:12—a transition between who a disciple *is* to what a disciple *does*.[2] Being a disciple does not simply refer to following Jesus in his words and deeds but also in being "an outward focused agent of the kingdom, inviting people to honor/glorify God" (5:16).[3] Everything that happens in this section of Matt 4:18–11:1 is designed to raise up disciples and prepare them for the work of healing the broken and calling the lost to true flourishing according to Jesus' vision of the righteous life (5:16, 48).

Signposts carefully placed in the narrative indicate the crowds as the subjects of Jesus' compassion and the focus of his mission, and these signposts also carefully bracket subsections of the larger narrative section. After calling his first disciples, Jesus heals those among the crowds (4:23–25), and then he teaches his disciples in their hearing (5:1–2). The neutrality of the crowds is established; they are distinguished from the disciples (cf. 13:36), but they are not in league with Jesus' opponents (cf. 9:33–34, 15:1–12, 23:1). Instead they are intrigued, and anyone with ears

2 Similar is Dale C. Allison Jr., *Studies in Matthew: Interpretation Past and Present* (Grand Rapids: Baker Academic, 2005), 180–81, who argues that Matt 5:13–16 is a transitional passage but that the beatitudes are best understood as eschatological blessings rather than descriptions of a disciple. The transition is between "the blessed future" and "the demands of life in the present" or from "gift" to "task." The purpose and meaning of the beatitudes is discussed in the section below.

3 Jonathan T. Pennington, *The Sermon on the Mount and Human Flourishing: A Theological Commentary* (Grand Rapids: Baker Academic, 2017), 163.

to hear has the opportunity to join the number of Jesus' disciples.[4] After the sermon, the crowds are astonished at Jesus' teaching and continue to follow him (7:28–8:1). Then, after healing many among the crowds, Jesus has compassion for them as sheep without a shepherd (9:36) and sends his disciples only among "the lost sheep of the house of Israel" (10:5–8). The crowds play a prominent role at the beginning and end of each subsection (teaching, 5:1, 7:28, and healing, 8:1, 9:36). The following outline illustrates the brilliance of Matthew's embedded structure when pointing toward important themes in the narrative:

- 4:18–22—Jesus calls his first disciples
  - 4:23—Summary statement that Jesus teaches and heals among the crowds
    - 4:25—The crowds follow Jesus
      - 5:1–7:27—Details of Jesus' teaching ministry
        - 7:28—The crowds are amazed at Jesus' teaching
    - 8:1—The crowds follow Jesus
      - 8:2–9:33—Details of Jesus' healing ministry
        - 9:33—The crowds are amazed at Jesus' healings
  - 9:35—Summary statement that Jesus teaches and heals among the crowds
- 9:36–11:1—Jesus sends his disciples out to the lost sheep of the house of Israel

That this section ends with Jesus' description of the crowds as "sheep without a shepherd" is an important detail. This is a clear indictment of the leaders of the Jewish community, leaders who have failed the people and left them lost.[5] Jesus is establishing two competing modes of discipleship: within the sermon he states that the righteousness of his disciples must exceed that of the scribes and Pharisees (5:20) and after the discipleship subsection concludes with 11:1 the antagonism of the Jewish leaders becomes a major plot point in the story (Matt 11:16–19; 12:1–14, 24–45; 15:1–14; 16:1–12). Jesus' appeals to the crowds intensify, and they are increasingly tasked with the need to decide (Matt 11:7–30, 12:43–50,

4 Amy-Jill Levine, *Sermon on the Mount: A Beginner's Guide to the Kingdom of Heaven* (Nashville: Abingdon, 2020), 3, "The message is explicitly for his disciples, but they are not the only ones welcome to receive it."

5 Matthew's writer understood the differences between various groups among the Jewish leadership (Sadducees, Pharisees, scribes, etc.), but within the narrative they are treated as one amalgamated character: false shepherds who are leading Israel astray. See the important discussion regarding Matthew's depiction of the Jewish leaders, especially the Pharisees, in the introduction.

15:10–20).[6] The crowds are under the authority of the Jewish leaders, but Jesus offers a compelling and competing vision against their authority.

This competing vision is illustrated by yet another bracket: the beatitudes in 5:3–12 and woes in 23:1–36. The relationship between these passages is not always recognized,[7] but there is an intrinsic connection between makarisms and woes found prolifically throughout Jewish literature,[8] and there are a number of parallels in Matthew's beatitudes and woes that establish their connection. In fact many of the parallels between the two chapters appear in precisely the same order: qualifications for the kingdom of heaven (Matt 5:3, 23:13), a concern for mercy (Matt 5:7, 23:23), a call for purity (Matt 5:8, 23:25–26), the persecution of God's faithful (Matt 5:10–12, 23:34), and an accusation regarding the mistreatment of the prophets (Matt 5:12, 23:34).[9] Pennington notes that a contrast between these two motifs is expected: makarisms describe flourishing, and woes provide an expected counterexample of dispositions that do not result in flourishing but in grief and destruction. Jesus' disciples are to be pure in heart (Matt 5:8), but the Jewish leaders are hypocrites who pursue external righteousness without purity of heart (Matt 15:6–20, 23:25–28). The Jewish leaders are whitewashed tombs that appear beautiful on the outside but are internally unclean (Matt 23:27–28).[10]

This contrast between Jesus' ideal disciples on one end and the scribes and Pharisees on the other is further established by Jesus' statement in Matt 5:20 that one's righteousness must exceed that of the scribes and Pharisees in order to enter the kingdom of heaven. The kingdom belongs to those who exhibit the beatitudes (Matt 5:3, 10), but the scribes and

[6] See Konradt, *Gospel*, 3.

[7] See, for example, Robert A. Guelich, "The Matthean Beatitudes: 'Entrance Requirements' or Eschatological Blessings?" *JBL* 95 (1976): 419; Donald A. Hagner, *Matthew 1–13*, WBC 33A (Dallas: Word, 1993), 89; R. T. France, *The Gospel of Matthew*, NICNT (Grand Rapids: Eerdmans, 2007), 162, who explicitly mention the connection between makarisms and woes in Luke but state that Matthew makes no such connection; and David E. Garland, *The Intention of Matthew 23* (Leiden: Brill, 1979), who in a study on Matt 23 does not make a connection between Matthew's makarisms and woes.

[8] See, for example, Isa 3:10–11; Qoh 10:16–17; Luke 6:20–26; 1 En 99:10–16; 1 En 103:5–6; 2 En 52:1–15; and 2 Bar 10:6–7.

[9] Davies and Allison, *Matthew 1–7*, 440–41, note these parallels but argue that they are not strong enough to guarantee that Matthew's writer intended them to be read together.

[10] Pennington, *Sermon*, 84.

Pharisees have rejected the kingdom and are guilty of leading others away as well (Matt 23:13). In Matthew's Gospel, the righteous person is the one who follows Jesus and does God's will both externally and from within the heart (cf. Matt 7:21–24, 12:50).[11] Righteousness refers to "whole-person behavior that accords with God's nature, will, and coming kingdom."[12] As Roland Deines writes, Jesus offers access to "the eschatological, overflowingly rich righteousness" that "opens the way into the kingdom of God" for those who obey Jesus' call to discipleship. Conversely, "the righteousness of the scribes and Pharisees misses the goal" because they do not acknowledge Jesus as the Messiah who fulfills the Scriptures and who makes eschatological righteousness possible in the present.[13] Jesus' call to righteousness conflicts with the hypocritical behavior of the scribes and Pharisees, who tie up heavy burdens on the shoulders of others but are unwilling to practice what they teach (Matt 23:3–4, 28).[14]

Although the usual pattern of makarisms and woes places them in direct comparison (cf. Luke 6:20–26), Matthew's separation of the makarisms and woes on opposite ends of the text does not negate their function as a literary pair. The beatitudes of Matt 5 and the woes of Matt 23 serve as brackets around the conflict between Jesus and his opponents that accelerates throughout the narrative. The makarisms open Jesus' first teaching block, the Sermon on the Mount, which describes the ethics of the kingdom. The woes come at the start of the final teaching block in Matthew and at the end of Jesus' public ministry. Although the woes are addressed *to* the scribes and Pharisees, they are not *for* them; Jesus' judgment of his opponents has been rendered. Instead Matt 23:1 indicates that Jesus is speaking to the crowds to offer them one final chance to enter into discipleship and reject the hypocrisy of the scribes and Pharisees. The crowds are mentioned for the first time in Matt 4:25, just before the dispositions

[11] On the view that righteousness in Matthew refers to right conduct, see Benno Przybylski, *Righteousness in Matthew and His World of Thought*, SNTSMS 41 (Cambridge: Cambridge University Press, 1980).

[12] Pennington, *Sermon*, 91.

[13] Roland Deines, "Not the Law but the Messiah: Law and Righteousness in the Gospel of Matthew—An Ongoing Debate," in *Built upon the Rock: Studies in the Gospel of Matthew*, ed. Daniel M. Gurtner and John Nolland (Grand Rapids: Eerdmans, 2008), 80–81.

[14] This point, that the leaders of the Jewish people are presented in Matt 23 as the antithesis of Jesus' disciples, is made by Sjef van Tilborg, *The Jewish Leaders in Matthew* (Leiden: Brill, 1972), 26, 98, and Garland, *Intention*, 118.

of the makarisms are revealed, but the last time Jesus addresses this group is here, in Matt 23:1. Jesus addresses the crowds and the disciples when pronouncing woes against his opponents, but hereafter he only directly addresses his disciples (Matt 24:1, 3; 26:1, 8, 10, 20–21, 26, 31, 36, 38, 45). K. C. Hanson argues that this places an *inclusio* around Jesus' public ministry; there is an antithetical character to the makarisms and woes that encapsulates Jesus' entire ministry toward offering the crowds two competing visions of righteousness. True disciples will be "sons of God" (Matt 5:9), but the scribes and Pharisees are instead "sons of hell" (Matt 23:15).[15] Jesus' judgments against his opponents are tremors of the coming climax of the conflict and the social upheaval Jesus faces in his final week. The crowds must choose, and once the final pronouncement of woes has been made, Jesus focuses on his disciples through his final block of teaching (Matt 24–25) and the final portions of the narrative (Matt 26–28).[16]

15 K. C. Hanson, "How Honorable! How Shameful! A Cultural Analysis of Matthew's Makarisms and Reproaches," *Semeia* 68 (1994): 81–111.

16 Pennington, *Sermon*, 143, "The hearing, understanding, and obeying moves one from being part of the crowd to being a disciple." There is the matter of the crowds' reaction to Jesus in Matt 27:20; the Jewish leaders are portrayed as persuading the crowds in their favor. Matthias Konradt, *Israel, Church, and the Gentiles in the Gospel of Matthew*, trans. Kathleen Ess (Waco, Tex.: Baylor University Press, 2014), 159–66, makes a careful distinction between the crowds in Jerusalem versus the crowds Jesus interacted with more often throughout the narrative. The exception of 27:20 does not invalidate the general rule that the crowds are viewed positively in Matthew. The crowds in the passion narrative serve as a cautionary tale of those who allow themselves to be convinced by the failed Jewish leaders and therefore follow the wrong path.

2

The Character of Jesus' Beatitudes in Matthew

μακάριος appears seventy times in the LXX. It is the standard rendering of אשׁרי (*'ašrê*), which refers to a state of being blessed, happy, or fortunate.[1] Makarisms have their foundation in wisdom texts,[2] where they initially appeared as single sentences or groupings of two, referring mainly to those who have a right relationship with God,[3] and offering earthly blessings, prosperity, and a wise life to those who trust in God and keep his commandments.[4] While makarisms continued to appear in wisdom

[1] See Eugene H. Merrill, "אשׁר," in *NIDOTTE*, ed. William A. VanGemeren (Grand Rapids: Zondervan, 1997), 1:561. The LXX, or Septuagint, is the earliest Greek translation of the Hebrew Bible. It consists of the Greek texts of Israel's Scriptures (commonly referred to as the Old Testament in a Christian context) that served as the primary literary texts for the writers of the New Testament, but the New Testament writers often show signs of being aware of the Hebrew version, so they likely would have had knowledge of many of the Hebrew terms that served as the theological background for the Greek renderings. Understanding the Hebrew terminology behind their Greek translations provides information about how the Hebrew Bible was understood at the time the LXX translators were working, which then provides helpful information regarding what the New Testament writers might have meant by the use of certain terms. See Karen H. Jobes and Moisés Silva, *Invitation to the Septuagint* (Grand Rapids: Baker Academic, 2015), 4–5.

[2] Especially the Psalms (twenty-five times) and Sirach (eleven times). Cf. Sir 14:1–2, 20–27; 25:8–9.

[3] See "μακάριος," in *NIDNTTE*, 2nd ed., ed. Moisés Silva (Grand Rapids: Zondervan, 2014), 3:207.

[4] See Klaus Koch, *The Growth of the Biblical Tradition: The Form-Critical Method* (London: Adam & Charles Black, 1969), 7, who states that makarisms in the wisdom literature of the Hebrew Bible refer to "worldly well-being" for those who live in "conformity with the principles prescribed by God and the wise." See also Robert A. Guelich, "The Matthean Beatitudes: 'Entrance Requirements' or

texts in the Second Temple period, they increasingly began appearing in prophetic-apocalyptic contexts as well. Klaus Koch states that prophetic-apocalyptic beatitudes are directed at those who will be saved in the last judgment "and who will participate in the new world because they have remained true to their faith."[5] Whereas wisdom makarisms are focused on ethics and human flourishing, the prophetic-apocalyptic makarisms are focused on consolation and assurance through a future reversal of unfortunate circumstances.[6]

That makarisms in Jewish tradition are found in varied contexts has prompted scholars to evaluate the form and content of Matthew's and Luke's lists. Do these beatitudes call the reader/hearer to a life of flourishing and ethical conduct, cultivating certain dispositions or behaviors? Or do they describe downtrodden and struggling people and offer consolation and the hope of rescue in the future age?[7] Most scholars argue that Luke's list fits the prophetic-apocalyptic style in both form and content. This includes Luke's second-person construction, its direct address to people in specific situations (as opposed to addressing humankind in general), and a more obvious reversal of unfortunate conditions (poverty, hunger, weeping, persecution).[8] Luke's beatitudes were written to offer confidence that for the forlorn, earthly misfortunes will be reversed in the new age.[9]

The character of Matthew's beatitudes is harder to pin down. Their form is not easily placed within either wisdom or prophetic-apocalyptic

---

Eschatological Blessings?" *JBL* 95 (1976): 416–17, and Korinna Zamfir, "Who Are (the) Blessed? Reflections on the Relecture of the Beatitudes in the New Testament and the Apocrypha," *SS* 5 (2007): 75–100, especially 78.

5 Koch, *Growth*, 7, refers to these as "apocalyptic blessing," and cites Dan 12:12; 1 En 81:4, 82:4; 2 Bar 10:6, 11:6, 14:10; Tobit 13:14; Ps. Sol. 14:26, 17:50, 18:6; 2 En 42:6–14, 52:1–16.

6 Thinking about "wisdom" and "apocalyptic" as "genre" can be misleading. In many cases, it is better to think of these as styles or modes of discourse rather than genres of entire texts. Typically, wisdom includes writings that seek to instill knowledge and provide a foundation for a flourishing life. Apocalyptic material often concerns the supernatural world, promises or descriptions of future events, declarations concerning the reign of God, dualistic descriptions of good and evil, and a focus on divine revelation rather than worldly wisdom.

7 For an early such examination, see Julius Wellhausen, *Das Evangelium Matthaei: Übersetzt und Erklärt* (Berlin: Georg Reimer, 1904), 12–16.

8 See Eduard Schweizer, "Formgeschichtliches zu den Seligpreisungen Jesu," *NTS* 19 (1973): 121–26, and Guelich, "Matthean Beatitudes," 417–19.

9 See Thomas Hoyt Jr., "The Poor/Rich Theme in the Beatitudes," *JRT* 37 (1980): 31–41, especially 37.

traditions. Matthew's list appears to preserve an element of eschatological focus in the makarisms it shares with Luke, but its third-person address, elaboration of lines (e.g., "poor in spirit" rather than "poor"), and aspects of virtue instruction also places Matthew's beatitudes in the path of wisdom instruction.[10] When compared with other beatitudes throughout Jewish tradition, Matthew's list is unique in that it shows affinities with both wisdom and eschatology and features a convergence of the two traditions.[11] Rather than a direct address to people in a static condition, Matthew's third person construction serves as a call for respondents to a future kingdom that has broken into the present and is available to those who embody Jesus' ideals. Luke's concern for the poor and hungry is recalibrated as a call for meek peacemakers to be pure of heart and hunger for righteousness.

Although Matthew's approach is idiosyncratic, many scholars still place the Matthean beatitudes into one of two categories: either they describe entrance requirements for the kingdom (ethical) or eschatological blessings/reversals in the midst of unfortunate circumstances (apocalyptic). Recent trends have argued that Luke fits nicely into the apocalyptic tradition, and that Matthew "ethicized" Luke's makarisms, modifying them to include wisdom instruction.[12] Rather than reversing the fortunes of Luke's "poor," Matthew's "poor in spirit" became an ideal to be emulated.[13] For many years, entrance requirements to the kingdom and eschatological reversals were the only two options that scholars entertained, though recent years have seen more nuances brought into the discussion.[14] There are now at least seven major possibilities addressed in

[10] See Hans Windisch, *The Meaning of the Sermon on the Mount* (Philadelphia: Westminster, 1951), 175–76, who argues that Matthew's first four makarisms refer to the hope of salvation in the age to come, and the second set of four refers to a religious attitude in line with wisdom instruction. On the relationship between wisdom and eschatology in Matthew's beatitudes, see also Hans Dieter Betz, *Essays on the Sermon on the Mount*, trans. L. L. Welborn (1985; repr., Minneapolis: Fortress, 2009), 17–36; Joachim Gnilka, *Das Matthäus-Evangelium* I, HTK I/1 (Freiburg: Herder, 1986), 116–17; and Georg Strecker, "Die Makarismen der Bergpredigt," *NTS* 17 (1970–71): 255–75.

[11] See Eduard Schweizer, *The Good News according to Matthew* (Atlanta: John Knox, 1975), 81.

[12] Ulrich Luz, *Matthew 1–7*, Hermeneia (Minneapolis: Fortress, 2007), 190.

[13] See the discussion in W. D. Davies and D. C. Allison, *Matthew 1–7*, ICC (London: T&T Clark, 1988), 439–40.

[14] Jonathan T. Pennington, *The Sermon on the Mount and Human Flourishing: A Theological Commentary* (Grand Rapids: Baker Academic, 2017), 62,

recent scholarship integrating form and content toward interpreting the Matthean beatitudes. A brief description of each of these seven possibilities is helpful toward establishing the character of Matthew's list.

1. Entrance Requirements

Proponents of this view argue that Matthew's beatitudes refer to ethics. However, the beatitudes are not simply ethical exhortations; they list requirements for those who wish to enter the kingdom of heaven.[15] The list functions as a standard of initiation, a way of getting into the community of Jesus' disciples, and details the sort of righteousness that describes the total makeup of the kingdom community. The beatitudes establish a social consciousness, and they set parameters for those who pursue greater righteousness.

2. Eschatological Reversals

Rather than ethical standards for the kingdom, many scholars argue that Matthew's beatitudes promise future blessings through the eschatological reversal of negative personal and social circumstances.[16] Advocates of this view allow that some of the beatitudes include implied ethical expectations, such as purity in heart (5:8) and peacemaking (5:9), but that others, such as mourning (5:4) and persecution (5:10), describe hardship, and the

---

recognizes the problems in limiting our scope to a sharp distinction between entrance requirements and eschatological blessings. Calling for more nuance, Pennington argues that this simple dichotomy, "like most dichotomies in complex situations, proves to be false." Scholars who appear to entertain only these two options for Matthew's makarisms include Davies and Allison, *Matthew 1–7*, 439; Guelich, "Matthean Beatitudes," 419; Charles H. Talbert, *Reading the Sermon on the Mount: Character Formation and Decision Making in Matthew 5–7* (Grand Rapids: Baker Academic, 2004), 47; Warren Carter, "Narrative/Literary Approaches to Matthean Theology: The 'Reign of the Heavens' as an Example (Mt 4:17–5:12)," *JSNT* 67 (1997): 25. See also C. H. Dodd, *More New Testament Studies* (Manchester: Manchester University Press, 1968), 4–5, who argues that Luke's makarisms "announce an impending reversal of conditions," while Matthew's list "brings exclusively into relief the ethical quality of the martyr's sufferings."

[15] On this view, see Betz, *Essays*, 26–34; Windisch, *Meaning*, 26–27, 87–88; Georg Strecker, *The Sermon on the Mount: An Exegetical Commentary* (Edinburgh: T&T Clark, 1988), 25–61; and Hoyt, "Poor/Rich," 32.

[16] See, for example, Leonhard Goppelt, *The Theology of the New Testament*, vol. 1: *The Ministry of Jesus in Its Theological Significance* (Grand Rapids: Eerdmans, 1981), 68; Davies and Allison, *Matthew 1–7*, 440; and Talbert, *Reading*, 47.

overall tenor of the beatitudes is to provide hope for a future where all that is wrong will be made right, where the poor, the sick, the helpless, and the oppressed will be exalted and vindicated.[17] Matthew's beatitudes do not contain any actual commands until 5:11–12, where the reader/hearer is called to rejoice and be glad, and they close with the reality of persecution as a state of suffering—a condition that cannot easily be entered into through intentional effort. Rather than requirements to enter the kingdom and the community of Jesus' disciples, the beatitudes serve to bless the disciples as they are already—as those living out the difficulties of day-to-day life and need hope for the eschatological reversal of their misfortune.[18] In this view, the first clauses of the makarisms describe the burdens of those who struggle in this life, and the second clauses proffer hope that God will intervene to overturn the broken values of the present world.[19] The second clauses are bracketed by the promise of the kingdom (Matt 5:3, 10), which is conveyed in the present tense: although the reward is yet future, it is secured because the kingdom already belongs to the blessed.[20] The present kingdom, made manifest in the life of Jesus, is the guarantee that God's promises for the future are trustworthy.

Davies and Allison, who are prominent advocates for this view, argue for an important supporting feature. They point out that Matthew's beatitudes are sandwiched between Matt 4:23–5:2, in which Jesus heals before he instructs, and 5:13–16, which separates the beatitudes from the explicit commands of the rest of the Sermon on the Mount. In their view, this structure suggests that the function of the beatitudes is to "put grace before imperative, greeting before confrontation, blessing before demand" and that the comforting words of the beatitudes serve as compensation to those who are about to be confronted with the realities of

17 Mark Allan Powell, "Matthew's Beatitudes: Reversals and Rewards of the Kingdom," *CBQ* 58 (1996): 460–79, splits Matthew's list into two stanzas of four makarisms each and argues that the first four promise eschatological reversals.

18 Davies and Allison, *Matthew 1–7*, 439–40.

19 So Günther Bornkamm, *Jesus of Nazareth* (London: Hodder & Stoughton, 1960), 76, the audience of the beatitudes are "beggars before God," who "do not fit into the structure of the world and therefore are rejected by the world"; and Norman Perrin, *The Kingdom of God in the Teaching of Jesus* (London: SCM Press, 1963), 85, the beatitudes "could be pictured as the complete reversal of the existing order of things."

20 Allison, *Sermon*, 42.

kingdom-oriented commitment described by the rest of the sermon.[21] This argument, that God's favor is upon the disciples, is similar to the next interpretive option, which views Matthew's beatitudes as neither ethics nor reversals but as descriptions of God's good favor toward his people.

3. Evidence of God's Favor

This position is similar to the eschatological reversals view. Both views reject the idea that the first clauses of Matthew's makarisms present "entrance requirements" into the kingdom of God, both views understand the second clauses as "divine passives" that place the reader/hearer under the grace of God, and both views understand God's favor as the motivating factor in the reception of his blessings. However, advocates of the "evidence of God's favor" perspective argue that the main point of the beatitudes is neither ethics nor eschatological reversals, but rather, the central point is that the readers/hearers understand that because Jesus has opened new pathways for a relationship with God, they have God's good favor upon them and a right and secure position as his children. The beatitudes are less concerned with the precise nature of a person's status or cultural condition than with the condition of being loved and blessed by God as a member of the covenant community. The beatitudes have an ethical flavor, but that is not their primary characteristic; rather than describing entrance requirements, they describe the character and conduct of those who have already been accepted by God and presented as Jesus' disciples. The disciples are qualified for rewards based on God's grace, and therefore they will live ethically in light of their position. Jesus brings the eschatological future into the present and, with it, the hopeful expectation of the realization of God's promises. This new kingdom reality motivates kingdom-oriented conduct and enables one to do God's will.[22]

[21] See Davies and Allison, *Matthew 1–7*, 440, and Dale C. Allison, *The Sermon on the Mount: Inspiring the Moral Imagination* (New York: Crossroad, 1999), 44.

[22] Advocates of this view embrace either the ethical aspects of the beatitudes or the apocalyptic, or both, but emphasize these characteristics differently. The important thing about their presentation is that God's grace and favor toward his people take precedence over all other considerations. The beatitudes are relational and describe the state of those who are "in" already. In this case the first clauses could describe ethical exhortations for disciples or unfortunate circumstances to be reversed. See Guelich, "Matthean Beatitudes," 429–30; Donald A. Hagner, *Matthew 1–13*, WBC 33A (Dallas: Word, 1993), 91; Charles L. Quarles, *Sermon on the Mount: Christ's Message to the*

4. The Wages of the Imminent Kingdom

Advocates of this view argue that Jesus' entire conception of ethics, including the beatitudes, is driven by the idea that repentance prepares one for the imminent coming of the kingdom. As Albert Schweitzer writes, "Whosoever, therefore, preached the nearness of the kingdom must also teach the righteousness pertaining to the kingdom."[23] The kingdom is close, and the beatitudes describe the character and conduct of those who will be found to belong to it. A similar view is argued by Nathan Eubank,[24] who recognizes the ethical scope of Matthew's list and illustrates how the beatitudes correspond to ethical demands made in the rest of the narrative (e.g., the poor in spirit and meek in Matt 5:3, 5 corresponds to the need to become childlike in 18:1–4 and renounce possessions in 19:16–30). The beatitudes proclaim blessedness for those who follow Jesus' teachings, so their ethical dimensions make it unlikely that Matthew's writer had simple consolations in mind. However, the beatitudes are not imperatives, so the usual dichotomy between ethical demands and eschatological reversals does not properly explain their function.

Eubank reads the beatitudes through the summary of Jesus' teaching found in Matt 4:17, "Repent, for the kingdom of heaven has come near." The nearness of the kingdom introduces a new situation that requires a specific response based on the times. The beatitudes "describe the way of life that is necessary in light of the nearness of the kingdom." Blessedness is proclaimed for those who follow Jesus' teaching and example, but they are pronounced blessed not because of what they do but because of what they receive; "the beatitudes quiver with apocalyptic expectation." God's will is about to be done on earth as it is in heaven, which inaugurates the kingdom and brings with it mercy, comfort, and so forth. Therefore, the righteous will be repaid for living in light of the nearness of the kingdom.

Modern Church (Nashville: B&H Publishing, 2011), 39–44; Carl R. Holladay, "The Beatitudes: Happiness and the Kingdom of God," in *The Bible and the Pursuit of Happiness*, ed. Brent A. Strawn (Oxford: Oxford University Press, 2012), 141–68; and Scot McKnight, *Sermon on the Mount*, SGBC (Grand Rapids: Zondervan, 2013), 36.

[23] Albert Schweitzer, *The Mystery of the Kingdom of God: The Secret of Jesus' Messiahship and Passion*, trans. Walter Lowrie (Amherst, N.Y.: Prometheus, 1985), 53–55.

[24] Nathan Eubank, *Wages of Cross-Bearing and Debt of Sin: The Economy of Heaven in Matthew's Gospel*, BZNW (Berlin: De Gruyter, 2013), 74–77.

Eubank highlights the promise of wages in Matt 5:12.[25] Jesus endures persecution, and those who follow him in this "possess wages in the heavens that are about to be repaid by God."[26] In Eubank's view, other views regarding the beatitudes are insufficient because they do not take into account the direct circumstances faced by Jesus' followers. Ethical demands are in view, but the nearness of the kingdom dictates which demands are appropriate for the immediate state of affairs.

5. Virtue-Ethics

As Eklund describes, some form of a virtue-ethics approach has been around since the earliest times of Matthean interpretation.[27] For example, the Didache (ca. 95–100), which likely used Matthew as a source,[28] records Matt 5:5 in the form of a command: "And be meek, since the meek will inherit the earth" (Did 3:7). This interpretation moves beyond implicit exhortation and into the realm of explicit expectation. Meekness is not a circumstance to be avoided but a virtuous disposition to be pursued.[29] Eklund points out that prior to the eighteenth century, it is rare to find interpreters who did not believe that the beatitudes referred to virtues. However, these virtues were not "requirements" for entrance into the kingdom, but rather they described "the path to true happiness and flourishing laid down by God."[30] Matthew's beatitudes served as invitations to a Christ-patterned way of life that led to true well-being.

[25] The Greek term here is μισθός (*misthos*), usually translated as "rewards." Eubank, *Wages*, 68, argues that the term in Matthew refers to a divine recompense for those who follow Jesus and is therefore a "wage" rather than a reward.

[26] That rewards are not just a comfort to sufferers but an actual repayment for suffering is also argued by Martin Luther, *Luther's Works*, vol. 21: *The Sermon on the Mount*, ed. Jaroslav Pelikan (St. Louis, Mo.: Concordia, 1956), 292.

[27] Rebekah Eklund, *The Beatitudes through the Ages* (Grand Rapids: Eerdmans, 2021), 35.

[28] Several theories regarding the relationship between Matthew and the Didache have been proposed. The problem is complex, but the theory that the writer(s) of the Didache knew and used Matthew's Gospel is still the best accounting of the evidence. See, for example, Christopher M. Tuckett, "Synoptic Tradition in the Didache," in *The Didache in Modern Research*, ed. Jonathan A. Draper (Leiden: Brill, 1996), 92–128.

[29] Similarly, see 2 En 50:2, "Live in meekness for the number of your days, so that you may inherit the endless age that is coming."

[30] Eklund, *Beatitudes*, 35.

Pennington is a recent, persuasive advocate of the virtue-ethics perspective. He analyzes the beatitudes through the nexus of two cultural horizons—Jewish and Greco-Roman—and argues that the terms and ideas in Matthew's list reflect a virtue-ethics background from within both traditions. Concerning the Jewish background, Pennington argues that the old dichotomy between makarisms found in the wisdom writings and those found in prophetic writings is irrelevant to the character of Jesus' beatitudes in Matthew. In Israel's historical, literary, and theological story, both the wisdom and prophetic writings aimed at the same basic goal: to describe the trustworthiness of God to bring about the redemption of his people and lead them into a flourishing life.[31] By the Second Temple period, wisdom and eschatological motifs began integrating into new strands of tradition, where wisdom's concern for human flourishing and practical instruction was paired with eschatology's hope for restoration.[32] This bond served to reinforce moral instruction through the outlook of the end of the age. The anticipation of God's good future galvanized God's people and stimulated their commitment toward repentance and a life of virtue. By the time of the first century, there had already been a cross-pollination between wisdom and prophetic traditions to form hybrid traditions where these backgrounds informed each other and could no longer be pulled apart or easily distinguished. These traditions had become "inextricably interwoven"[33] so that human flourishing in the present was informed by the future in-breaking of God to reverse all in the world that had been brought to ruin. Therefore, the dichotomy between ethical demands and eschatological reversals is too rigid. Matthew's version of Jesus' beatitudes reflects this cross-pollination and refers to virtue formation inspired by eschatological hope.[34]

31 Pennington, *Sermon*, 25, on this point cites Exod 15:1–18; Isa 51:3, 11; 52:7; 54:10; 55:12–13; 65:17–25; 66:12; Ezek 34:25; 36:35; 37:26.

32 This is especially true of 4QInstruction, 1 Enoch, and certain texts found among the Dead Sea Scrolls. For a discussion on the trajectories of wisdom and apocalyptic in the Second Temple period and the integration of the two strands of tradition into a hybrid tradition, see my *God's Will and Testament: Inheritance in the Gospel of Matthew and Jewish Tradition* (Waco, Tex.: Baylor University Press, 2021), 6–18.

33 Pennington, *Sermon*, 63

34 Pennington, *Sermon*, 66, the entire Sermon on the Mount "presents itself as an eschatological wisdom teaching on virtue." That Matthew's Gospel features a prolific use of both wisdom and apocalyptic motifs and themes has been

Pennington argues that Greco-Roman ideas of virtue-ethics are also present in Matthew's beatitudes. One key point of connection is the relationship between the term μακάριος with the term τέλειος (*teleios*), which is found in Matt 5:48. τέλειος in Matt 5:48 is usually translated "perfect"[35]—Jesus calls his disciples to "be perfect, therefore, as your heavenly Father is perfect." However, τέλειος is a Greek ethics term that, rather than perfection as we might think of it today, often connotes the concepts of wholeness and completion. Many New Testament scholars have noted the connection between these terms and another Greek virtue-ethics term, εὐδαιμονία (*eudaimonia*), which is not found in the New Testament. This term connotes the idea of human flourishing.[36] Pennington argues effectively that these three terms—μακάριος, τέλειος, and εὐδαιμονία—all share common connotations and were used to illustrate the same basic ideas regarding the intentional pursuit of virtue and learned practical wisdom.[37]

---

argued by many scholars, although with different nuances and emphases. See, for example, M. Jack Suggs, *Wisdom, Christology and Law in Matthew's Gospel* (Cambridge, Mass.: Harvard University Press, 1970); Daniel Marguerat, *Le jugement dans l'évangile de Matthieu* (Geneva: Labor et Fides, 1981); Donald Hagner, "Apocalyptic Motifs in the Gospel of Matthew: Continuity and Discontinuity," *HBT* 7 (1985): 53–82; Celia Deutsch, "Wisdom in Matthew: Transformation of a Symbol," *NovT* 32 (1990): 13–47; Christopher Rowland, "Apocalyptic, the Poor, and the Gospel of Matthew," *JTS* 45 (1994): 504–18; David C. Sim, *Apocalyptic Eschatology in the Gospel of Matthew* (Cambridge: Cambridge University Press, 1996); John Kampen, "Aspects of Wisdom in the Gospel of Matthew in Light of the New Qumran Evidence," in *Sapiential, Liturgical and Poetical Texts from Qumran*, ed. Daniel K. Falk, Florentino García Martínez, and Eileen Schuller (Leiden: Brill, 2000), 227–39; Ben Witherington III, *Matthew* (Macon, Ga.: Smyth & Helwys, 2006); Grant Macaskill, *Revealed Wisdom and Inaugurated Eschatology in Ancient Judaism and Early Christianity*, SJSJ 115 (Leiden: Brill, 2007), 253–58; Daniel M. Gurtner, "Interpreting Apocalyptic Symbolism in the Gospel of Matthew," *BBR* 22 (2012): 525–45.

35 RSV, NRSV, NIV, ESV, KJV, NLT.

36 See, for example, Betz, *Essays*, 32. Also Luz, *Matthew 1–7*, 190, who suggests that the relationship between μακάριος and εὐδαιμονία is so close that the two terms can hardly be distinguished one from the other. William C. Mattison III, "The Beatitudes and Moral Theology: A Virtue-Ethics Approach," *Nova et Vetera* (English ed.) 11 (2013): 822–23, notes the connection between μακάριος and εὐδαιμονία and argues that for anyone schooled in classical culture, they would have understood the makarisms "in the context of the enduring question of how to live a happy life."

37 Pennington, *Sermon*, 31–35.

According to Pennington, in both traditions, the Jewish wisdom-apocalyptic and Greco-Roman virtue traditions, the circumstances in which a person finds themselves are less important than the choices they make. Living a life of virtue leads to flourishing. In ancient Jewish texts, it is God alone who is tasked with conquering evil and bringing restoration to his people, but his people are called to live in alignment with his will. Jesus' beatitudes in Matthew reflect this dynamic and therefore render the dichotomy between wisdom and eschatology problematic. Jesus' beatitudes reflect both a coming restorative kingdom *and* the expectation that ideal disciples will live presently in light of the coming future restoration. As Pennington writes, "Jesus is offering a vision for a way of being in the world that will result in true human flourishing, precisely in the context of forward-looking faith in God eventually setting the world to rights."[38] This makes the best sense of the relationship between the makarisms' first and second clauses. The first clauses of each makarism describe those who flourish in the kingdom, and it is they who stand to receive the eschatological blessings of the second clauses.[39] The makarisms are not "entrance requirements," but they are still ethical. They are not merely an "evidence of God's favor" because they describe dispositions that must be cultivated in order to thrive. They do not describe "eschatological reversals" because it's precisely those who cultivate these dispositions who stand to be rewarded with God's good blessings.

6. Jesus the Priest

Nicholas Perrin makes the argument that Jesus saw himself as the eschatological high priest, who subordinated his royal identity to his priestly one, and that Jesus identified his movement as a priestly movement.[40] It is in this frame that Perrin interprets the beatitudes. Emphasizing that the jubilary text of Isa 61 serves as a key intertextual source for Matthew's list, that jubilee invokes the Day of Atonement, and that the Day of Atonement featured the delivery of the Aaronic blessing, Perrin argues that Jesus offered the beatitudes as an Aaronic blessing. Since Jesus serves as the priest who has surpassed Aaron, he updates the Aaronic blessing and declares the final jubilee, as would be the natural prerogative of his office as high priest.[41]

38 Pennington, *Sermon*, 63–64.

39 Pennington, *Sermon*, 66.

40 Nicholas Perrin, *Jesus the Priest* (Grand Rapids: Baker Academic, 2018), 7–13.

41 Perrin, *Jesus*, 133–34.

Perrin's arguments require that Matthew's writer(s) made the connection from Isa 61 to the Day of Atonement, to the Aaronic blessings, without making these connections either explicit or even helpfully implicit in the internal logic of his text. Although possible, this is far from certain. However, setting aside this difficulty, Perrin also relies on a view that Matthew's makarisms are in fact blessings, which are paired with corresponding curses, and he notes parallels with passages such as Num 6:23–29 and Deut 10:8.[42] If "blessed" is not the best translation of μακάριος and the makarisms do not actually function as blessings, then Perrin's argument is dealt a fatal blow. The translation of μακάριος is discussed below.

The six interpretive options discussed above all tend to present the beatitudes as a harmonious unit. However, there are two further options that should be mentioned that view the beatitudes as a complex list lacking uniformity. According to these two options, Matthew's list features different kinds of beatitudes, and so the whole list cannot be cleanly categorized by the five options discussed so far. The first of these options breaks the beatitudes into stanzas, while the second views each makarism individually and disregards the notion of a consistent thematic formula for the whole list.

7. Dividing the Beatitudes into Stanzas

Several options have been presented regarding the possibility that Matthew's beatitudes are a coherent, structured, and uniform arrangement but that they are designed with different stanzas that each have their own character and intent. The most common of these options requires that Matthew's list be divided into two stanzas of four beatitudes each, for a total of eight beatitudes. In this view, the phrase "kingdom of heaven" in Matt 5:3 and 10 form an *inclusio* around the full list, which sets Matt 5:3–10 as the limit of the structure and places 5:11–12 outside of it as an extension of the last beatitude. The first stanza is made up of Matt 5:3–6, and the second is made up of 5:7–10. Several features are addressed by those who support this two-stanza structure:

(1) Each stanza possesses exactly thirty-six words in Greek, suggesting an intentional, symmetrical poetic structure.

(2) The last beatitude in each stanza honors righteousness.

> 5:6—those who hunger and thirst for righteousness
> 5:10—those who are persecuted for righteousness' sake

[42] Perrin, *Jesus*, 132.

(3) In the first stanza, the subject in each of the first clauses is represented by a word that begins with the Greek letter π (*pi*), suggesting a poetic unity behind the character of these four beatitudes:

πτωχός (*ptochos*) = poor
πενθέω (*pentheo*) = mourn
πραΰς (*praus*) = meek
πεινάω (*peinao*) = hunger

Depending on one's interpretation, the two stanzas can be cleanly divided into sets of beatitudes that share a common purpose. In one interpretation, the first stanza refers to unfortunate circumstances to be reversed by God, while the second refers to the ethical dispositions that disciples must cultivate and the rewards offered to the virtuous.[43] In another reading, the first stanza refers to one's disposition toward God, while the second refers to one's demeanor toward others.[44]

This two-stanza model is insightful at points. The poetic structure of the eight beatitudes in Matt 5:3–10 is unmistakable. However, there is a fundamental problem with this approach—it requires precisely eight beatitudes. Allison makes a persuasive argument that Matthew's list features nine makarisms rather than eight.[45] Although it is the case that only the first eight feature the simple two-clause structure, 5:11 still begins with a ninth occurrence of μακάριος, indicating a ninth makarism in the list. Furthermore, Allison provides several examples of Jewish and Christian texts that feature a long, irregular member of a series to add emphasis to the final member.[46] Although the ninth beatitude disrupts the tidiness of the rest of the list, its awkwardness is not uncommon.

Other multistanza approaches have tried to account for Matthew's beatitudes featuring nine makarisms rather than eight. For example, Frederick Dale Bruner argues for three uneven stanzas. In this view, the first four beatitudes refer to need, the next three to acts of service, and the

43 See Powell, "Matthew's Beatitudes," 460.

44 See David E. Garland, *Reading Matthew: A Literary and Theological Commentary on the First Gospel* (New York: Crossroad, 1993), 54.

45 In fact, there is a wide variety of opinions regarding the number of beatitudes in Matthew, from as few as four to as many as ten. For a summary of the options, see Eklund, *Beatitudes*, 42–47.

46 Allison, *Sermon*, 29, lists 4Q525; 1 En 99:10–15; Matt 2:1–16, 23:13–36; Luke 6:24–26, 37–38; 1 Clem 13:2; Polycarp, *Letter* 2.3; Did 1:3–5; Acts of Paul and Thecla 5–6; 2 En 42:6–14 J.

final two refer to persecution and future reward.[47] Scot McKnight argues for an even three-stanza structure, where the first three beatitudes refer to humility, the second three refer to justice, and the last three refer to peace.[48] Before assessing these options, it is important to mention one last possibility—that Matthew's beatitudes feature no structure at all.

8. No Standard Structure

Typical of this position is Luz, who argues that Matthew's beatitudes do not possess a uniform character because they did not originate from the same sources. Luz argues that Matt 5:3, 4, and 6 are the most original and they refer to eschatological reversal of conditions. The remaining makarisms were added by Matthew's writer and were compiled from various sources; therefore, they have no unified meaning and are best viewed independently.[49]

Conclusions

The diversity of options elucidates the interpretive challenges and illustrates the point made in the introduction to this book: even when we have a stable text, all texts need to be interpreted, and this variable element is both assisted and disrupted by three layers of context. First, there is the context of the interpreter, who must navigate their own environment to analyze a text through its own historical, literary, narrative, and theological circumstances. Then there is the context of Matthew's writer, which is not identical to yet a third contextual layer, being that of Jesus and the events that Matthew's writer describes. In other words, the careful reader must interpret Matthew's interpretation of Jesus, knowing that Matthew's writer was also influenced by a particular cultural milieu and social circumstances. Although this interpretive matrix introduces considerable difficulties into the act and art of interpretation, I would argue that the varied perspectives of the beatitudes presented over the years have actually brought more clarity than confusion. The insights of readers from varied backgrounds and perspectives allows for a compounding and developing inventory of possibilities, and the plurality of options allows subsequent readers to find common threads in the interpretive discussions that help make sense of what is, in the case of Matthew's beatitudes, a deceptively complex passage. It is precisely the common threads in the various options

[47] Frederick Dale Bruner, *Matthew: A Commentary*, vol. 1: *The Christbook, Matthew 1–12* (Grand Rapids: Eerdmans, 2004), 155–56.

[48] McKnight, *Sermon*, 37–38.

[49] Luz, *Matthew 1–7*, 186–90.

discussed here that have convinced me that a hybrid of three approaches best reflects the dynamism of Jesus' words and the narrative and linguistic features of Matthew's version.

Matthew's emphasis of Jesus' concern for righteousness is the deciding factor on my interpretation of the beatitudes. In contrast to Mark and Luke, Matthew is particularly fond of righteousness and its word group, and as I discussed above in relationship to Matthew's structure, the concepts of right living and discipleship are central to Jesus' concerns in the First Gospel. Jesus' followers are called to be salt and light (Matt 5:13–16), to "shine before others," and they are to stand apart from the scribes and Pharisees by practicing a greater righteousness (Matt 5:20). God's grace certainly permeates the narrative as Jesus shows mercy to the crowds (Matt 4:23–25), but there is no grace-versus-works dichotomy in Matthew that forces us to choose between them. Matthew's beatitudes are an exposition on the nature of those who possess the kingdom, but there are no imperatives other than "rejoice and be glad" (Matt 5:12), so the list clearly does not function as entrance requirements into the kingdom. Matthew's beatitudes are not concerned with "how to get in." However, the abundance of virtue-ethics terminology makes it unlikely that the beatitudes only refer to unfortunate circumstances. My difficulty with the options discussed here for defining the character of Matthew's beatitudes is that they too often have difficulty fitting individual beatitudes into their structure, and they do not consider closely enough Matthew's concern with righteousness and discipleship, both in the Gospel as a whole and in the surrounding context.

It is in this way that the "evidence of God's favor" position also strikes me as insufficient. Prior to Jesus' teaching of the Sermon on the Mount, Jesus offers his first disciples a chance to "follow me" (δεῦτε ὀπίσω μου; *deute opisō mou*; Matt 4:19), and they leave their vocation to do so.[50] God's grace to the first disciples is proffered through Jesus when they are called to follow, and as they make the appropriate sacrifices, they are promised eschatological rewards as a result (Matt 5:3–12). Therefore, contained within the offer of following Jesus is God's grace in the form of *possibility*. Those who accept the call and follow Jesus and his teachings are then *described* by the virtuous dispositions contained within the makarisms,

[50] Jesus' call to "follow me" is made several times throughout Matthew (cf. Matt 8:22, 9:9, 10:38). The call to follow is made to the rich man in Matt 19:21 (δεῦρο ἀκολούθει μοι), and he does not respond favorably. The demand can be resisted and is understood as an offer to become a disciple of Jesus.

and it is to those so described that eschatological promises are made. God's grace does not *produce* righteousness as an inevitable result, but it does make obedience *possible* and *motivates* obedience to Jesus' teachings.

The virtue-ethics approach coupled with an eye toward eschatological renewal makes the best sense of the integrated threads of wisdom and eschatology, which incorporates the character of the disciples and the anticipation of eschatological rewards. The second clauses of the beatitudes call for a time when the dispositions of the first clauses will no longer be necessary; for a time when the humble will be exalted (Matt 23:12) and mourning will be no more (cf. Rev 21:4). The first clauses certainly describe virtues that are only necessary due to the grim conditions of a world far from God. But the aim for the disciples is not only that they will be blessed in the age to come but also that their hope will motivate their active participation with Jesus. The first clauses of the beatitudes might describe conditions only necessary on this side of heaven, but they are dispositions to be cultivated and embraced rather than lamented or feared. Of course, one must establish that phrases and terms such as "poor in spirit," "mourn," and "meek" refer to ethical dispositions, and the commentary in part 2 attempts to establish as much. But I'm convinced that in these beatitudes, Jesus is concerned with the character of those who follow him and the ways that his followers exceed the scribes and Pharisees in their obedience to God according to the standards of the kingdom.

While I posit that ideas from both the virtue-ethics approach and the eschatological renewal approach are equally necessary to fully appreciate the dynamics of Jesus' teaching, I am also convinced that the core of Schweitzer's imminency argument is correct, even if I disagree with many of the outer layers. The problems with Schweitzer's view are ably described by Perrin, who notes that in Schweitzer's own conception of the imminent kingdom, Jesus' beatitudes (and other ethical teachings besides) amount to little more than an "interim ethics"—temporary measures that are *only* relevant to a transitory period in the immediate aftermath of their proclamation. They are emergency tactics designed to navigate inevitable suffering for only a brief time. In Perrin's view, the ethics of Schweitzer's Jesus are "makeshift norms" with little to no relevance to Schweitzer's time, or ours, and are therefore consigned to theological irrelevance. As Perrin argues, Schweitzer's Jesus was motivated by "contingent crises," and the beatitudes only served to prepare those whose imminent expectations saw decisive fulfillment within a matter of months, rather than years, or even centuries.[51]

[51] Perrin, *Jesus*, 3.

Although I am convinced that Jesus intended his beatitudes (and his ethics more widely) to exhibit and maintain a potent and ongoing relevance for as long as it takes, until the ultimate renewal of all things, and that they serve as kingdom norms in any time and place, I am also convinced that a *posture* of imminent expectation was germane to Jesus' presentation and to the content of the beatitudes. Whether the consummation of the fullness of the kingdom took months or millennia, Jesus' disciples are to live in *preparation* for the imminent kingdom—*they are to live as though the kingdom will be fully consummated at any moment*. In this way, imminency is an important part of the interpretive matrix.

Take, as analogy, a baseball game with no outs and runners at first and third. In the early innings, the defense will typically line up their middle infielders at double play depth and surrender the run at third to clear the bases and "limit the damage." However, in the bottom of the ninth, this same strategy would lose the game, so the infielders are forced to stand at the edge of the infield grass, which limits one's reaction time on hard hit balls, in order to make a desperate play at the plate. The two-minute drill in a football game is a comparable analogy. If a team is down by one score or less and has limited time on the clock, they will have practiced an entirely different set of plays and a different pace of play in order to score as quickly as they can. Keeping up the pace and momentum of a two-minute offense would not be possible for an entire game, but in the final minutes, with everything on the line, this strategy becomes necessary. The beatitudes are an ethics for a discipleship community that lives every moment as though it's the bottom of the ninth or the final two minutes of a closely contested game.

There are passages in the New Testament that seem to suggest a slow and steady discipleship—one in which Jesus' followers have the space to settle into normative and formative patterns and cultivate embedded traditions and slowly won spheres of influence.[52] Discipleship is, in many ways, a habit-forming endeavor, and it often takes years of discipline to establish a Christlike cadence to life's daily rhythms. However, more common are passages that evince, if not an imminent consummation of the final kingdom, a posture of expectation to that effect. A disciple behaves not as one who is consumed with the precise timing of Jesus' return but as one who is eager and hopeful and who realizes that

[52] See, for example, 1 Thess 4:11–12, "to aspire to live quietly, to mind your own affairs, and to work with your hands, as we directed you, so that you may behave properly toward outsiders and be dependent on no one."

the stakes for Christ-patterned living are high. Whether we might call this a "posture of expectancy" or "cautious anticipation," ideal discipleship can be creative, calm, measured, patient, and self-controlled, but it is never not suspenseful.

This posture of expectancy is evident in the eschatologically oriented passages in Matthew's final discourse section. There is no uniformity to Matthew's depictions of final judgment (cf. Matt 13:41–42, 49; 16:27; 19:28–29; 24:9–14, 29–31; 25:31–46), but if there's one thing that's clear about the trilogy of parables in Matt 24:45–25:30, it's that they serve as a vision of accountability for the disciples for their own acts of service for the kingdom. The trilogy of parables serves as a warning to the disciples—the timing of the *Parousia* is uncertain, but the necessity for watchfulness regarding its imminence (24:36–44) heightens the need for the disciples to be diligent.[53] Following Jesus' teaching concerning the nearness of the kingdom (Matt 4:17), this same urgency is established prior to the teaching of the beatitudes, placing them within this same frame of expectation—suffering is inevitable (Matt 5:10–12), but there is a manner of flourishing that prepares ideal disciples for what's to come. The beatitudes have served faith communities well for centuries, but in their first instance they served as both ethical instruction and words of comfort for those facing imminent trials. As Perrin argues, Jesus' ethics implicate their hearers "in a crisis of decision, demanding urgent response." Therefore, there is "no room for aloof detachment or hedging deferment"[54]—the beatitudes are situated in a gospel rife with immediacy and calls for absolute self-surrender (cf. Matt 19:28–30).

Translating μακάριος

Now that we've reviewed the interpretive options regarding the character of the beatitudes, we're better prepared to discuss the translation issue surrounding μακάριος. Although "blessed" is still the way that μακάριος is translated the majority of the time,[55] it implies a divine favor by God

[53] See W. G. Kümmel, *Promise and Fulfilment: The Eschatological Message of Jesus* (London: SCM Press, 1961), 55, who argues of the parables in Matt 24:45–25:30 that "the undoubted meaning of this imagery is that the disciples must at all times be ready for the arrival of the Lord. . . . These parables are intended to urge preparedness for the day of the appearance of the Parousia which may occur at any time and is therefore pressing."

[54] Perrin, *Jesus*, 6.

[55] See, for example, Quarles, *Sermon*, 42; and McKnight, *Sermon*, 36.

and passivity on the part of the disciple that misses the ethical dimensions of Jesus' beatitudes. R. T. France points out that rather than the Hebrew term ברוך (*barak*), meaning "blessed by God," the Hebrew equivalent of μακάριος is אשרי, meaning "happy, fortunate."[56] This is an important distinction because in the Hebrew Bible, when אשרי is featured in makaristic formulas, it does not simply describe those who are blessed or happy in their circumstances but those who are in a happy state specifically due to their wise choices. Makarisms do not refer to wise choices themselves but are observations about those who make wise choices and flourish because of them.[57] Pennington states that due to the relationship between אשרי and μακάριος, "it becomes clear that something other than a pronouncement of divine blessing is at hand." Matthew is making an appeal "for what true well-being looks like in God's kingdom."[58]

Pennington argues that makarisms, when properly understood, do not function as blessings.[59] Instead makarisms (e.g., Ps 1) often function as implicit invitations to pursue wisdom and living a certain way.[60] This is highlighted by the relationship between makarisms and their corresponding negatives. In ancient Near Eastern literature, the corresponding negative to a blessing is a curse. However, makarisms are not contrasted with curses but rather with woes.[61] The relationship between Matthew's

56 R. T. France, *The Gospel of Matthew*, NICNT (Grand Rapids: Eerdmans, 2007), 160–61.

57 See Pennington, *Sermon*, 49; and K. C. Hanson, "How Honorable! How Shameful! A Cultural Analysis of Matthew's Makarisms and Reproaches," *Semeia* 68 (1994): 84.

58 Pennington, *Sermon*, 47. Similar is Craig S. Keener, *The Gospel of Matthew: A Socio-rhetorical Commentary* (Grand Rapids: Eerdmans, 2009), 165, who states that the makarisms declare, "It will go well with the one who . . . for that one shall receive."

59 Pennington, *Sermon*, 50. See also Hanson, "How Honorable!" 81–85, who argues that English Bible translations have blurred the distinction between blessings and makarisms. He provides a brief review of scholars who have failed to understand the distinction, and argues similarly to Pennington and France that אשרי and μακάριος are related to but distinct from the concept of blessing.

60 See, for example, Prov 3:13, "Happy are those who find wisdom, and those who get understanding."

61 See Hanson, "How Honorable!" 85–89, who analyzes the relationship between blessings and curses and offers numerous examples from the Hebrew Bible and Second Temple literature. Similar to Pennington, Hanson concludes that despite some important similarities, makarisms and woes function differently than blessings and curses.

makarisms and woes is discussed earlier in this chapter. Matthew's writer uses these terms as expected: to contrast the flourishing life with a life that lacks wisdom and leads to a path of destruction.

Important for Pennington's argument is the relationship between μακάριος and two other Greek ethics terms, τέλειος and εὐδαιμονία.[62] Rather than "perfect," as τέλειος is often translated in Matt 5:48, he suggests that a better gloss would be "whole," "complete," or "virtuous." The term τέλειος has an organic relationship with εὐδαιμονία, which many scholars translate as "flourishing."[63] This "teleiosity" or "flourishing" described in Matt 5:48 runs like a thread through the Sermon on the Mount, which consistently calls for a greater righteousness for those who enter the kingdom of heaven (Matt 5:17–20). The Pharisees, described as hypocrites, live in the opposite direction of this sort of flourishing, and this is epitomized by the opposite visions of Godward virtue presented in Matt 5:3–12 and 23:1–36.[64] In this way, the makarisms are meant to describe not entrance requirements or the reception of blessings but rather a "wholehearted orientation toward God."[65] The makarisms begin the Sermon on the Mount

[62] Hanson, "How Honorable!" 93, produces an important example from Josephus' *Antiquities*, in his account of Judah Maccabeus' speech to his troops, which places μακάριος and εὐδαιμονία in near synonymous relationship, by describing the honor and prosperity that comes from following laws and ancestral customs; "Since, therefore, at the moment it lies in your power either to recover this liberty and regain a prosperous (εὐδαιμονα) and honorable (μακάριον) life—by this he meant one in accordance with the laws and ancestral customs—or to endure the shame, and to leave your people without descendants by being cowardly in battle. You yourselves must fight, then, since those who do not fight will also die; believing that suffering for such great causes—freedom, patrimony, laws, worship—secures you perpetual honor" (*Ant.* 12.7.3).

[63] This begins with Aristotle, who related τέλειος, the complete attainment of a goal, with εὐδαιμονία, the flourishing that results in such an attainment. See John M. Cooper, *Reason and Human Good in Aristotle* (Cambridge, Mass.: Harvard University Press, 1975), 89–92. Cooper notes that many scholars of Greek philosophy have translated εὐδαιμονία as "happy" but that this translation falls short because εὐδαιμονία is not a subjective, emotional, or recurrent psychological state. It is not about brief moments in time but rather sustainable living in light of a bright future. Cooper connects εὐδαιμονία to τέλειος and explains that "teleiotation" is the "ultimate end," and εὐδαιμονία is the flourishing life that leads one there. Therefore, Cooper translates εὐδαιμονία as "human flourishing."

[64] See McKnight, *Sermon*, 30, who argues that Matthew's makarisms provide "a list of the good guys" and that Matt 23 provides "an alternate list of bad guys."

[65] Pennington, *Sermon*, 74–80.

by detailing the character dispositions of those who stand to live in light of the moral imagination that the sermon aims to inspire.[66] Those who flourish are those who are poor in spirit, those who mourn over the state of God's people, those who are meek, and so forth, and it is those who flourish in these ways who can observe the greater righteousness of the sermon (Matt 5:20) and be whole as their heavenly Father is whole (Matt 5:48). Due to these factors, Pennington offers "flourishing" as a translation for μακάριος. His arguments are convincing enough to determine that "flourishing" better captures the virtue-ethical character and intent of the makarisms than alternatives such as "blessed" or "happy"; therefore, this study adopts the translation of "flourishing" and its corresponding virtue-ethics approach for Matthew's makarisms.

66 The phrase "moral imagination" is taken from Allison, *Sermon*, which features in the subtitle of his book and runs as a theme throughout.

3

Reading Jesus' Beatitudes in Matthew

Jesus uses his proclamations of the kingdom and his healings to draw the crowds (e.g., Matt 4:24, "So his fame spread throughout all Syria"; Matt 8:1, "When Jesus had come down from the mountain, great crowds followed him"), and before introducing them to the ethics of this kingdom, he details for them examples of the character traits, or "dispositions," that aid ideal disciples in their efforts to live in light of kingdom norms. The first clause in each beatitude describes the dispositions of ideal disciples, while the second clauses motivate the disciples by describing the eschatological blessings that await them. It's important here to clarify what I mean by "dispositions" and the way in which I envision these dispositions functioning within the Matthean narrative.

The best way to understand the virtue-ethics context of the Matthean beatitudes is through a distinction between *virtuous dispositions* and *virtuous decisions*. Dispositions are qualities achieved through initiative, often in the face of obstacles. They are norms that describe a person's inherent characteristics that serve as indicators of behavior, and they are so embedded into a person's constitution that they predict future decisions and motives. Dispositions are not simple "personality traits." For example, a person might be either introverted or extroverted, but as personality traits, these qualities are both natural and amoral. They are not intentional and do not predict the virtuous value of a person's choices. Conversely, virtuous dispositions lead to virtuous decisions that are intentional on the part of the individual.[1]

This predictability might be compared to the disposition of physical objects. For example, if a glass is brittle, brittleness is its disposition. If it

1 See Hugh Sockett, "Dispositions as Virtues: The Complexity of the Construct," *JTE* 60 (2009): 291–303.

breaks, it did not do so because it was brittle but because some outside force acted on it to cause it to break. Brittleness is only a disposition that predicted it would break under certain conditions.[2] The situation with virtuous dispositions is similar except that people, as active agents, can cultivate their dispositions and develop their character. This developed character helps to explain why a person made certain decisions at certain times and explains how they might react when faced with obstacles or moral dilemmas. A person can behave in a way that appears selfless but with entirely selfish motives. Stable, virtuous character traits are independent of choices and actions, but virtuous dispositions that can be identified are more likely to lead to consistently virtuous behavior and choices. Virtuous dispositions are those that a person must develop to flourish and live well consistently.

This is why it is so significant that Jesus' beatitudes introduce the ethics of the kingdom found in the Sermon on the Mount. The sermon refers to particular dilemmas such as anger, adultery, divorce, retaliation, almsgiving, greed, and judgment. The beatitudes describe the dispositions of those who are flourishing according to kingdom values and aid the disciples in their ability to live out the ethics of God's kingdom. The phrase "theirs is the kingdom of heaven" in Matt 5:3 and 10 serves as a bracket around all of the dispositions described; those who are humble, who mourn, who are meek, who hunger and thirst for righteousness, who are merciful, who are pure in heart, who are peacemakers, and who are able to rejoice in the midst of persecution are those who are able to love those who persecute them (Matt 5:44) and live in light of kingdom-oriented righteousness (Matt 5:20). Those who live out the kingdom dispositions are able to imitate Jesus and be whole, as God is whole (Matt 5:48). This wholeness leads to good decision-making and predicts how ideal disciples will act in any and all circumstances where humility, meekness, peacemaking, and so on are the only appropriate responses. The cultivation of virtuous dispositions leads to consistent virtuous decision making.

Desirable dispositions must be identified, and not all moral philosophers will agree on which ones are best for human flourishing. Despite their countercultural and counterintuitive nature, the beatitudes are

2 See Stephen Mumford, *Dispositions* (Oxford: Oxford University Press, 1998), 5–7.

offered by Jesus as those that are suitable for kingdom living.[3] The connection between makarisms and woes is again worth addressing. The beatitudes in Matthew are in a third-person construction, which allows anyone among the crowds to accept Jesus' call, and the second clauses of the beatitudes honor those who respond favorably. Conversely, the woes are in the second person and are directed toward certain people. In Matt 23, Jesus explicitly identifies several behaviors of the scribes and Pharisees that are opposed to the values expressed in Matt 5:3–12. Jesus wants his followers to be merciful, but the scribes and Pharisees lack mercy (23:23). Jesus wants purity, but the scribes and Pharisees are hypocrites (23:25–26). The scribes and Pharisees persecute God's messengers (23:32–35), but Jesus wants disciples who will pray for those who persecute them. Jesus, in his position as Messiah and unique son of God, authorizes his beatitudes, and they serve to delineate the values of the kingdom. Conversely, the woes serve as their antithesis, attributing disrepute to those who were supposed to be trustworthy but instead led God's people along the wrong path.[4] Part 2 will engage with each beatitude to better understand the nature of each of these contrasting dispositions.

3 See Francois P. Viljoen, "Righteousness and Identity Formation in the Sermon on the Mount," *HTS* 69 (2013): 1–10, who writes, "By revealing this new way of life, the beatitudes affect moral behavior. The addressees have to respond with adequate attitudes, actions and thoughts that are different to conventional ways of behavior. Therefore, the set of beatitudes describes the way of life of faithful disciples of Jesus."

4 See K. C. Hanson, "How Honorable! How Shameful! A Cultural Analysis of Matthew's Makarisms and Reproaches," *Semeia* 68 (1994): 95–96.

Part II
Commentary on Matthew's Beatitudes

Jesus' beatitudes serve as a call to cultivate kingdom-oriented dispositions for those who would be his *ideal disciples.* As my colleague Scott Hoezee once said, Jesus sent his disciples "on a beatitude-shaped journey through life." Although these dispositions are countercultural and counterintuitive and they are counterpoints to the misguided ways of the scribes and Pharisees, they are not counterpointing to Jewish tradition or the story of Israel as God's covenant people. The scribes and Pharisees did not honor the ancient paths that led to communion with God but instead were blind guides who left Israel as sheep without a shepherd.[1] Jesus opposed the Jewish leaders not because he was moving away from his heritage but because they had. The end of Matthew opens the call to discipleship to the nations (Matt 28:19–20), but the nations are invited into a kinship with God's people through the work of the Jewish Messiah; a Messiah who fulfilled the Jewish Scriptures, honored the prophets (Matt 23:37–39), and incorporated ancient teachings into his own.

There is also an important difference between Matthew's and Luke's beatitudes that highlights an important feature of Matthew's version. Luke's list is directed at the second-person plural, "you." According to Luke, Jesus speaks to his disciples and says, "*yours* is the kingdom of God," "*you* will be filled," and so forth. The crowds are present, but Jesus appears particularly concerned to pronounce God's good future to people in specific circumstances. In Matthew's version, Jesus speaks to his disciples, but the crowds look on, and Jesus addresses the beatitudes in the third-person plural: "*theirs* is the kingdom of heaven," "*they* will be comforted," and

1 This claim, which has become somewhat controversial in recent scholarship, is discussed in the introduction.

so forth. Matthew's beatitudes are the "whosoever" beatitudes. They are directly addressed to the disciples, but they function as invitations to the crowds to follow Jesus and enter into the path of ideal discipleship. This is an important aspect of the way that the beatitudes point to the contrast between ideal disciples and the failed path of the Jewish leaders.

There is much about Jesus' beatitudes that feels startling and new—a careful reading forces us to reevaluate our common values. But the beatitudes are also saturated with ancient ideas and are indebted to sources that permeated Jewish culture and instruction. Jesus utilized some of these sources intentionally, with a combination of creativity and fidelity. Other ancient Jewish sources might not be cited or alluded to intentionally by Jesus or the Gospel writers, but their language and ideas had fused with the popular teaching of the time and their influence can still be felt. A recognition of these background sources is, along with Matthew's own narrative agenda, essential to understanding the meaning and intent of each beatitude and the unit as a whole. A particular feature of this commentary is to highlight and understand the ways that antecedent Jewish traditions might have influenced Jesus' beatitudes in their themes, word choices, structure, and aims.

The majority of background traditions discussed in this commentary are addressed when they are relevant from one beatitude to the next. However, Isa 61:1–7 is often recognized as the dominant subtext of the entire list. At least linguistically, it is likely that Jesus had many of the ideas of Isa 61 in mind when he proclaimed the beatitudes. Both Isa 61:1–7 (LXX) and Matt 5:3–12 refer to the poor (πτωχός, Isa 61:1; Matt 5:3), both refer to mourning (πενθέω, Isa 61:2; Matt 5:4), both refer to righteousness (δικαιοσύνη, *dikaiosynē*, Isa 61:3; Matt 5:6), and both refer to the inheritance of the earth as an eschatological fulfillment (κληρονομήσουσιν τὴν γῆν, *klēronomēsousin tēn gēn*, Isa 61:7; Matt 5:5).[2] Matthew explicitly mentions Jesus' role concerning Isaianic prophetic fulfillment (Matt 4:14–16), and Isaiah's promises permeate Matthew's entire Gospel.[3] The

[2] W. D. Davies and D. C. Allison, *Matthew 1–7*, ICC (London: T&T Clark, 1998), 436–37, list other potential parallels, but those listed here are the most relevant and compelling.

[3] See Richard B. Hays, *Echoes of Scripture in the Gospels* (Waco, Tex.: Baylor University Press, 2016), 175–85, who notes Isaiah's influence on Matthew's universal themes, and Jonathan T. Pennington, *The Sermon on the Mount and Human Flourishing: A Theological Commentary* (Grand Rapids: Baker Academic, 2017), 145–46, who briefly summarizes the connections between Isaiah

content of Isa 61 lends itself toward jubilee and deliverance, and Jesus uses this same passage that way in Luke 4:16–21. In Matthew's beatitudes, the linguistic cues are subtler, but Pennington is right to suggest that Matthew's beatitudes combine Isa 61 with the makaristic context to "simultaneously invite Jesus' disciples into these flourishing virtues and comfort them with the promise of God's deliverance and setting of the world to right."[4] Invoking Isaiah's terminology brings together discipleship and the good news of deliverance, and these are the central ideas encompassed by the beatitudes.

and a number of Matthean passages. See also Jonathan T. Pennington, *Reading the Gospels Wisely: A Narrative and Theological Introduction* (Grand Rapids: Baker Academic, 2012), 14–16.

4 Pennington, *Sermon*, 146.

Matthew 5:3

> Μακάριοι οἱ πτωχοὶ τῷ πνεύματι, ὅτι αὐτῶν ἐστιν ἡ βασιλεία τῶν οὐρανῶν.
>
> Flourishing are those who are poor in spirit, because theirs is the kingdom of heaven.[1]

Matthew's first makarism (5:3) states, "Flourishing are those who are poor in spirit, because theirs is the kingdom of heaven." The corresponding makarism in Luke (6:20) is slightly different and reads, "Flourishing are the poor, because yours in the kingdom of God." Well known are the differences in form, and debate continues on the sources of these differences and the effect of these differences for the meaning of each. The three principal differences are as follows:

(1) Whereas Luke's makarism is addressed to the second-person plural, Matthew's addresses the third-person plural.
(2) Whereas Luke's makarism refers to the poor, Matthew's refers to the poor τῷ πνεύματι, or "poor in spirit."
(3) Whereas Luke's makarism refers to those who possess the "kingdom of God," Matthew's refers to those who possess the "kingdom of heaven."

Debate continues regarding the sources for this beatitude, including whether one can be said to be more "original" than the other. Although this puzzle is interesting, it is also highly speculative, and in my view, solving it is not necessary to understand the meaning of Matthew's version. The differences in form and meaning have also been explained by various

1 The translations of individual beatitudes are my own. However, I chose the term "flourishing" as the first word in each beatitude based on the suggestion of Jonathan T. Pennington, *The Sermon on the Mount and Human Flourishing: A Theological Commentary* (Grand Rapids, Baker Academic, 2017), 143–44. See part 1 of this study for a discussion on translation.

appeals to antecedent traditions in the Hebrew Bible and Second Temple literature, and so exploring possible parallels, allusions, and echoes in the antecedent literature provides some of the most fruitful insights into Jesus' goals. This section will detail some of the possible backgrounds to Matt 5:3 and will also briefly compare it with Luke 6:20 to better understand how the nuanced differences between them affects our comprehension of the meaning and the aspirations Jesus has for his disciples that are particular to Matthew's version.

Flourishing Are Those Who Are Poor in Spirit

Who, exactly, are "the poor," and how is this group qualified by the prepositional phrase "in spirit"? In ancient Greek literature the term πτωχός (poor) refers exclusively to economic poverty and constituted that one was a beggar. In Jewish and Christian literature πτωχός, and many of the Hebrew words the LXX uses πτωχός to translate, maintained economic connotations but often came to include metaphorical poverty referring to those in special need of God's help. These terms became a self-designation for the meek, humble, and oppressed people of God.[2] Understanding the near parity between the term "poor" in Matt 5:3 and the term "meek" in Matt 5:5 sheds considerable light on Jesus' possible meaning and the dynamics of the relationship between those beatitudes. The relationship between πτωχός (poor, humble) and πραΰς (meek, humble) is incredibly close.[3] It is often compared to the relationship between the Hebrew terms ענו (*ʿānāw*) and עני (*ʿānî*), which many scholars argue are virtually synonymous,[4] though the terms have developed over time to carry distinct nuances.[5] The πτωχός of Isa 61:1 (LXX), which lies behind Matt 5:3, and the πραΰς of Ps 36:11 LXX (Ps 37:11 MT and English), which lies behind Matt 5:5, both have ענו behind them in the Hebrew. While in preexilic times the cognates ענו and עני applied to oppression and economic

2 For more on this, see the commentary below on Matt 5:5.

3 On πτωχός, see *NIDNTTE*, 4:181. On πραΰς, see *NIDNTTE*, 4:123.

4 Robert H. Gundry, *Matthew: A Commentary on His Handbook for a Mixed Church under Persecution* (Grand Rapids: Eerdmans, 1994), 69. See also Robert A. Guelich, "The Matthean Beatitudes: 'Entrance Requirements' or Eschatological Blessings?" *JBL* 95 (1976): 425, the terms in the Hebrew Bible are "essentially synonymous, each sharing a socio-economic as well as religious meaning," but this close relationship broke down in later Judaism, especially in rabbinic literature. He states, "It is all but impossible to pinpoint when such a shift took place."

5 See W. J. Dumbrell, ענו, *NIDOTTE*, 3:455.

exploitation, the exile widened the range of meaning so that in post-exilic literature these terms came to refer to Torah observance and submission to the will of God.[6] As H. Benedict Green argues, with ענו as the term behind both Matt 5:3 and 5:5, and considering the development of the term by the time it was used in Isaiah and the Psalter, the root meaning of these terms is "humble."[7]

Religious poverty seems to be supported by similar phrases in the Dead Sea Scrolls. The phrase "poor in spirit" is found nowhere else in the Bible aside from Matt 5:3 (though the "contrite spirit" of Ps 34:18 comes close) but many scholars have argued that precedent for the phrase is found in the Qumran literature. 1QM XIV 7 and 1QS IV 3 feature the phrase poor/humble in spirit, and this phrase is contrasted in 1QS XI 1 with those who are "lofty in spirit." In these instances, the focus is not on those who are weak in character but rather refers to the person's relationship with God. As R. T. France states, the humble in spirit in the Qumran literature "is a positive spiritual orientation, the reverse of arrogant self-confidence."[8] Similarly, Craig A. Evans argues that the "poor" in 1QM XIV 7 refers to those who stand opposite of those with a hard or haughty heart. It is a way of referring to those who are righteous, who "rely upon God and not upon power, wealth, or reputation."[9]

The religious meaning does not require an exclusion of the economic, but rather the two often go together. For many in Jesus' audience, the religious state of poverty was likely matched by an outward condition. In the words of Davies and Allison, "They knew the meaning of need because they were poor in spirit and poor in fact."[10] It is often in this distinction

6 See H. Benedict Green, *Matthew: Poet of the Beatitudes* (Sheffield: Sheffield Academic, 2001), 182–83, who cites 1 QS V 7–11 and the Psalter as examples.

7 Green, *Matthew*, 184. See also *NIDOTTE*, 3:455. And Ben Witherington III, *Matthew* (Macon, Ga.: Smyth & Helwys, 2006), 121, who recognizes that "poor" and "meek" go back to the same Hebrew root and argues that these terms do not refer to weakness but to "total dependency on God."

8 R. T. France, *The Gospel of Matthew*, NICNT (Grand Rapids: Eerdmans, 2007), 165.

9 Craig A. Evans, *Matthew*, NCBC (Cambridge: Cambridge University Press, 2012), 104. For a more expansive list of similar phrases found in the Dead Sea Scrolls with possible relevance to this meaning, see Timothy D. Howell, *The Matthean Beatitudes in Their Jewish Setting: A Literary Speech Act Analysis*, SBL 144 (New York: Peter Lang, 2011), 133.

10 Davies and Allison, 443.

between economic and religious poverty that scholars situate Matthew's inclusion of the phrase "in spirit." Although Luke's use of πτωχός does not necessarily exclude the religious dimension of poverty, his beatitude and its corresponding woe exhibit a decidedly more economic flavor, and Luke is generally more concerned than Matthew with charity, economic disadvantage, and critiquing the rich. As Matthew's Gospel is more concerned with discipleship, ethics, and greater righteousness, specifically in contrast to the actions of the scribes and Pharisees, a religious emphasis of poverty is more in keeping with Matthew's overall message, and the addition of the phrase "in spirit" is often seen as a product of this emphasis.

That economic poverty is often qualified by an ethical and spiritual dimension in certain Jewish traditions is manifest in 4QInstruction (hereafter Instruction),[11] a nonsectarian text found among the Dead Sea Scrolls.[12] Although it would be difficult to demonstrate that Matthew's writer(s) knew Instruction in particular, many scholars have pointed to the thematic similarities between Instruction and Matthew, and these similarities make it evident that both compositions were written in a Jewish social and cultural milieu in which poverty was experienced and openly processed in both a literal and metaphorical manner. In other words, while it would be dubious to insist on some sort of explicit literary connection between Instruction and Matthew (though it's entirely possible that Jesus and/or Matthew's writer(s) knew and made use of Instruction), there are enough thematic and theological correlations to suggest that they can be

11 Extant manuscripts of the text have been found only at Qumran and consist of the manuscripts 1Q26, 4Q415–418, and 4Q423. It is known by many names, most often 4QInstruction. 4QInstruction can be a misleading title, due to the finding of a fragment in cave 1 at Qumran and the fact that most scholars now regard the text as originating prior to its use at the Qumran site. For this reason, I follow John Kampen, *Wisdom Literature*, ECDSS (Grand Rapids: Eerdmans, 2011), 38, in using the title Instruction. For publication of the Hebrew text with early extensive analysis, see John Strugnell, Daniel J. Harrington, and Torleif Elgvin, *Discoveries in the Judaean Desert XXXIV: Sapiential Texts Part 2, 4QInstruction* (Oxford: Clarendon, 1999).

12 Some scholars have argued that the text was a product of the Qumran community. For a brief survey of scholars who have argued along these lines, see Matthew J. Goff, *The Worldly and Heavenly Wisdom of 4QInstruction* (Leiden: Brill, 2003), 222–24. Most scholars now regard the text as a product from outside of the community but suggest that the texts were popular among the sectarian group at Qumran in a way similar to 1 Enoch and Jubilees. Most scholars date the composition to the late third or early second century BCE.

viewed as two points along a trajectory of ideas within a common thought world.[13] The nuanced views of poverty found in both compositions help to establish their common perspective.

Instruction was written by a teacher to a student, and it has much to say about poverty and its relationship to a disciplined life. The addressee of Instruction is consistently reminded that he is poor (e.g., 4Q416 2 ii 20; 4Q416 2 iii 2; 4Q416 2 iii 8; 4Q416 2 iii 19).[14] There is no doubt that in some passages, material poverty is in view,[15] but poverty throughout the composition also connotes humility (4Q417 2 i 14), lowly status (4Q416 2 iii 15–16), and at times it represents an ethical ideal rather than an economic one.[16] The addressee is facing material hardship, but the refrain to remember his poverty does not only signify his economic reality. The consistent reminder that he is poor also signifies his need to maintain an ethical disposition and a posture of humility and reverence for God *despite and in the face of his economic position.*

Instruction is deeply concerned with something called "the mystery of existence." Although the nature of this mystery is difficult to pin down and

13 See, for example, Grant Macaskill, *Revealed Wisdom and Inaugurated Eschatology in Ancient Judaism and Early Christianity*, SJSJ 115 (Leiden: Brill, 2007), who places 1 Enoch and Instruction in conversation with Matthew and 2 Enoch. See also Loren T. Stuckenbruck, "4QInstruction and the Possible Influence of Early Enochic Traditions: An Evaluation," in *Wisdom Texts from Qumran and the Development of Sapiential Thought*, ed. Armin Lange, Charlotte Hempel, and Hermann Lichtenberger (Leuven: Leuven University Press, 2002), 245–62; Matthew J. Goff, "Discerning Trajectories: 4QInstruction and the Sapiential Background of the Sayings Source Q," *JBL* 124 (2005): 657–73; and Kampen, *Wisdom*, 28–29. It has been argued by some scholars that Instruction and Matthew are two of the few compositions in the Second Temple period that best illustrate the trajectory of sapiential and apocalyptic elements converging on each other to establish a particular Jewish worldview influenced deeply by both traditions. For a more detailed description of the various linguistic, thematic, and theological parallels between Instruction and Matthew, see my *God's Will and Testament: Inheritance in the Gospel of Matthew and Jewish Tradition* (Waco, Tex.: Baylor University Press, 2021), 294–301.

14 For studies on poverty in Instruction, see C. M. Murphy, *Wealth in the Dead Seas Scrolls and in the Qumran Literature*, STDJ 40 (Leiden: Brill, 2001), 163–209, and Goff, *Worldly*, 127–67.

15 See Samuel L. Adams, *Social and Economic Life in Second Temple Judea* (Louisville: Westminster John Knox, 2014), 197–98.

16 See Benjamin G. Wold, *Qumran Wisdom and the New Testament: Exploring Early Jewish and Christian Textual Cultures* (Cambridge: Cambridge University Press, 2023), 129–48.

much debate continues regarding everything from the mystery's content, to its method of communication, and even to the best translation of the Hebrew phrase,[17] it can be summarized as the pursuit of knowledge and wisdom in relation to God's creative work and plan for the cosmos, including humankind's place within God's plan for all things. It signifies the content of learning that must be the focus of the addressee. The addressee is to study it, gaze on it, examine it, meditate on it, and grasp it.[18] It is to be the object of study and devotion, with benefits passed to the addressee as a reward for proper learning and observance. It allows for correct decision making, opens an awareness of eschatological judgment, and guarantees an eternal reward.[19] It is the content of heavenly wisdom that directly affects human behavior and is the key to a human understanding of the ways of truth and the order of the cosmos. By incorporating the past creation of God, the present behavior of humans, and the future judgment, the mystery is wisdom instruction that provides a meeting place for the heavenly and earthly realms.

Both economic and metaphorical poverty are directly linked to the pursuit of the mystery throughout Instruction. Material poverty brings with it hardships, and the addressee is warned that the pursuit of wealth and the reversal of misfortune could too easily distract from the far more valuable pursuit of the mystery of existence (4Q416 2 ii 8–9). Instead of pursuing economic relief, the addressee is to trust God to fulfill basic needs, and he must be satisfied with what God has provided. The addressee's responsibility is to pursue wisdom and observe the mystery of existence. Although there is some debate regarding the exact social position of the addressee of Instruction, I have argued elsewhere that his most important role is that of a student in the process of becoming a sage.[20] The addressee is on the path to an elevation of status as one who serves God. The composition is not concerned with poverty for its own sake but with the effect that poverty might have on the addressee as he pursues his vocation. His

[17] The Hebrew phrase, רז נהיה (*raz nihyeh*), has been variously translated as "the mystery of existence," "the mystery that is to come," and "the mystery that is to be." To a great extent, the translation choice has a lot to do with the way in which we should best understand the pedagogical and theological connotations of the phrase.

[18] See Matthew J. Goff, "The Mystery of Creation in 4QInstruction," *DSD* 10 (2003): 163–86.

[19] Samuel L. Adams, *Wisdom in Transition: Act and Consequence in Second Temple Instructions*, SJSJ 125 (Leiden: Brill, 2008), 247.

[20] See my *God's Will and Testament*, 197–202.

economic poverty drives him toward a spiritual and ethical poverty that forces him to express radical reliance on God, and setting aside the need for economic advancement allows the addressee to focus on his vocation. Economic worry amounts to spiritual distraction, but pursuit of wisdom leads to Godward devotion.

The parallels between Instruction and Matthew are striking. Jesus' disciples are those who pursue greater righteousness, and counterintuitively, this is made easier when one is free from the constant need to pursue economic interests. To accept one's position, and to rely on God for one's needs (Matt 6:25–34), allows one to become firmly established in the vocation of discipleship. Jesus' ideal disciples flourish when they rely on God in nonideal circumstances. In both Matthew and Instruction, the reader/hearer can flourish in the eyes of God while appearing not to flourish in the eyes of others. Instruction describes those who pursue wisdom as "people with a spirit" and those who fail to pursue wisdom as those of "fleshly spirit." Those who pursue wisdom are those who are humble and lowly. The addressee is exhorted not to exchange his glory for a price (4Q416 2 ii 6), meaning he is not to pursue wealth or become embroiled in financial entanglements that would distract him from the mystery or disqualify him from devoting himself to his vocation, which, in his case, refers to his path toward becoming a sage and liturgical leader within the community. In Matthew, wealth and its pursuit are likewise viewed as a distraction from embracing one's full vocation as a disciple.

The disadvantage of wealth is presented clearly in the story of "The Rich Young Ruler" (Matt 19:16–30). A wealthy young man is instructed by Jesus to sell his possessions, give his money to the poor, and follow Jesus as a disciple. As the young man goes away grieving due to his concern for his great wealth, Jesus instructs his disciples on the difficulty wealthy people face in devoting themselves fully to God and entering his kingdom (19:24). That the rich young ruler was not simply "greedy" but also likely concerned with reasonable broader social interests is described well by David Crump. Crump shows a degree of sympathy for the rich young ruler not typically found in popular teaching on the passage and recognizes that the young ruler would have been faced with anxiety-inducing levels of uncertainty regarding his social position and the future of his kin and others who relied on his business interests.[21] Although Jesus often offers opportunities for people to follow him, he never seems to do so

[21] David Crump, *Encountering Jesus, Encountering Scripture: Reading the Bible Critically in Faith* (Grand Rapids: Eerdmans, 2013), 51–69.

in a way that removes uncertainty. Following Jesus requires a denial of self-interest, a surrender of autonomy, and a submission of one's life and resources to God's will. The uncertainty serves as a driver for the faith that is required, and although such uncertainty is often a terrifying aspect of discipleship, the beatitudes insist that disciples are rewarded with nothing less than God's very kingdom.

Jesus' kingdom is one in which its citizens must primarily be concerned not only with ultimate trust in the king rather than in their own means, but also with ultimate allegiance to the affairs of the king. In another place, Jesus tells his disciples, "If any wish to come after me, let them deny themselves and take up their cross and follow me. For those who want to save their life will lose it, and those who lose their life for my sake will find it. For what will it profit them if they gain the whole world but forfeit their life? Or what will they give in return for their life?" (Matt 16:24–26, NRSVue). The wealthy are not only settled in their self-reliance but are often also devoted to a myriad of other concerns related to commerce and their various vocations and social functions. Jesus the king requires complete surrender to the vocation of discipleship and service to the kingdom. While this is difficult for the wealthy, it is an elevation to the poor in spirit who find true wealth in following God resolutely.

The terminology of Instruction might be appropriate of the young ruler: that he "exchanged his spirit for a price" and surrendered an opportunity of a God-oriented vocation for one of financial advantage. This same theme is present in the beatitudes and throughout the Sermon on the Mount: a disciple of Jesus is not to be concerned with storing up treasures on earth (6:19–21), or being devoted to the pursuit of money (6:24), or searching for security by improving his or her financial position (6:25–34). Instead a disciple of Jesus is in a state of flourishing if he or she is poor in spirit (5:3), meek (5:5), pursuing righteousness (5:6), being salt and light (5:13–16), and relying on God alone. In Instruction, wealth is an unnecessary pursuit that may distract one from the vocation of becoming a sage. In Matthew, wealth is an unnecessary pursuit that may distract one from the vocation of being a disciple.

Johannes Baptist Metz, in his spiritual classic *Poverty of Spirit*, recognizes that Jesus faced the same demands that he placed on the rich young ruler but that Jesus successfully resisted the temptation of power and self-sufficiency. Metz connects Matt 5:3 with the wilderness temptation story in the preceding chapter (Matt 4:1–11) and argues that for Jesus to resist the devil, he needed to enter deeper into his poverty of spirit and reliance on the Father. Satan's temptation is "an enticement to strength, security and spiritual abundance; for these things will obstruct God's saving approach to humanity in the dark robes of frailty and weakness."[22] For Jesus to be fully human, he must enter into frailty, poverty of spirit, and suffering, and Satan does not want him to commit to this role, as it ultimately leads to the cross.[23] Metz argues that the placement of poverty of spirit at the head of the beatitudes is not an accident but illustrates its priority among the virtues: "without it there can be no Christianity, and no imitation of Christ."[24] The Pharisees were rich in spirit in vaunting their own brand of piety, and when comparing them with Jesus, the disciples and the crowds in Matthew are faced with a decision between the two. The rich young ruler, in confirming his adherence to the commandments (Matt 19:17–20), might have had confidence in his own position before God. However, Jesus knew that he lacked the poverty required for him to fully embrace God's kingdom.

Because Theirs Is the Kingdom of Heaven

The phrase "theirs is the kingdom of heaven" is an *inclusio* around Matt 5:3–10, which means that all of the second clauses of each beatitude between 5:3 and 5:10 are best understood not as disconnected eschatological promises but as benefits of the kingdom. Those who possess the kingdom will be comforted, they will inherit the earth, they will be filled, they will receive mercy, they will see God, and they will be called children of God; all of these benefits are aspects of the kingdom and none of them are identical to it. The kingdom is the greater reality of which these benefits are a part.

In many places where Mark and Luke feature the phrase "kingdom of God," Matthew features the phrase "kingdom of heaven." Such is the case when comparing Matt 5:3 with the parallel beatitude in Luke 6:20. Matthew uses the phrase "kingdom of heaven" thirty-two times, and the phrase is found nowhere else in all of Jewish and Christian literature.[25] For many years, most scholars argued that this was an honorary

22 Johannes Baptist Metz, *Poverty of Spirit* (Mahwah: Paulist, 1998), 11.

23 Cf. 2 Cor 8:9, "For you know the generous act of our Lord Jesus Christ, that though he was rich, yet for your sakes he became poor, so that by his poverty you might become rich."

24 Metz, *Poverty*, 21.

25 Jonathan T. Pennington, *Heaven and Earth in the Gospel of Matthew* (Grand Rapids: Baker Academic, 2009), 3.

circumlocution so that Matthew's writer could observe a Jewish tradition by avoiding the use of the name of God. However, because the term θεός (*theos*; God) appears in Matthew on several occasions, including the full phrase "kingdom of God" at least four times,[26] the honorary circumlocution argument is losing its popularity.

Pennington has demonstrated that although "kingdom of God" and "kingdom of heaven" refer to the same kingdom, Matthew's unique version of the phrase is not an honorary circumlocution but rather Matthew's way of highlighting theological aspects of the kingdom that are important to themes and ideas throughout the first Gospel. "Kingdom of heaven" is used by Matthew when it functions as a comparison or contrast with "the earth," and throughout Matthew heaven and earth function as a word pair to draw attention to these comparisons and contrasts. Matthew's use of heaven in the singular refers to the visible realm, but heaven in the plural refers to the divine and invisible realm and its bearing on the visible earth.[27] In Matthew's beatitudes, the kingdom of heaven is plural and is paired with the subsequent reference to the Father in heaven (Matt 5:16) to draw our attention to the contrast between the heavenly and earthly kingdoms.

Considering the way that the phrase "the kingdom of heaven" frames the rest of the beatitudes, it is important to understand the nature of the kingdom (βασιλεία; *basileia*) and the function of the genitive phrase "of heaven" (τῶν οὐρανῶν; *tōn ouranōn*). Beginning with the latter, there are a few valid options for understanding the genitive qualifier. The phrase "kingdom of God," found more in Mark and Luke, denotes both possession (the kingdom that belongs to God) and source (the kingdom that derives from God). However, in Matthew, heaven does not "possess" the kingdom. It is best, then, to understand the kingdom of heaven as that which belongs to God,[28] but Matthew's phrase "of heaven" then carries its

[26] Matt 12:28; 19:24; 21:31, 43. France, *Matthew*, 101, states, "Since Matthew seems to have no inhibitions about speaking of God by name elsewhere, this is hardly an adequate explanation." See also Gundry, *Matthew*, 43, who disregards the circumlocution argument, instead arguing that Matthew's writer was influenced by Dan 3:31–4:34 in order to highlight "God's universal dominion."

[27] Pennington, *Heaven*, 140–42.

[28] See Wesley G. Olmstead, *Matthew 1–14: A Handbook on the Greek Text* (Waco, Tex.: Baylor University Press, 2019), 42, who argues in favor of the subjective genitive because, before looking at "of heaven," we must first think of kingship and ask, "Whose reign?" The phrase "kingdom of heaven" in the first instance expresses God's sovereignty over earthly kingdoms.

own unique connotations regarding God's kingdom. The phrase does not mean that the kingdom is "in" heaven, as one would expect the dative, such as we find in Matt 6:9 regarding God, "our father who is in heaven" (Πάτερ ἡμῶν ὁ ἐν τοῖς οὐρανοῖς, my translation). This reference to the Father's location in Matt 6 is immediately followed by the prayer that the Father's kingdom would come "on earth as it is in heaven" (Matt 6:10), signifying the contrast between the heavenly and earthly realms, the heavenly quality of the kingdom, and the incoming influence of the heavenly realm on the earthly one. In Matt 4:17, using the same genitive phrase found in Matt 5:3 and 10, Jesus proclaims that "the kingdom of heaven has come near," indicating that the kingdom is "at the point of arrival"[29] as a dynamic force that is now breaking into the world.[30] This heavenly inbreaking fosters an urgency that necessitates the beatitudinal dispositions Jesus expects from his disciples. The inbreaking of the kingdom of heaven on the earth means that its presence, influence, and expression on the earth is both one of source—the kingdom that derives from heaven; and attribution—God's kingdom is of a heavenly nature.[31]

If God's heavenly kingdom is coming to bear on the earth, then what of substance can we say about the kingdom? Apparently, we can say a great deal, as the kingdom of God has been the subject of considerable academic discussion for more than a century.[32] Space precludes a deep dive into various debates and reconstructions, but it is important here to provide at least a sketch of what Jesus had in mind when he announced the coming of his kingdom.

First, if there is one thing that has reached a near consensus among interpreters, it's that the kingdom refers to God's *reign* over all things. In Matthew's depiction, there is a very real sense in which Satan expressed some measure of dominion on the earth when he offered the kingdoms of the earth to Jesus in exchange for worship (Matt 4:8). Satan's measure of

29 Howell, *Matthean*, 128.

30 Frederick Dale Bruner, *Matthew: A Commentary*, vol. 1: *The Christbook, Matthew 1–12* (Grand Rapids: Eerdmans, 2004), 87.

31 See Pennington, *Heaven*, 296, "we are not forced to make an either-or choice between the source genitive and the attributive genitive."

32 To include a list of even only the most influential studies on the kingdom would be unwieldy in length and still somehow reductive. As the twentieth century was the zenith of kingdom research, a good place to begin sifting through the most relevant work on the subject is the helpfully brief survey found in Wendell Willis, ed., *The Kingdom of God in 20th-Century Interpretation* (Peabody, Mass.: Hendrickson, 1987).

control is what makes the temptation tangible for Jesus. However, we can also say with confidence that Jesus resisted this temptation not because he was unconcerned with the status of the kingdoms of the earth, as though Satan might have had a better chance had he offered Jesus something even more enticing. No, Satan certainly chose wisely—Jesus was concerned with his earthly authority (Matt 28:18). But Jesus resisted because he knew that his mission was to wrestle control away from Satan and establish himself firmly as the true and only king. God's reign through Jesus is established and demonstrated through Jesus' teaching and even more dramatically through his miracles, as Jesus' ability to heal and restore is an emphatic movement of compassion for those affected by evil and an attack against forces of oppression. Jesus' life serves as a declaration of God's rule and the revelation of the nature of his kingdom. The miracles are instances of the reign of God overruling royal pretenders, pushing back against evil, and the beginning point in the process of reversing all that has been made wrong.[33] The crucifixion of Jesus the king, then, is the ultimate act of wrong, and yet it stands above all other acts—Jesus becomes a victim of human corruption and enters into human suffering so that through the resurrection, he can conquer it. The cross and resurrection serve as the culmination of Jesus' mission to demonstrate God's control and substantiate the potency of his kingdom over all others.

Some scholars have argued that the kingdom in Matthew refers *only* to God's reign and that the concept of *realm* is not indicated by the phrase.[34] However, Pennington makes a strong case that the heaven and earth word pair logically necessitates a spatial territory over which God reigns.[35] This

[33] This is not to oversimplify the miracle stories, as though they have only this purpose. Wendy J. Cotter, *The Christ of the Miracle Stories: Portrait through Encounter* (Grand Rapids: Baker Academic, 2010), 9, argues well that the miracle stories are fuller expressions of Jesus' virtue and demonstrate the nature of his heart toward others. Matthew Thiessen, *Jesus and the Forces of Death: The Gospels' Portrayal of Ritual Impurity within First-Century Judaism* (Grand Rapids: Baker Academic, 2020), 184, argues that Matthew links the kingdom of heaven with healings "because the heavenly realm cannot tolerate the ritual impurities and illnesses associated with the human mortal condition." Jesus' miracles accomplish many things, but the central idea behind them is Jesus' concern to set right all that has been made wrong.

[34] See, for example, Gundry, *Matthew*, 44, who argues that the kingdom of heaven in Matthew refers to God's sovereign, universal rule but "does not have to do with his general control over creation."

[35] The territorial aspect of the kingdom in Matthew is discussed in greater detail below, in the section on Matt 5:5 and the use of the phrase "inherit the earth."

combination of reign and realm heightens the contrast between the ways of heaven and the ways of earth; "the social order of the kingdom of heaven is very unlike the present earthly order,"[36] and although "the renewal" is eschatologically envisioned (Matt 19:28), the presence of heavenly power and values creates a dissatisfaction with common earthly values. In other words, the present experience of Jesus' teaching, authority, and power creates a longing for the future renewal of the cosmos and motivates the disciples to live now in light of the future. God's ways are not our ways, but Jesus emphatically demonstrates that God's ways are better. Although the ways of heaven fundamentally transcend the ways of earth, heaven breaks into earth, and the heaven and earth theme introduces social tension and "emphasizes the universality of God's dominion."[37]

What can we say about the timing of the kingdom? This has long been a puzzle and a topic of considerable debate in the twentieth century.[38] At points, the kingdom is portrayed as a present reality, such as when Jesus describes his exorcisms as evidence of the presence of the kingdom (Matt 12:28). At other times, it is evident that there is an anticipation of a future fulfillment of the kingdom, such as when, at the Passover, Jesus describes a future meal with his disciples in his father's kingdom (Matt 26:29). In the beatitudes, the present tense verb ἐστιν (*estin*) occurs (Matt 5:3, 10): "theirs *is* the kingdom of heaven." Many commentators have argued that this implies the present reality or experience of the kingdom. However, caution must be taken concerning the use of ἐστιν in these verses; it is possible that this is a proleptic present, meaning a present tense verb used not to describe a present reality but rather the definitive certainty of a future reality or event. In other words, it's possible that Matt 5:3 and 10 describe the present experience of the kingdom. However, considering the future tense of the second clauses of all of the other beatitudes, the present tense ἐστιν could refer only to the present assurance of the fulfillment of the promises and the eschatological reality of the kingdom.[39] The kingdom *is as good as theirs*.[40]

36 Pennington, *Heaven*, 323.

37 Pennington, *Heaven*, 343.

38 See, for example, the first four essays in Willis, *Kingdom*, 1–65.

39 See Rebekah Eklund, *The Beatitudes through the Ages* (Grand Rapids: Eerdmans, 2021), 95.

40 Examples of prolepsis can be found throughout the biblical texts. Consider 2 Tim 1:10, which says that Jesus "abolished death." The ramifications of death have been abolished, but the fuller abolition of physical death remains an eschatological expectation.

That the beatitudes anticipate a future kingdom fulfillment is indicated not only by the future tense verbs found in the other promises (Matt 5:4–9) but also in the way that Matthew's use of "kingdom of heaven" echoes the apocalyptic context of the book of Daniel. Scholars have long recognized Daniel as the theological and linguistic background of Matthew's use of the phrase.[41] In Daniel, God's kingdom activity took place in heaven but with an eschatological view toward earthly restoration:

Dan 2:44: And in the days of those kings the God of heaven will set up a kingdom that shall never be destroyed, nor shall this kingdom be left to another people. It shall crush all these kingdoms and bring them to an end, and it shall stand forever.

Dan 4:26: As it was commanded to leave the stump and roots of the tree, your kingdom shall be re-established for you from the time that you learn that Heaven is sovereign.

Dan 7:27: The kingship and dominion and the greatness of the kingdoms under the whole heaven shall be given to the people of the holy ones of the Most High; their kingdom shall be an everlasting kingdom, and all dominions shall serve and obey them.[42]

Daniel's portrayal of conflict between heaven and the kingdoms of the earth is fulfilled in Matthew not through violence but through the presence of Jesus, who inaugurates the kingdom and demonstrates its power in his teaching and miracles. In this sense God's rule arrived with Jesus, but the full manifestation of the kingdom on earth still awaits future consummation.[43]

Although there is a sense in Matthew in which the kingdom of heaven is eschatologically oriented, its presence is clearly experienced by the disciples in their active participation with Jesus. Jesus' proclamation of the kingdom (Matt 4:23, 9:35) is characterized by his ethical instruction (Matt 5–7) and miracles (Matt 8–9), which are present experiences passed along to the disciples (Matt 10:7).[44] Once again, thematic parallels with Instruction are illuminating. 4Q416 2 iii, lines 11–12 tell the addressee that he has had his head lifted above his poverty and that he has been given a seat

[41] See Howell, *Matthean*, 127.

[42] See Howell, *Matthean*, 127.

[43] See Klyne R. Snodgrass, *You Need a Better Gospel: Reclaiming the Good News of Participation with Christ* (Grand Rapids: Baker Academic, 2022), 80–83.

[44] See Ron Farmer, "The Kingdom of God in the Gospel of Matthew," in *The Kingdom of God in 20th-Century Interpretation*, ed. Wendell Willis (Peabody, Mass.: Hendrickson, 1987), 119–30.

among "the nobles." As one seated among the nobles, the addressee has been given authority by God to do God's will. Several scholars have argued effectively that in this fragment, the term "nobles" refers to angels.[45] In the midst of the constant reminders that the addressee is poor, he is told that he can walk in righteousness (l. 10) because God has seated him among the angels and lifted him from poverty into an inheritance of glory. The poverty described here is metaphorical; the addressee's material lack continues, but he has received a greater status than wealth—namely, a seat among the angels.

An elevation of status for the disciples is also in view in Matthew's beatitudes. The disciples in Matt 5:3–12 have been given a reward in heaven (5:12) and a place within the kingdom of God (5:3, 10); therefore, both Instruction and Matthew insist that the reader/hearer should behave in a way befitting one who holds a heavenly status. In Matthew, the kingdom is a gift that demands a new kind of response, where kingdom subjects hand out forgiveness and exhibit radical forms of mercy. Jesus envisions a participation with heaven for those who enter into their role as a disciple, and this participation is an inaugurated aspect of future glory and promises. The fullness of the kingdom remains future, but as Davies and Allison argue, "only overly sceptical dissection or misrepresentation can remove from Jesus' preaching of the kingdom either its future or its present elements." The kingdom, then, is not a moment but a series of events, as the kingdom is both inaugurated in Jesus and also in the process of being realized.[46] As kingdom subjects and active agents, the disciples demonstrate the heavenly ideals of the kingdom not only as recipients but also as participants whose lives contrast with typical earthly values.

Reflections on Matthew 5:3

Luke's beatitudes are written to the second-person plural: "because *yours* is the kingdom of God." There is a sense in which these lines are spoken directly to those in need—directly to the broken. Matthew's beatitudes are instead addressed in the third-person plural, "theirs" (αὐτῶν; *autōn*).

[45] Matthew J. Goff, *4QInstruction* (Atlanta: SBL, 2013), 105; Benjamin G. Wold, *4QInstruction: Divisions and Hierarchies*, STDJ 123 (Leiden: Brill, 2018), 85–90; Kampen, *Wisdom*, 76.

[46] Davies and Allison, *Matthew 1–7*, 390, point to Jubilees 23 and the Apocalypse of Weeks (1 En 93+91:12–17) as examples of eschatological processes entering into history one step at a time. This suggests that a "now/not yet" eschatology is in harmony with Jewish thinking at the time.

These beatitudes might be called "whosoever" beatitudes—they imply a sense of invitation. Whosoever enters into the position of poverty of spirit has a share in the kingdom of heaven and is invited to participate in it alongside the king.[47] This invitation orientation is consistent with Jesus' frequent calls throughout Matthew to "come, follow me" (Matt 4:19, 8:22, 9:9, 10:38, 16:24, 19:21). Jesus demands repentance from his followers (Matt 4:17) and proclaims the types of dispositions that disciples must possess to participate in the urgency of the kingdom, to teach and to heal, and to take part in the beginning stages of kingdom renewal on the earth. This poverty of spirit—this complete dependence on God—is the first of these vital dispositions and therefore might be the one disposition that makes the others possible. It is only when one relies on God in all circumstances that one can devote themselves fully to God's call on their life.

Yiu Sing Lúcás Chan describes well the idea that poverty of spirit is not just a condition but a disposition to be practiced and outwardly expressed. Chan writes that poverty of spirit refers to

> the renunciation of whatever separates us from God—especially spiritual pride. In practical terms, such renunciation or self-emptiness points to detachment. . . . Detachment does not mean "not caring"; on the contrary, it cares for things, though in a way different from how avaricious people do. We learn to see God in all things and love them in accordance with God's will. . . . Detachment does not simply mean the giving up of things but, more importantly, the giving up of the "obsessive" desire for them. When we are able to do so, we grow in freedom.[48]

The story of the rich young ruler appears to suggest that Chan is onto something. As a disposition, poverty of spirit enables ideal disciples to loosen the reins of all that hinders their fidelity to the one who reigns. It's a disposition that frees one from earthly concerns that contradict and conflict with heavenly values. According to Matt 5:3 fidelity to the king is awarded with a share in the kingdom, both now and in its future consummation.

[47] See Olmstead, *Matthew 1–14*, 76, the genitive pronoun αὐτῶν is loosely possessive and signals a share in heaven's reign.

[48] Yiu Sing Lúcás Chan, *The Ten Commandments and the Beatitudes: Biblical Studies and Ethics for Real Life* (Lanham, Md.: Rowman & Littlefield, 2012), 165.

Matthew 5:4

μακάριοι οἱ πενθοῦντες, ὅτι αὐτοὶ παρακληθήσονται.

Flourishing are those who mourn, because they will be comforted.

Like Matt 5:3, the Isaianic jubilee provides the linguistic foundation for Matt 5:4. In Isa 61:1–7, Israel has been oppressed, and its cities have been destroyed (Isa 61:4), but the Israelites anticipate a time of "everlasting joy" (Isa 61:7). The Israelites mourn (πενθέω; *pentheō*) because they suffer, but good news is being proclaimed to the poor (Isa 61:1), and in the year of jubilee, comfort (παρακαλέω; *parakaleō*) will be brought to those who mourn (Isa 61:2). Most scholars correlate Matt 5:4 with Luke 6:21, but Matthew's use of "mourn" and "comfort" are different than Luke's "weep" and "laugh," indicating that even if these beatitudes parallel each other and reflect a similar idea, Matthew's language is influenced by the passage in Isaiah. Strikingly similar language is also found in the Thanksgiving Hymns from Qumran, where God's compassion is proclaimed to the poor and the broken of spirit, and everlasting joy is proclaimed to those who mourn (1QH[a] XXIII 14–15).[1]

Flourishing Are Those Who Mourn

What does Jesus mean, in Matt 5:4, by "mourning," and how is it that those who mourn are flourishing in some way? According to Davies and Allison, mourning is not about flourishing because Matthew "can hardly be encouraging his readers to mourn." They mourn because they are in

1 These lines are fragmented, but the general ideas are clear enough. Timothy D. Howell, *The Matthean Beatitudes in Their Jewish Setting: A Literary Speech Act Analysis*, SBL 144 (New York: Peter Lang, 2011), 137, concludes that even if there is no evidence that Jesus and/or Matthew made use of the Thanksgiving Hymns, there is "an uncanny literary likeness" between them and Matthew's beatitudes, which at the very least demonstrates a transference of thoughts and ideas.

sorrow and are anticipating a time when God will turn their sorrow into joy. Davies and Allison argue that the context in Matthew is essentially the same as that in Isaiah—the kingdom has not arrived in its fullness, the son of man has not arrived in his glory (cf. Matt 24:29–31), and God's will is not yet done on earth as it is in heaven (Matt 6:10). The righteous mourn because the eschatological reversal has not yet taken place, and they are not content with the status quo.[2] Several other reasonable proposals have been put forth, including the sorrow of the disciples over their own sin,[3] mourning over all that they have left behind when they chose to follow Jesus,[4] a general mourning over the trials of life,[5] mourning over their state of poverty described by the previous beatitude (Matt 5:3),[6] or mourning over the persecution they face at the hands of their enemies (Matt 5:11–12).[7]

Although it's possible that mourning includes a multitude of viable referents and is therefore general in nature, I propose that the key to understanding the Matthean vocabulary lies within the specific narrative of Matthew's Gospel. As I argue in part 1, Matthew's beatitudes, while separated from the woes on opposite ends of the text, are still connected

2 W. D. Davies and D. C. Allison, *Matthew 1–7*, ICC (London: T&T Clark, 1988), 449, list several passages that demonstrate that the theme of God turning sorrow into joy is common in Jewish tradition (e.g., Isa 60:20, 66:10; Jer 31:13; Bar 4:23; Ps 126:2–6; Rev 21:4). See also Yiu Sing Lúcás Chan, *The Ten Commandments and the Beatitudes: Biblical Studies and Ethics for Real Life* (Lanham, Md.: Rowman & Littlefield, 2012), 171, who argues that this beatitude is "hardly an exhortation or an imperative" and that no one is being told to mourn.

3 Rebekah Eklund, *The Beatitudes through the Ages* (Grand Rapids: Eerdmans, 2021), 101–4, demonstrates that this was the dominant view of interpreters from the early church clear up until the Reformation. She provides a helpful survey of interpreters who commented on this beatitude to this effect. The idea that grief over sin leads to repentance is found elsewhere in the New Testament (2 Cor 7:10; Jas 4:8–10), and these passages influenced early interpreters of Matt 5:4.

4 St. Augustine, *The Lord's Sermon on the Mount*, ACW 5 (New York: Paulist, 1948), 14.

5 John Calvin, *Sermons on the Beatitudes*, trans. Robert White (Edinburgh: First Banner of Truth, 2012), 28–29.

6 Charles H. Talbert, *Reading the Sermon on the Mount: Character Formation and Decision Making in Matthew 5–7* (Grand Rapids: Baker Academic, 2004), 51, the second beatitude is a variation on the first. Those who mourn are dependent on God and in need of his help.

7 Davies and Allison, *Matthew 1–7*, 448.

to the woes through their contrasting images. The beatitudes describe the ideal disciples, while the woes describe the Jewish leaders who have failed to follow God well and to lead God's people into flourishing. After pronouncing the woes and describing the scribes and Pharisees as blind guides for God's people (Matt 23:13–16), Jesus is seen lamenting over Jerusalem, the city that "kills the prophets and stones those that are sent to it" (Matt 23:37). Although the term πενθέω does not occur in Matt 23, a sense of mourning over the state of Jerusalem is clearly present in the passage.

Jesus' mourning over Jerusalem is anticipated throughout the narrative progression of the First Gospel. Matt 1:21 appears in the midst of Jesus' *Jewish* genealogy and provides an early mission statement for the whole Gospel—Jesus came to save his people, the Jewish people, from their sins. Before Jesus' conflicts with the Jewish leaders hit their zenith, Jesus sends his disciples not to the gentiles but only initially to "the lost sheep of the house of Israel," where they are commanded to proclaim the good news of the kingdom and demonstrate the power of the kingdom through miracles of mercy and compassion (Matt 10:5–8). Those within the house of Israel are "lost sheep" because their guides are blind and good laborers are hard to come by—Jesus' fellow Jews are "sheep without a shepherd" (Matt 9:35–38). The supposed shepherds of Jerusalem, which, for Matthew, appear to include all teachers and leaders regardless of group designation (the chief priests, scribes, Pharisees, etc., are all amalgamated in Matthew's Gospel),[8] have failed God's people. Therefore Jesus, in his concern and compassion for God's people, has raised up disciples for the purpose of providing direction and care for those who have been led astray.

This narrative progression reaches a turning point in Matt 21:33–45. The details of the so-called Parable of the Wicked Tenants are controversial, but I have argued elsewhere that rather than presenting all of Israel as the wicked tenants, Jesus targeted only the Jewish leaders for their poor stewardship over the vineyard. The vineyard has not failed, but only its workers have failed in their task at cultivating the vineyard. Due to this failure, Jesus declares that God will replace the workers, who have lost their share in the kingdom, and the kingdom will be given to others who

8 See Matthias Konradt, *Israel, Church, and the Gentiles in the Gospel of Matthew*, trans. Kathleen Ess (Waco, Tex.: Baylor University Press, 2014), 37, 45, 75–77, 90–91, 102, 114–18, who argues that the Jewish leaders, as shepherds, have failed (Matt 10:6, 15:24) and Jesus has replaced them as the shepherd of Israel.

will produce its fruits. These "others," I argue, are the ideal disciples who are being sent out to proclaim God's true kingdom and shepherd God's people properly.[9]

This narrative progression features another contrast between Jesus' shepherding heart and results of Israel's failed leaders. In Matt 11:20–24, Jesus reproaches the cities that did not repent when they experienced his ministry. Jesus pronounces woes and the expectation of judgment. Then, during his lament over Jerusalem and following his woes against the scribes and Pharisees, Jesus mourns and describes his desire to gather the people of Jerusalem "as a hen gathers her brood under her wings" (Matt 23:37). Not quite a shepherding metaphor, but the inclination behind the imagery is the same. Jesus came to save his people from their sins, but many who had been led astray by false shepherds obstinately rejected him.

So how do we connect Jesus' mourning to that of those who mourn in the second beatitude? I argue above, in the discussion regarding Matt 5:3, that the phrase "theirs is the kingdom of heaven" refers not only to possession of the kingdom or the reception of its benefit but also to *participation* in the kingdom—participation in the kingdom's values and in the mission and ministry of its king. Several of these beatitudes indicate a manner of participation with the king and his kingdom, and Matt 5:4 is no different. Mourning is less about sorrow in the personal experience of the mourner and more about mourning along with Jesus. In other words, *ideal disciples mourn that which their Lord mourns.* Ideal disciples enter into Jesus' own experience and his concerns become their concerns. As Jesus mourns over the state of God's people, his disciples join him in his lament, but this does not stop at simple identification—mourning then becomes the fuel for mission. The blind guides and false shepherds of the house of Israel have made a mess of things, but the disciples join Jesus in guiding the lost and healing the broken. The offer of the kingdom was always meant to extend to gentiles (Matt 28:18–20), but Jesus' concern for the Jews meant that the mission of the kingdom needed to begin with them.

This is not to suggest that the second beatitude must be completely empty of personal application for the mourners. As Eklund argues, the notion that mourning refers to "anything that breaks the heart" runs the risk of becoming "too vague to be helpful," but various biblical traditions

9 See my *God's Will and Testament: Inheritance in the Gospel of Matthew and Jewish Tradition* (Waco, Tex.: Baylor University Press, 2021), 321–37.

do evince mourning in a variety of contexts.[10] For example, Matthew's chosen term, πενθέω, occurs in the LXX to indicate grief in the face of death (e.g., Gen 23:2, 37:34–35, 50:3; 2 Sam 14:2, 19:1) as well as mourning over death (e.g., Ps 34:14, 77:63). The exile "suggests a wide variety of griefs (the potential loss of the covenant with God, foreign domination, starvation, loss of land and home, death)."[11] Furthermore, Matthew's Gospel provides an early example of mourning in the form of Rachel, who weeps for her children (Matt 2:18).[12] Even the beatitudes end with the expectation of persecution, which is a very real experience that even the most righteous disciples would face with trepidation unless they be quite unlike their master, who, in the garden of Gethsemane, struggled with the trials that awaited him (Matt 26:36–46). Also possible is the role of the mourners to mourn not only with Jesus or for their own concerns but also with others who mourn.[13] Although not present in the immediate context in Matthew, early Christian literature is teeming with exhortations to bear the burdens of others (Gal 6:2), console others (2 Cor 1:4), and "weep with those who weep" (Rom 12:15). Jesus would certainly endorse the impulse to mourn over any form of brokenness, whether it be personal or in the interest of others.

Although mourning over personal and general circumstances is laudable and not necessarily excluded by the second beatitude, it is likely that Jesus' lament over the state of his people and his conflicts with the Jewish leaders are foregrounded in his teaching that those who mourn are those who flourish. It is in this idea that mourning becomes flourishing—it is this disposition that allows the ideal disciples to share in Jesus' own grief and therefore become motivated to join him in his mission to show mercy and compassion to Israel's lost sheep. The second beatitude is not in the imperative form, but it describes a virtue of those who share the kingdom's values and therefore still describes an expectation for the disciples. If the master laments and the disciples share his inclinations, then they will mourn as well. Mourning in Matt 5:4 is not a condition from

10 Eklund, *Beatitudes*, 110.

11 Eklund, *Beatitudes*, 104.

12 These biblical references, among others, are provided by Eklund, *Beatitudes*, 100, 105.

13 So Scot McKnight, *Sermon on the Mount*, SGBC (Grand Rapids: Zondervan, 2013), 40, those who mourn grieve their own experiences and the experiences of others; "they suffer and they love those who suffer."

which to be rescued but a condition to enter into that fuels participation in kingdom renewal.

As it happens, mourning over the state of Israel is also found in Jewish traditions antecedent to Matthew. Tobit assumes that Israel's disobedience led to the exile, he mourns Israel's exilic circumstances, and he longs for the day when God will no longer hide his face from his people (e.g., Tob 13). The prophets associate Israel's afflictions with God's judgment and depict God as a shepherd who will redeem his people (e.g., Jer 31:10–11). Jeremiah 31:13 declares that God will turn their mourning into joy and that he will comfort them. Even within Matthew, in the aforementioned mourning of Rachel, Matthew draws on Jer 31:15, and Rachel's weeping serves as an allegory for the exile that is then fulfilled in Herod's massacre of the infants.[14] These same prophets, who longed for Israel's redemption, are invoked by Jesus (Matt 23:29–36). In the same way that Israel rejected and killed many of the prophets, the scribes and Pharisees are guilty of rejecting Jesus, and later in the narrative, the chief priests and elders of the people will be complicit in Jesus' death, too (Matt 26:1–5). In the Matthean narrative, Matt 5:4 likely anticipates the cross so that Jesus' ideal disciples do not only mourn *with* Jesus but also *over* Jesus in the midst of his own trials. If this is the case, then the First Gospel also bears witness to the difficulty of mourning well—when Jesus faces trials in the garden, his disciples fall asleep (Matt 26:40–46), and Peter later denies him (Matt 26:69–75). However, some of Jesus' followers, such as Joseph of Arimathea (who is called a disciple in Matt 27:57), along with Mary and Mary, perform clear rituals of devotion and mourning over Jesus' death (Matt 27:57–61). In this sense, mourning certainly includes personal sorrow, but ideal disciples also flourish when their kingdom-oriented dispositions lead them to godly responses.

Because They Will Be Comforted

The second clause of the second beatitude is clearer than some of the other second clauses. Matt 5:4 begins the series of future tense verb forms (from Matt 5:4–5:9); those who mourn *will be* comforted. This comfort likely begins with the resurrection, which brought "great joy" (Matt 28:8) and motivated further mission (Matt 28:18–20). Many scholars argue that παρακληθήσονται is a "divine passive," which implies that God is

14 See Craig A. Evans, *Matthew*, NCBC (Cambridge: Cambridge University Press, 2012), 65–66.

the one who comforts.[15] This is certainly the primary idea, and insofar as God is the one who comforts, the now and not yet of the kingdom is relevant: a measure of comfort arrives with Jesus, through his ministries of mercy and compassion, and yet, total and thoroughgoing comfort awaits the renewal and the final consummation of the kingdom. A measure of comfort is possible now for those who trust in God and take joy in the resurrection, and a greater comfort is on the horizon, when the conditions for mourning will be removed, grief will be no more, Jesus' mission of salvation and renewal will be complete, and all that is wrong will be made right. Although I argue that for ideal disciples, mourning is a virtue, it is a virtue for a season, a virtue in a time of sorrow, and disciples can take comfort in the eschatological promise that such a virtue will not remain all-consuming.

Although God is the ultimate comforter, Chan insightfully points to the role solidarity plays in providing comfort among God's people. Those who mourn together, through that act, provide comfort to one other. Mourning is, in many ways, an "others-oriented" endeavor so that through identifying with others and through an openness and subordination to their suffering, we can sense the needs of another, which is the first step toward meeting those needs. Mourning precedes consoling so that accompanying the sufferer becomes an expression of virtue. Chan writes,

> Mourning is actually another form of the virtue of humility—a humility that is about and aimed toward the other and points to the surrendering of one's desires altogether for the sake of the other. . . . We let go of our own desires even to the point of discomfort for the sake of bringing God's love to others.

When through solidarity, mourning becomes a communal experience, it becomes a comforting one.

Reflections on Matthew 5:4

John Calvin, in his sermons on the beatitudes, ties Matt 5:3 and 5:4 together under the synonymous theme that he calls "the broken blessed." Although Calvin does not conceive of the nature of the beatitudes in the same ways that I'm presenting here, his understanding of the disciples as "the broken blessed" is evocative and insightful. For Calvin, the disciples are to "renounce self, and take up our cross." This implies that "everyone should

15 See Wesley G. Olmstead, *Matthew 1–14: A Handbook on the Greek Text* (Waco, Tex.: Baylor University Press, 2019), 77.

carry with him his own gallows," to accept death as their own companion, to willingly be vilified and slandered and spit on—that disciples can only follow Jesus if they enter into Jesus' own experience. Disciples can only be comforted if they are willing to surrender comforts, be condemned from every side, and live a life of purposeful and meaningful weakness.[16] Solidarity with Jesus, and a willingness to be associated with him in all his trials, is a necessary condition for disciples to celebrate with Jesus in his glory and receive a share in his kingdom. Mourning is likely multifaceted and includes mourning over personal experiences and, in solidarity, the experiences of others, but mourning with Jesus is likely the precondition to expressing mourning as a kingdom-oriented ideal.

16 Calvin, *Beatitudes*, 19.

Matthew 5:5

μακάριοι οἱ πραεῖς, ὅτι αὐτοὶ κληρονομήσουσιν τὴν γῆν.

Flourishing are those who are meek, because they will inherit the earth.

It is argued above that the phrase "poor in spirit" in Matt 5:3 refers not only to an economic condition but is also a self-designation for those who express their reliance on God, submit to his will, and recognize their dependence on God's grace and rule. For many scholars, Matt 5:5 was added, either by Matthew's writer or by pre-Matthean tradition, to provide a parallel to Matt 5:3 and further explicate its meaning.[1] In this view, πραΰς (the meek) is synonymous with and explicates the meaning of πτωχός (poor), and "inherit the earth" is synonymous with and explicates the meaning of "theirs is the kingdom of heaven."[2] There are problems

1 Robert A. Guelich, "Matthean Beatitudes: 'Entrance Requirements' or Eschatological Blessings?" *JBL* 95 (1976): 423–26. Matt 5:5 was added to parallel Matt 5:3 to interpret it and protect its religious meaning. See also W. D. Davies and D. C. Allison, *Matthew 1–7*, ICC (London: T&T Clark, 1988), 449.

2 Dale C. Allison, *The Sermon on the Mount: Inspiring the Moral Imagination* (New York: Crossroad, 1999), 47. "Poor in spirit" and "meek" are both ways of describing those who avoid hubris and are powerless in the eyes of the world. "The kingdom of heaven" and "inherit the earth" are terms relating to the future state. See also Guelich, "Matthean Beatitudes," 425–26; Davies and Allison, *Matthew 1–7*, 449; Donald A. Hagner, *Matthew 1–13*, WBC 33A (Dallas: Word, 1993), 92. H. Benedict Green, *Matthew: Poet of the Beatitudes* (Sheffield: Sheffield Academic, 2001), 181–82, argues that Matthew's makarisms feature synonymous parallels through alternating pairs and that Matt 5:3 and 5:5 are paired within this structure. According to Green, although Matt 5:3 and 5:5 are synonymous parallels and there is a great deal of similarity between "poor in spirit" and "meek," the two verses are not identical twins, as their second clauses provide different emphases. See also Robert H. Gundry, *Matthew: A Commentary on His Handbook for a Mixed Church under Persecution* (Grand Rapids: Eerdmans, 1994), 69, who argues that the two are not synonymous but that 5:5

with this view, as there are several reasons to read Matt 5:5 as a unique beatitude with its own important nuances.

Flourishing Are Those Who Are Meek

As discussed above regarding Matt 5:3, the relationship between πτωχός (poor, humble) and πραΰς (meek, humble) is incredibly close. The πτωχός of Isa 61:1 (LXX), which lies behind Matt 5:3, and the πραΰς of Ps 36:11 LXX (Ps 37:11 MT and English), which lies behind Matt 5:5, both have ענו behind them in the Hebrew. I argue above that the Hebrew term ענו, which lies behind both Matt 5:3 and 5:5, maintains its economic connotations of oppression and social alienation but that due to shifts in the use of the term over time, it also comes to refer to humility in the face of trials. In other words, Matthew's use of the term πραΰς in Matt 5:5 has more to do with one's response to their circumstances than to the circumstances themselves. This reading is further confirmed by the Matthean motif of applying each of the makarisms to Jesus at later points in the Gospel. In light of this motif the term "meek" would correlate with the references to Jesus' humility (πραΰς) in Matt 11:29 and 21:5.

Not all scholars correlate πραΰς in Matt 5:5 with the concept of humility. Davies and Allison argue that instead of seeking to avoid hubris, the term refers to those in the world who are powerless.[3] Similar is Mark Allan Powell, who argues that ענו refers not to the humble but to the humiliated, the oppressed, and the powerless. Because the use of ענו in

---

does explicate the meaning of 5:3. Meekness implies an acceptance of the lowly position indicated by poor in spirit. The possibility of parallelism is somewhat complicated by the fact that although most manuscripts have the order "poor in spirit," "mourn," and then "meek," as in Matthew, some manuscript witnesses flip the second and third makarisms, placing 5:3 and 5:5 together. Guelich, "Matthean Beatitudes," 427, argues that despite the parallelism between 5:3 and 5:5, the common order preserves the order of its source in Isa 61:1–7, which refers to the poor (Isa 61:1) and those who mourn (Isa 61:2) before Isa 61:7, which shared a common bond with Matt 5:5. Conversely, Allison, *Sermon*, 48, argues that the synonymous nature of 5:3 and 5:5 implies that there is "a good chance that that was the original sequence." Bruce M. Metzger, *A Textual Commentary on the Greek New Testament* (Stuttgart: UBS, 1994), 10, argues the unlikelihood that a scribe would divide the rhetorical antithesis of heaven (5:3) and earth (5:5) and that it is more likely that second-century copyists, believing that 5:3 and 5:5 were synonymous, reversed the order of 5:4 and 5:5 to bring together "poor in spirit" and "meek." The question regarding the original order remains open, and solving it is not necessary for interpretation.

3 Davies and Allison, *Matthew 1–7*, 449.

Ps 37:11 stands in the background of πραΰς in the Greek translation in Ps 36:11 LXX, which is quoted in Matt 5:5, the Matthean beatitude has the same connotations in mind. In this case those who are meek are those who are alienated from privilege on the earth and disadvantaged in present times. Those who will inherit the earth are the dispossessed who are awaiting their share in the future age. When God's rule is firmly established, "the weak and powerless will receive what God wants them to have."[4] Although I agree with these scholars that the meek are likely dispossessed and awaiting future recompense, I do not agree that this is what meekness means.

At least two important points of contention can be raised with the view that πραΰς in Matt 5:5 refers to the oppressed and dispossessed. First, this view does not consider the semantic range of ענו or the development of its meaning over time, nor does it consider the many nuances of the term πραΰς when it serves as a translation of ענו. For example, these terms are used in Num 12:3 when Moses is referred to as the humblest person on the face of the earth. In Zeph 2:1–3, those who are עני/πραΰς are those who obey God's commandments and seek righteousness and humility, and by doing so they set themselves apart from the arrogant of that generation. The humility spoken of refers to behavior that God commands and which the godly must pursue.[5] Most important, in Ps 37, the section from which Jesus quotes in Matt 5:5, the meek are those who refrain from anger and wrath and show patience for God's timing (Ps 37:8–9). Those who are generous and avoid the ways of the wicked shall inherit the land (Ps 37:22). The entire Psalm is a contrast between the righteous and the wicked, and the inheritance is offered only to those who obey God and pursue righteousness. As with Matthew's beatitudes, the inheritance of the land is offered as a refuge in a time of trouble (Ps 37:39–40), but this does not eliminate the ethical dimensions of meekness as a desired behavior for God's people.

Second, the view that the meek in Matt 5:5 refers to the oppressed and dispossessed does not consider the use of the term πραΰς within Matthew and in the wider Greek context. Although Matthew is a thoroughly Jewish text, it still interacts with Greek and Roman language and demonstrates conversance with the Hellenistic thought world. To be clear, Powell does argue that because two out of three instances of πραΰς in Matthew are

4 Mark Allan Powell, "Matthew's Beatitudes: Reversals and Rewards of the Kingdom," *CBQ* 58 (1996): 460–79, here 466–67.

5 See W. J. Dumbrell, ענו, *NIDOTTE*, 3:455.

quoted from the LXX (Matt 5:5 from Ps 36:11; Matt 21:5 from Zech 9:9), Matthew has the Hebraic connotations in mind. However, as we just saw, this still does not eliminate the ethical dimensions. This also ignores the fact that Matthew's use of πραΰς, even when quoted directly from the Jewish Scriptures, is placed into a new context where the ethical dimensions become more apparent. For example, Matt 5:5 is taken from its original context and placed in a makaristic formula and paired with other beatitudes that feature ethical language. Similarly, Matt 21:5 is taken from Zechariah and recast to describe Jesus as a king in the midst of a Roman cultural environment. Matthew honors his Jewish heritage by appealing to the Jewish Scriptures, but care must be taken to understand the new context within Matthew's Gospel and Jesus' cultural circumstances.

Deirdre Good compellingly argues that Matthew's use of πραΰς engages with Greek and Roman ideas of meekness. Good demonstrates that the concept of πραΰς was intimately connected to the Hellenistic concept of kingship. Rulers were expected to be meek: to be unbothered by troubling circumstances, to resist tyranny, and to show benevolence and compassion toward citizens. Hellenistic kings were expected to offer forgiveness rather than retribution and demonstrate forbearance rather than despotism or anger. Anger in particular is the primary negative subdomain of virtue, and meekness is its primary opposite. At its core πραΰς is "the quality of a benevolent rather than a tyrannical king."[6] Meekness is a virtue that should be practiced by kings and all moral agents and sits alongside what is good, kind, just, holy, perfect, humble, gentle, blessed, and merciful.

Matthew opens with the example of King Herod who, although used in the immediate context as a counterpart to pharaoh in Matthew's exodus typology,[7] is also an example of a Roman client king who modeled his court after a Hellenistic monarchy.[8] As Josephus explains, Herod was given to frequent outbursts of anger and suffered from instability.[9] He

6 Deirdre J. Good, *Jesus the Meek King* (Harrisburg, Pa.: Trinity Press International, 1999), 14–15. Throughout her study, Good cites several passages from Greek writers to build a definition of πραΰς in a Hellenistic context.

7 See Dale C. Allison Jr., *The New Moses: A Matthean Typology* (Eugene, Ore.: Wipf & Stock, 1993), 140–65.

8 See Victor Tcherikover, *Hellenistic Civilization and the Jews* (Grand Rapids: Baker Academic, 1999), 253, who writes, "Thus the Hasmoneans went the way of Hellenization and began to resemble the normal type of Hellenistic monarch; Herod later trod the same road and trod it till the end." On the design of a Hellenistic court and Herod's application of it, see Good, *Jesus*, 55–60.

9 Josephus, *Antiquities of the Jews*, 15.7.

held grudges, slaughtered his enemies and members of his own family, and deprived his opponents of political power. In Matthew's Gospel, Herod is enveloped in a rage-filled jealousy concerning the birth of the king of the Jews, and he orders the merciless slaughter of all infants in and around Bethlehem in an attempt to destroy the infant Messiah (Matt 2:1–18).[10]

Conversely, Jesus is called the "meek king" (Matt 21:5), and when he has a chance to describe himself with virtue language, he chooses "meek" (πραΰς) and "humble" (Matt 11:29). Whereas Herod finds children expendable (Matt 2:16), Jesus welcomes children and proclaims that the kingdom is theirs (Matt 19:13–15). Jesus explains that Hellenistic rulers dominate as tyrants, but he came to serve. Herod did everything he could to hold on to his power, including taking the lives of others, while Jesus came to give his life as a ransom for many (Matt 20:24–28). Jesus was offered the kingdoms of the world by the tempter, and he rejected this temptation to rely instead on his father (Matt 4:1–11). As king of the Jews, Jesus was as a meek king who served and suffered and surrendered his life for his people (Matt 27:32–56). It is only Jesus the meek king who is vindicated through resurrection and is able to declare, "All authority on heaven and earth has been given to me" (Matt 28:18).

Although there is no abstract definition of πραΰς in Matthew, the term is clearly applied to Jesus in a way that positions him within the Roman imperial context as the ideal king. He resists tyranny and retribution and surrenders himself in nonviolence (Matt 26:52–56). That the meekness of Jesus is both a virtue and a thing to be modeled by his followers is found in other early Christian texts. For example, in 1 Cor 4:14–21, Paul, as an expression of his imitation of Christ, resists the arrogance of his opponents and says that he will come to the Corinthians not "with a stick" but with "love in a spirit of gentleness" (πραΰτης, *prautēs*, a cognate of πραΰς). In 2 Cor 10:1, Paul states that he writes to them "by the meekness (πραΰτητος) and gentleness of Christ." In his leadership, Paul exercises meekness rather than harshness, patience rather than anger, all with Jesus' meekness as the model.

Not all of Jesus' followers have real-world power to be tamed. In fact, the beatitudes were likely written for early disciples who were subjects of persecution and had little earthly influence, affluence, or authority. The meek disciples, as post-exilic Jews, were among the dispossessed who awaited vindication in the future age. The second clause of the beatitude offers a vision for this. However, it is in the opposition to anger and retribution

[10] Good, *Jesus*, 55–60.

that meekness is applied as a virtue to any and all of Jesus' followers, and this sets the interpretive framework for meekness as a virtue in the beatitudes. Again we must note that Matt 5:5 quotes Ps 36:11 LXX (Ps 37 in MT and English) almost verbatim, while placing it into a makaristic formula. It is in that Psalm, just a few lines before the quote in question, that the meek are instructed to "refrain from anger, and forsake wrath." Doing this allows God's people to commit themselves to God's ways, be patient for God's timing, and allow God to vindicate them (Ps 36:5–8, 37:5–8 MT).

The meek in Matt 5:5 is a plural adjective (πραεῖς), indicating that meekness is to be found in the life of the community. Cultivating virtues promotes and sustains community life, and meekness is best understood in relationship to the model of Jesus as a meek king who eschews anger toward his people and instead serves in mercy, sacrifice, and forgiveness. In this way we see the important differences between Matt 5:3 and 5:5, between "poor in spirit" and "meekness." Whereas the poor in spirit are those who recognize their dependence on God's grace and rule, the meek are those who cast aside aggression, anger, and retribution for the sake of building a kingdom-oriented community. This lack of aggression also relates to the second clause in this beatitude. In Matt 11:12, Jesus states that "the kingdom of heaven has suffered violence, and the violent take it by force." In Matt 5:5, it is those who resist such aggression who will inherit the earth, for the kingdom of heaven is theirs.[11]

Because They Will Inherit the Earth

The second clauses of Matt 5:3 and 5:5 are also often viewed synonymously. And like the first clauses, there are similarities, but they are best not viewed as synonyms. Instead it is better to view the inheritance of the earth as *an aspect* of the reception of the kingdom. As described above regarding Matt 5:3, the phrase "theirs is the kingdom of heaven" is an *inclusio* around Matt 5:3–10, which means that all of the second clauses of each beatitude between 5:3 and 5:10 are best understood not as disconnected promises but as eschatological benefits of the kingdom. Those

[11] Matt 11:12 is an infamously difficult verse to interpret. Frederick Dale Bruner, *Matthew: A Commentary*, vol. 1: *The Christbook, Matthew 1–12* (Grand Rapids: Eerdmans, 2004), 512–14, surveys the history of interpretation. I follow the suggestion by Matthias Konradt, *The Gospel according to Matthew: A Commentary*, trans. M. Eugene Boring (Waco, Tex.: Baylor University Press, 2020), 176, that Jesus has his opponents among the Jewish leadership in mind. The meekness of the disciples is, then, yet another contrast between the Jewish leaders and Jesus' ideal disciples.

who possess the kingdom will be comforted, they will inherit the earth, they will be filled, they will receive mercy, they will see God, and they will be called children of God; all of these benefits are aspects of the kingdom and none of them are identical to it. The kingdom is the greater reality of which these benefits are a part.

This is supported by Pennington's research regarding the heaven and earth word pair as discussed in the section above regarding Matt 5:3. God's heavenly kingdom is very different from the earthly kingdoms. The promise to inherit the earth is future tense and eschatological; as the kingdom of heaven comes to bear on the earth, those presently participating in the heavenly kingdom will inherit the earth as a result. The values presented in Jesus' beatitudes are in opposition to the ways of the Jewish leaders and the Roman world.[12] Those flourishing in the heavenly kingdom are the poor in spirit who are elevated to a heavenly status and the meek who will inherit the earth in the future age. The inheritance of the earth is yet future because the values of the kingdom must come to bear on the earth before it can be fully handed over to Jesus' disciples (Matt 6:10), and the heaven and earth theme "provides solace and hope for the disciples" while they await the time when the realities of heaven will come to bear on the earth.[13] While they wait, Jesus' followers are called to live within God's ethical standards, which are both counterintuitive and countercultural when compared with the standards of the earth.[14]

Rather than viewing the kingdom of heaven and the inheritance of the earth as virtual synonyms, Matt 5:5 is better viewed as a functioning addition to the heaven and earth word pair where the inheritance of the earth is an eschatological, spatial, and this-worldly reward for present kingdom participation. With Matthew's heaven and earth word pair in view, it is best to recognize both that Matt 5:3 and 5:5 carry similar connotations while also recognizing that Matt 5:5 carries its own theological weight. "Inherit the earth" is a rare phrase, but it has an important history in Jewish texts and in its trajectory toward Jesus' use of the phrase and carries important, specific, and identifiable concepts not found in most of the second clauses of the other beatitudes, which use terms and phrases with less specific referents. For this reason, it is worth taking more time here

[12] Jonathan T. Pennington, *Heaven and Earth in the Gospel of Matthew* (Grand Rapids: Baker Academic, 2009), 343, "The heaven and earth theme *emphasizes the universality of God's domain*" (emphasis original).

[13] Pennington, *Heaven*, 344.

[14] As described by the rest of the sermon and in contrast to the ways of the scribes and Pharisees. Pennington, *Heaven*, 346–47.

than I will take with the other beatitudes to provide details of the history of this specific and meaningful phrase "inherit the earth."[15]

Inheritance Traditions in the Background of Matthew 5:5

What does it mean to "inherit the earth"? The concept of inheritance has a rich history in ancient Judaism. The noun נחלה (*naḥ*ª*lâ*) and verbal forms from the root נחל (*nāḥal*) are the main words for inheritance in the Hebrew Bible.[16] The noun is used 220 times, and the verb is used 59 times. A second term that often refers to inheritance is the verb ירשׁ (*yāraš*), which appears in the Hebrew Bible 232 times, though this term often refers to possession or disinheritance, often by force.[17] In the LXX, the Greek noun for inheritance is κληρονομία (*klēronomia*), and the verbal form is κληρονομέω (*klēronomeō*). The meaning of these Greek terms mirrors the Hebrew terms quite closely. Their usage serves to demonstrate the largely synonymous way that ירשׁ and נחלה were received by the LXX translators and demonstrates that when interpreting inheritance in both Hebrew and the LXX, נחלה and κληρονομία function in a relatively synonymous fashion.[18] Typically, especially in the Hexateuch, the inheritance of Israel refers to the promised land (e.g., Exod 23:30–31; Num 34:13–29). God owns the land (Lev 25:23) and bestows it to his people as a gift (Deut 4:21). The precise nature of the land inheritance shifts over time and from one textual tradition to another, so it is important to identify which traditions likely had the greatest influence over Jesus' word choices and theological ideas. I propose that the following contexts are the most likely detectable influences, and each speaks to our ability to interpret the use of the phrase "inherit the earth" in Matt 5:5.

[15] Because inheritance was the subject of my previous book, *God's Will and Testament*, much of the information here is taken from there, though it is edited down considerably. See pages 282–302.

[16] See Christopher J. H. Wright, נחל, *NIDOTTE*, 3:77.

[17] See Christopher J. H. Wright, ירשׁ, *NIDOTTE*, 2:539.

[18] For more on statistics and translations, see κληρονομία, *NIDNTTE*, 2:693–96. It is the case that there are difficulties at times and in individual instances of justifying the translation choices of the LXX translators. There may be instances where Greek terms for "inheritance" are used to translate נחלה and ירשׁ when other terms may be more appropriate, but these statistics demonstrate the volume of instances where the Hebrew and Greek terms for inheritance line up, revealing that for the LXX translators, these terms were viewed largely as synonyms. For more on the dynamics of the LXX as a translation of Hebrew, see Karen H. Jobes and Moisés Silva, *Invitation to the Septuagint* (Grand Rapids: Baker Academic, 2015), 86–102.

1. Isaiah 61:7

The relevance of Isa 61:1–7 to the beatitudes is discussed above; it remains here to consider the potential influence of verse 7 on Matt 5:5. Both verses feature the phrase κληρονομήσουσιν τὴν γῆν (they will inherit the earth) in the future tense, a phrase that is extremely rare in extant Greek Jewish and Christian compositions but that is also found in Isa 60:21.[19] In both Isaiah passages κληρονομέω translates ירש rather than the more common נחל. In this instance the meanings are synonymous and may be nothing more than stylistic, as ירש also stands behind κληρονομήσουσιν γῆν throughout Ps 36 LXX (vv. 9, 11, 22, 29) as well as κληρονομήσει γῆν in Ps 24:13, while the noun κληρονομία translates נחלה in Ps 36:18 to the same basic effect.[20] In Isa 60:21, the righteous will "inherit the land forever."

[19] In compositions that were written in Greek, or in those translated into Greek and in which the Hebrew vorlage is now unknown, the phrase appears with the article only three times in 1 En 5:6–8 (κληρονομήσουσιν τὴν γῆν), and once in Matt 5:5 (κληρονομήσουσιν τὴν γῆν). It appears without the article in Tob 4:12 (κληρονομήσει γῆν). See also a similar use of the phrase in Jub 17:3, 22:14, and 32:19. κληρονομέω appears in close connection with γῆν a number of times in the LXX (thirty-seven times, according to Ulrich Luz, *Matthew 1–7*, Hermeneia [Minneapolis: Fortress, 2007], 186) when translating both נחל and ירש in conjunction with ארץ, but these instances are rarely in construct form in Hebrew. The vast majority of instances are found in the Hexateuch, in the aorist tense, when referring directly to the inheritance of the land as a promise or result of the conquest (cf. LXX, Gen 15:7, 28:4, 47:27; Exod 23:30; Lev 20:24; Num 21:35, 26:53; Deut 1:8, 2:31, 3:12, 4:1). Some instances appear in the future tense, still clearly in relationship to the conquest (cf. LXX, Num 14:24, 31; 18:20; 26:55; 34:17; Deut 4:22; 5:33). The precise phrase κληρονομήσουσιν τὴν γῆν, in the future, active, indicative, third-person, plural construction, when a prophetic-eschatological intention is present in the context, is found only in 1 En 5:6–8, Matt 5:5, and Isa 60:21 and 61:7. Psalm 36:11 (LXX), from which Matt 5:5 draws most directly, features κληρονομήσουσιν γῆν without the article. The phrase "inherit the earth" appears just once in the Hebrew Bible in construct form with נחל, in Isa 57:13 in reference to the land of Israel. "Inherit the earth" appears more often as a construct with ארץ and the root verb ירש, though it is still rare. It appears in Lev 20:24, where "land" is preceded by the direct object את in reference to the land belonging to the Canaanites, whom the Israelites are to dispossess from the land. The construct with ירש is found four times in Ps 37 (vv. 9, 11, 22, 29), while the root נחל is found in verse 18 of that chapter but not in construct with ארץ.

[20] Although note Davies and Allison, *Matthew 1–7*, 450, who argue that with ירש as the background, inheritance is possibly best rendered as "possess" or "acquire."

It is widely recognized that Isaiah stands in the background of Matthew's entire narrative. Isaiah's universalist eschatological vision is tied tightly to its presentation of inheritance concepts (cf. Isa 2:2–4; 14:1–2; 19:16–25; 49:1–8; 56–57), and as Richard B. Hays observes, Isaiah's universalist vision lies in the background of multiple Matthean passages (cf. Isa 60:1–6 with Matt 2:1–12; Isa 8:23–9:1, 42:1–7 with Matt 4:12–17, 12:15–21).[21] Since it is likely that Isa 61:7 influenced Matt 5:5, and it is possible that Isa 60:21 did as well, it is important to see how these passages fit into the overall narrative regarding inheritance in the final chapters of Isaiah.

In Isa 64–66 God's "people" are no longer delineated by birthright; they are those who seek God from within Israel, but also those who seek him from among the nations. The book of Isaiah often includes non-Israelites with Israelites as those that gather to worship at the mountain of God (Isa 11:11–12, 56:1–8); Isa 66:18–21 famously expands on this theme, as God sends the survivors of his judgment to gather the nations and give them standing in his eschatological kingdom.[22] The people of the nations facilitate the return of diaspora Jews, some of whom are made priests and Levites.[23] Isa 66:22–23 then states that in the new heavens and the new earth, "all flesh" shall worship before God. As Joseph Blenkinsopp notes, "One aspect of this eschatological scenario is that all humanity will worship the one true God, the God of Israel, in Jerusalem."[24] God declares his intention to create a new heaven and a new earth. Isa 65 features the term ארץ (*ʾereṣ*, land/earth), but its pairing with שמים (*šāmayim*, heavens) encompasses the universe and the divine realm, so the entire earth rather than Israel alone is in view.[25] Although Isa 60:21 and 61:7 refer to the eschatological renewal of the land, the climax of Isaiah promises an entirely new creation, illustrated by the heaven and earth word pair (Isa 65:17).[26] God's new people comes with a new vision of temporal space. In the same way that in Gen 1:1 God created the heavens and the earth, in Isa 65:17 he declares his intention to create new heavens and a new earth. Isa 65

[21] Richard B. Hays, *Echoes of Scripture in the Gospels* (Waco, Tex.: Baylor University Press, 2016), 175–85.

[22] Joseph Blenkinsopp, *Isaiah 55–66*, AB 19B (New York: Doubleday, 2003), 313.

[23] John D. W. Watts, *Isaiah 34–66*, WBC 25 (Nashville: Thomas Nelson, 2005), 940.

[24] Blenkinsopp, *Isaiah 55–66*, 316.

[25] See Christopher J. H. Wright, ארץ, *NIDOTTE*, 1:512, the heaven and earth word pair "expresses the totality of the created order."

[26] See Luz, *Matthew 1–7*, 195, n. 94, who argues that the wording of Isa 60:21 and 61:7 is that of the "cosmic expansion of the promise of the land."

describes an idyllic existence reminiscent of Eden, where the creation is at harmony and humans experience life at an optimum level: with the absence of violence and distress.[27]

Matthew 5:5 draws on these themes—the heaven and earth word pairing between Matt 5:3 and 5:5 suggests that τὴν γῆν (the land/earth) in Matt 5:5 refers not to the land of Israel alone but to the earth and the eschatological renewal of all things. This is supported within Matthew by the anticipation of cosmic renewal (Matt 19:28), and the fact that in the majority of instances in Matthew, γῆ (*gē*) appears to refer to the earth rather than the land of Israel (cf. Matt 5:18, 35; 6:10, 19; 9:6; 11:25; 12:42; 16:19; 18:18–19; 23:9; 24:30; 28:18).[28] The use of the heaven and earth word pair, as well as Matthew's consistent use of γῆ to refer to the earth, suggests that Matt 5:5 makes use of Isa 60:21 and 61:7 by drawing on their themes but doing so within the wider presentation of eschatological renewal within the final portions of Isaiah. In other words, the trajectory of the universalism is featured within Isaiah itself.[29] The latter portions of the book look to a future, renewed earth. The themes of Isa 60:21 and 61:7 are present in Matthew and have been appropriated to describe a future inheritance for Jesus' disciples.

2. *Psalm 37:11 (36:11 LXX)*

Ps 32:12 (LXX) features the term κληρονομία in a makarism.[30] Although this might have been known to Matthew's writer(s), it is another Psalm, Ps 37 in Hebrew and our English Bibles but Ps 36 in the LXX, from which Jesus quotes. The affinities are obvious:

> **Ps 36:11a: οἱ** δὲ **πραεῖς κληρονομήσουσιν γῆν**.
>
> **Matt 5:5:** μακάριοι **οἱ πραεῖς**, ὅτι αὐτοὶ **κληρονομήσουσιν** τὴν **γῆν**.

27 Blenkinsopp, *Isaiah 55–66*, 287, points out the difficulty in establishing a dependence of this passage on Gen 1–3. Later interpreters have made the connection by way of similarity, but there are differences that make the argument for dependence questionable.

28 With Matt 27:45 as an exception. See Davies and Allison, *Matthew 1–7*, 450.

29 See James M. Scott, *Paul and the Nations* (Tübingen: Mohr Siebeck, 1995), 13–14, 73, who argues that Isaiah, in many passages, stands among a tradition of Hebrew Bible texts that present a positive eschatological expectation for all nations.

30 See Ps 32:12 (LXX), 33:12 Hebrew and English, λαός, ὃν ἐξελέξατο εἰς κληρονομίαν ἑαυτῷ (the people whom he has chosen as his own inheritance).

The Psalm uses the phrase "inherit the earth/land" five times (36:9, 11, 22, 29, 34), and the noun "inheritance" one time (36:18). The Psalm describes the contrast between the righteous and the wicked, and it is concerned with the perception that the wicked prosper while those who follow God are left to suffer. The Psalmist states that the righteous Israelites need not worry about the wicked, as they will soon fade like the grass (36:1). They will be cut off (36:9–10), and the righteous will be saved. The text fits the post-exilic circumstance that found the Israelites alienated from the land and no longer in control of it. The inheritance is a future promise, indicated by the use of the future tense verb "will inherit." The Psalm is an anthology of wisdom sayings concerning a moral and God-fearing life. The inheritance referred to is the land of Israel, as opposed to "the earth," but rather than Israel as a whole, the inheritance is promised to those within Israel seeking to honor God. Relatively ignored in scholarship regarding Matthew's possible use of this Psalm is the shift in meaning that this Psalm took on late in the Second Temple period. In the Psalms Pesher, a commentary found among the Dead Sea Scrolls, the text downplays the wisdom aspects of Ps 37 and interprets it eschatologically.[31] Rather than Israel alone, the Pesher concludes that the righteous will inherit "the whole earth," introducing an important point of connection with Matt 5:5.[32]

3. *The Abrahamic Promise*

As discussed previously in this study, Jesus' genealogy begins with the declaration that Jesus is "the son of Abraham" (υἱοῦ Ἀβραάμ). The writer's goal is to situate Jesus as the culmination of a particular trajectory. Konradt summarizes this idea when he states, "The history of salvation, which began with the calling of Abraham, leads up to its culmination in Jesus."[33] By invoking Abraham, Matthew's writer draws attention to the Abrahamic promises: Jesus is included among Abraham's descendants, is therefore an heir to the inheritance, and consequently plays a role in being a light to the nations.[34] That all three aspects of the Abrahamic promise had long

[31] See George W. E. Nickelsburg, *1 Enoch 1*, Hermeneia (Minneapolis: Fortress, 2001), 162, and Craig A. Evans, *Matthew*, NCBC (Cambridge: Cambridge University Press, 2012), 105.

[32] See Evans, *Matthew*, 106.

[33] Matthias Konradt, *Israel, Church, and the Gentiles in the Gospel of Matthew*, trans. Kathleen Ess (Waco, Tex.: Baylor University Press, 2014), 25.

[34] Cf. Gen 17:4–6; Exod 32:13; Isa 49:1–8. Konradt, *Israel*, 26, 265–67, recognizes that some scholars have argued that the references to Abraham in Matt

been tied both to gentile and "whole earth" inheritance is demonstrated by Sir 44:21, where the inheritance is not the land of Israel alone but the whole earth, just as in Matt 5:5. Abraham is situated near the beginning of Sirach's account of Israel's heroic ancestry (44–50), where it states that Abraham's descendants would be as numerous as the dust and that the nations "would be blessed by his offspring." This blessing comes about for the "nations" (ἔθνη; *ethnē*) as "an inheritance" from sea to sea and from the Euphrates "to the ends of the earth." As an heir to Abraham the promises are now mediated through Jesus, which includes the inheritance itself with a view toward universalism.[35]

4. Jesus as David's Heir

Jesus, as the son of David (υἱοῦ Δαυὶδ, Matt 1:1), is the heir to David's throne.[36] In the Hexateuch, God maintains perpetual ownership of the inheritance, which he gives to his people as a gift. In 1–2 Samuel, God

---

1:1, 2, 17 may refer only to Jesus' role in the salvation story of Israel or to Jesus as the "ideal Israelite." However, Konradt argues, based on references to Abraham in Matt 3:9 and 8:11, that gentile inclusion is in view regarding references to Abraham in Matthew's Gospel. He states, "Matthew sought to indicate the universality of salvation in Jesus in 1:1 as well as with the reference to his Abrahamic ancestry" (267). In this regard Matthew's use of the Abrahamic tradition is in line with representations in other early Christian texts (Acts 3:25; Rom 4; Gal 3). See also Davies and Allison, *Matthew 1–7*, 158, that son of Abraham "probably also serves to announce the evangelist's interest in the salvation of the Gentiles"; and Luz, *Matthew 1–7*, 85, who connects the four gentile women to Abraham in the genealogy as clues to a universalistic undertone. Speaking of the connection between Abraham and Jesus in the genealogy, Luz states, "The movement of Israel's salvation to the Gentiles, a dominant theme of the Gospel of Matthew, is already declared in its opening text."

35 Evans, *Matthew*, 106, recognizes this in part when he relates the inheritance of Matt 5:5 to the inheritance aspect of the Abrahamic promise in Gen 15:7 and 28:4. He states that Matt 5:5 "recalls God's promise to Abraham" as well as the inheritance of the land in Exod 23:30 and Deut 4:1. However, Evans does not recognize Jesus' relationship to Abraham and therefore Jesus' role as the heir and mediator of the inheritance.

36 See Dale C. Allison Jr., "The Embodiment of God's Will: Jesus in Matthew," in *Seeking the Identity of Jesus: A Pilgrimage*, ed. Beverly Roberts Gaventa and Richard B. Hays (Grand Rapids: Eerdmans, 2008), 122, "David" is the key term in the genealogy. It brings royal connotations to the fore, occurring at 1:1, 6, and 17. It lets the reader know that the kingdom belongs to Jesus, that he sits on the throne, and that he will judge and rule (19:28; 25:31–40). See also Konradt, *Israel*, 23–49; Luz, *Matthew 1–7*, 70; Hagner, *Matthew 1–13*, 9;

mediates the inheritance through Saul (1 Sam 10:1) and then all kings who come after Saul. God entrusts his own inheritance (his people and his land) to a king for oversight, and to be cut off from God's inheritance is to be cut off from relationship with God as well as God's people. These themes are relevant to inheritance contexts throughout Matthew, as Jesus the messianic king and heir to the Davidic dynasty is now the one through whom the inheritance is gifted and obtained.[37] This is evident in Matt 21:37–38, which describes Jerusalem as an inheritance that belongs to Jesus and that the Jewish leaders attempt to take by force. And this is evident in Matt 19:29 in which Jesus describes the inheritance of eternal life as that which is only given to those who follow him. In Matt 5:5 it is Jesus who has the authority to declare that the meek will inherit the earth and that by doing so, they shall also have a share in the kingdom of heaven (Matt 5:3, 10).[38] Jesus is the meek Davidic king, and the inheritance is mediated through him in this role.

5. *God as Father*

The fatherhood of God is established early on in Jewish literature and is intimately tied to inheritance contexts. The father-son relationship between Yahweh and his people is manifested at both the national[39] and individual level,[40] and God is depicted as the chief ancestor who provides an inheritance to his children. Marianne Meye Thompson emphasizes God's activity as the provider of an inheritance as a vital aspect of his role as Father throughout the Hebrew Bible, Second Temple literature, and the New Testament. She argues that God as the giver of an inheritance makes the "God as Father" concept more ubiquitous than is usually argued, as the term for "father" need not be present to view God as father in a given

---

R. T. France, *The Gospel of Matthew*, NICNT (Grand Rapids: Eerdmans, 2007), 32; and Davies and Allison, *Matthew 1–7*, 156–57.

[37] See Joel Willitts, "The Twelve Disciples in Matthew," in *Jesus, Matthew's Gospel and Early Christianity: Studies in Memory of Graham N. Stanton*, ed. Daniel M. Gurtner, Joel Willitts, and Richard A. Burridge, LNTS 435 (London: Bloomsbury, 2011), 167, as the son of David, "Matthew's Jesus is the king over an eschatologically restored kingdom of Israel who will rule both Israel and the nations."

[38] Similar themes are found in other New Testament writings. For example, Haley Goranson Jacob, *Conformed to the Image of His Son: Reconsidering Paul's Theology of Glory in Romans* (Downers Grove, Ill.: IVP Academic, 2018), 82, 138–39, argues that in Romans, the inheritance belongs to Jesus, and to receive a part in the inheritance is to participate with Jesus in his reign as a coheir.

[39] See, for example, Exod 4:22; Deut 32:5, 6, 18, 19; Hos 11:1; and Jer 31:9.

[40] See, for example, Deut 14:1.

context. Anytime God is depicted providing an inheritance, one can argue that he does so as a father to his people even when he is not explicitly described as such.[41]

The connections between God's fatherhood and his people as his children are explicit in the beatitudes. God is never called "father" in the beatitudes, but God is referred to as a father to his people in the sermon immediately following: those who let their light shine before others give glory to their Father in heaven (Matt 5:16), and those who forgive their enemies behave as their heavenly Father (Matt 5:48). Matt 5:9 declares that those who exhibit the beatitudes will be called "children of God" (υἱοὶ θεοῦ), and it is these children who receive an inheritance in Matt 5:5.[42] In both the Hexateuch and Jesus' beatitudes, the inheritance is guaranteed by God himself as a gift. In the Hexateuch this is illustrated by the consistent use of the verb נתן (*nātan*, to give) in conjunction with inheritance contexts; in the beatitudes, this is illustrated by the use of the divine passive. Regardless of the involvement of God's people in participating in the acquisition of their inheritance, such inheritances would be unattainable without God's favor and role as the divine giver. The permanence of the inherited and renewed earth ensures the permanence of the relationship between God and his people.

Matthew's Gospel makes use of a series of relational genitives to describe the quality of these connections. In Matt 1:1, Jesus is the son *of* Abraham and son *of* David, which speaks to his role as Messiah and the guarantor of the promises. Throughout the Gospel, Jesus is the Son *of* God who mediates God's kingdom (e.g., Matt 4:3, 6; 8:29; 14:33; 16:16; 26:63; 27:40), which gives him authority over the inheritance and the responsibility to offer it universally. And in Matt 5:9, those who become children *of* God are those who receive the inheritance (Matt 5:5). The connection between the children of God and their inheritance is considered more below, in the analysis on Matt 5:9.

6. *Inherit the Earth in the Second Temple Period*

Although Jesus quotes Ps 37:11 directly in Matt 5:5, it is important to understand how the phrase "inherit the earth" was used in Jewish

41 Marianne Meye Thompson, *The Promise of the Father: Jesus and God in the New Testament* (Louisville: Westminster John Knox, 2000), 39.

42 Davies and Allison, *Matthew 1–7*, 458–59, who state, "Believers in Jesus are, in Matthew, already sons of God (5:45), whom they call Father (6:9)." This guarantees both a degree of intimacy with God and a likeness to him.

traditions of the Second Temple period to see how the meaning of the phrase shifted over time. If the shift in meaning of the phrase resonates at all with themes found in Matthew, then it opens the possibility that these shifts in meaning resonated with Jesus and his immediate audience. When these other occurrences of the phrase are compared with Matthew's understanding of the coming of the new creation (Matt 19:28), some important similarities are found. Above I mentioned the interpretation of Ps 37 in the Psalms Pesher, a commentary found among the Dead Sea Scrolls. The commentary downplays the Psalm's original wisdom context and interprets it eschatologically.[43] The wicked are in control of Israel at the time of writing and are made up of both the violent ones of the nations and the wicked of Israel. The wicked will be cut off forever and exterminated. "The congregation of the oppressed" are God's elect who do his will. The biblical Ps 37 refers to those who will inherit "the land," but the pesher concludes that the righteous will inherit "the whole earth."[44]

The phrase κληρονομήσουσιν τὴν γῆν occurs three times in 1 Enoch. This exact construction of the phrase in Greek—featuring the future, active, indicative, third person, plural form of the verb κληρονομέω with the article before the noun—is extremely rare in extant literature. Other than Isa 61:7 and Matt 5:5, it is found only in 1 En 5:5–9. The linguistic connection between 1 En 5:5–9 and Matt 5:5 is strengthened by their share of certain associated themes with inheritance. For example, both 1 En 5 and Ps 36:22 (LXX) declare that those not included in the inheritance will be cut off. Ps 36:22 reads: "for those blessed by the Lord shall inherit the land (αὐτὸν κληρονομήσουσι γῆν), but those cursed (καταράομαι; *kataraomai*) by him shall be cut off." By comparison 1 En 5:7 reads: "For the chosen there will be light and joy and peace, and they will inherit the earth (αὐτοὶ κληρονομήσουσιν τὴν γῆν), but for the wicked there will be a curse (κατάρα; *katara*)." This juxtaposition—that those who experience God's favor will receive the inheritance versus those outside of God's favor

[43] See Nickelsburg, *1 Enoch 1*, 162.

[44] Compare 4Q171 1+3 4iii 10 with 4Q171 1+3 4 10–11. For an English translation integrating the manuscripts of the pesher, see Géza Vermes, *The Complete Dead Sea Scrolls in English* (London: Penguin, 2011), 521–22. For a critical edition of the *Psalms Pesher* see James H. Charlesworth, ed., *The Dead Sea Scrolls: Hebrew, Aramaic, and Greek Texts with English Translations*, vol. 6B: *Pesharim, Other Commentaries, and Related Documents* (Tübingen: Mohr Siebeck, 2002), 6–33. The comments on inheritance in the pesher primarily concern Ps 37:22, 34.

being cut off—is strongly implied in Matt 5:5, as the inheritance is promised only to those who follow Christ. This is also made explicit in each of Matthew's other inheritance contexts (19:29, 21:38, 25:34). In this way in each passage, to inherit the land/earth is to be included and to be found within the identity of those connected to God. To be left out from the inheritance is to be excluded from identifying with God's people.

1 En 5 and Matthew also fit, to some degree, with the post-exilic circumstance that found the Israelites alienated from the land and no longer in control of it. In both cases the inheritance is a future promise, indicated by the use of the future tense verb "will inherit." The lack of control of the land places the audiences of both compositions in a place of dependence on God for future vindication. The land was more than geographic space; it was a place of security and a signifier of the identity of God's people as those uniquely chosen by him. In contrast to the Hexateuch, which promises the inheritance to all of Israel over and against the Canaanite inhabitants of the land, the post-exilic context of both 1 En 5 and Matthew's Gospel places the conflict between those *within* Israel seeking to honor God and those *within* Israel who are not doing so. In 1 En 5 there are those prospering in the land by their disobedience to the law. In Matthew the conflict is with the Jewish leaders in particular, who have followed God in a way defined by hypocrisy. As the parameters used to define and identify God's people have shifted, the nature of the land inheritance has shifted as well, and it is in this way that both 1 En 5 and Matthew are likely influenced by Isa 56–66: both 1 Enoch and Matthew import Isaiah's vision of a new people in a new land into its social milieu in order to present the righteous with an apocalyptic hope. The inheritance of the earth in Matthew refers to a reconstitution of the people of God around Jesus as their messianic king, and this comes with a new vision of temporal space.

The second instance of the phrase "inherit the earth," which requires discussion, is found in Instruction. 4Q418 81+81a 14 states that those who are נוחלי ארץ (inheritors of the earth) יתהלכי (shall walk), which is followed immediately by a reference to שמים (heaven). The line is fragmented, and the full context is difficult to determine. The phrase might possess eschatological connotations, but the emphasis is on those who are already set to inherit in the present. The use of the imperfect hitpael verb from the root הלך (*hālak*; to walk) in line 14 likely has ethical connotations and, paired with the reference to heaven, likely means that those who inherit the earth are those who walk on the inherited earth in a way that accords with the heavenly realm. The addressees are being instructed on how to live in the present earth in the same way as those who are in heaven (angels), and their present inheritance of the earth then accords with their heavenly status. In Isaiah, 1 Enoch, and the Psalms Pesher, the phrase "inherit the earth" is most often an eschatological phrase that carries with it a universalism and a view toward this-worldly renewal. To a degree, this may be in view in Instruction, but the context here emphasizes the ethical aspect of the inheritance; those who inherit the earth are likely those who *walk according to heaven*.

Like 4Q418 81+81a, Matt 5:3–12 features the heaven-earth word pair in an ethical context. Both passages offer the inheritance of the earth universally, and both offer it to those who conduct themselves toward God and others in an ethical way. In Instruction, those who inherit the earth are those who are given authority over it as sages and liturgical leaders in the community, and although this is less immediately apparent in the context of Matt 5:5, it is relevant to the role of the disciples throughout Matthew, who are given authority on the earth (Matt 10:1). The important difference between these examples is that in Instruction, the inheritance of the earth is a reference to authority *in itself*, while in Matthew, those in authority participate with the kingdom of heaven in the present but are given the inheritance of the earth as an eschatological promise and reward.

There are some important common threads related to "inherit the earth" contexts. In each case the promise of the earth is made by one with ultimate authority over the earth (usually God but in the case of Matthew, Jesus acting on God's behalf). In all cases except for possibly Instruction, the earth is a renewed and reconstituted earth, and in all cases except for possibly Instruction, the promise of the inheritance of the renewed earth is largely eschatological but imbued with significance for the present day. In all cases, the inheritance of the earth is open to all of humanity universally, and in all cases, it is promised to those who follow God and live in an ethical way. In the cases of 1 Enoch, Instruction, and Matthew's Gospel, the phrase is found in contexts that contribute to the trajectory of the convergence of wisdom and apocalyptically oriented literature discussed in part 1 of this study.[45]

[45] Significant studies detailing the merger between wisdom and apocalyptic in Instruction include Matthew J. Goff, *The Worldly and Heavenly Wisdom of 4QInstruction* (Leiden: Brill, 2003), 28, 216–19, who argues that Instruction's author was steeped in the traditional wisdom of Israel but merged this wisdom with apocalyptic elements based on the influence of a trajectory of wisdom literature in the Second Temple period that finds other possible examples

Reflections on Matthew 5:5

Meekness does not initially strike one as a virtue. It reminds one of weakness or the sort of person that is easily imposed on. However, what the world sees as weak, Jesus demonstrates as true strength: the ability to lead not from coercion or imposition, not from tyranny or dominance, but from a gentle heart and full reliance on the will and providence of God. There is a notion in popular preaching on this verse that has developed into a well-known idiom that goes something like this: "meekness is not weakness; it is power under control." There is a sense in which, for Jesus, this is true. Jesus is the miracle worker who says that he could have appealed to his father and summoned legions of angels to assist him in his time of need (Matt 26:53), but instead, so that the Scriptures would be fulfilled, he submits to the crooked authorities and willingly goes to his own death. Jesus was not weak, but he surrendered himself to the will of his father to be placed in a weak condition.

Although Jesus placed his power under control, I'm not sure this is as applicable to his followers. Peter was told to sheath his sword, not because he was in a position of power and needed to control it but the opposite; he was in a vulnerable position, and relying on his own strength would have led to his destruction (Matt 26:52). The use of the idiom "meekness is not weakness; it is power under control" in modern preaching seems like an attempt to resist the countercultural nature of the beatitude. We do not want to imagine that we are actually weak—it sounds so much better to have power but utilize it wisely—that we convince ourselves that the real virtue here is our wise use of power. To those who have power, this is entirely applicable—they must follow Jesus' example and resist tyranny against those under their influence. But I'm not convinced this is what Jesus had in mind for the majority of his earliest followers. Rather than

---

in some Enochic literature and sectarian texts at Qumran. The apocalyptic worldview was used by the author to provide a theological context to how the text's addressees should understand life and acquire wisdom. See also Samuel L. Adams, *Wisdom in Transition: Act and Consequence in Second Temple Instructions*, SJSJ 125 (Leiden: Brill, 2008), 273–77, who analyzes Proverbs, Ecclesiastes, Sirach, and Instruction and argues for a steady "eschatologizing" of wisdom over time, toward a greater use of mystery language and concern for the afterlife and an otherworldly inheritance. John Kampen, *Wisdom Literature*, ECDSS (Grand Rapids: Eerdmans, 2011), 44, on the relationship of apocalyptic to wisdom, states, "All the evidence points to Instruction as an early and significant work in a particular trajectory of wisdom literature in Second Temple Judaism."

"power under control," it is more likely that Jesus was speaking to people with actual weakness. And rather than instructing his disciples to transcend their weakness and obtain power, he instructed them on flourishing in the midst of that weakness. Jesus was speaking to those who, like him, mourn over the state of Israel and feel powerless to produce a different result (Matt 5:4; 23:37–39), and those who, like him, are persecuted for the sake of righteousness (Matt 5:10). Rather than the proper use of power, Jesus was instructing them to live well within their circumstances, no matter what those circumstances produce—even if they produce hardship.

I don't think it's an accident that shortly after the beatitudes, among Jesus' first teachings in the Sermon on the Mount, he speaks about resistance to anger (Matt 5:21–26) and retaliation (Matt 5:38–48). The beatitudes are not about controlling power but resisting the need for it. They are about controlling the self and resisting the intuitive need to be in control of every outcome. Whereas culture tells us to take control of our circumstances by any means necessary, Jesus tells his disciples to make peace with their neighbors when in conflict, avoid retaliation, and even love their enemies (Matt 5:44). Rather than anger, seek reconciliation (Matt 5:24); rather than retaliation, turn the other cheek (Matt 5:39); rather than violence against their persecutors, love them and pray for them (Matt 5:44), and by doing this the disciples will "be children of your Father in heaven" (Matt 5:45).

Although the disciples hold out hope that one day they will be exalted, meekness is not best understood as an unfortunate condition related to poverty and oppression, but rather, it is a disposition that allows one to resist anger and retribution. Jesus, as the meek king, is the model for his followers. Jesus relies on the will of his father (Matt 26:39), and he is exalted (Matt 28:18). Those who follow Jesus can also expect exaltation (Matt 19:28–30). These meek are the ones who will "inherit the earth." Being meek is not an entrance requirement into the inheritance, nor is it simply a response to salvation; in fact, salvation is not the goal of the beatitudes at all. Meekness and the other dispositions are meant to describe "the kind of people who will make up the kingdom of heaven."[46] The meek are those who trust God and follow Jesus well regardless of their circumstances because their circumstances do not shape their character

[46] Rodney Reeves, *Matthew*, SGBC (Grand Rapids: Zondervan, 2017), 98, states as much regarding the entire Sermon on the Mount, but it is an apt description of those who exhibit the beatitudes.

or dictate their actions. Instead, like Jesus, they move in humility through a hostile environment while focused on the kingdom of God as their ultimate reward.

The inheritance of the earth is an aspect of that kingdom-oriented reward. The exact nature of the inheritance of the earth has been a matter of some debate among interpreters. There are scholars who have proposed that "inherit the earth" is best viewed as a spiritual rather than spatial/geographic reality. For example, Klaus Haacker does not mention Matt 5:5 but does refer to other Matthean passages regarding inheritance and argues that inheritance/entrance passages regarding the kingdom of God/heaven are used metaphorically. Haacker writes, "The kingdom of God is not a territory but an age to come" and is synonymous with "eternal life."[47] This is also the view of Davies and Allison, who argue that because the kingdom is already in some sense present, the kingdom is necessarily spiritualized and divorced from geography. They argue that in Matt 5:5, "to inherit the land" has been spiritualized and that the land in 5:5 is no more concrete than any other promises made in the beatitudes. Instead Matt 5:5 "is just another way of saying, 'The one who humbles himself will be exalted (in the kingdom of God).'" This argument is based on the view of Davies and Allison that Matt 5:3 and 5:5 are best viewed synonymously so that the kingdom and the inheritance are two ways of saying the same thing.[48]

The "spiritual fulfillment" view is surveyed by Joel Willitts.[49] Willitts critiques this view, arguing that Second Temple Jews and Matthew's Gospel retain a focus on actual territorial fulfillment. However, he specifically critiques a supersessionist version of the spiritual fulfillment perspective, which views the lack of focus on the land of Israel in Matthew as a result of the Jews losing their status as the people of God. Although Willitts rightly argues against a supersessionist perspective and in favor of a territorial fulfillment of the promises regarding the kingdom of God/heaven in Matthew, he argues in favor of "the land of Israel" as the target of that fulfillment. In Matthew, the land is extended to include its "ideal" northern border. Willitts connects this to Jesus' mission in Matt 10:5–7 regarding

[47] Klaus Haacker, "What Must I Do to Inherit Eternal Life? Implicit Christology in Jesus' Sayings about Life and the Kingdom," in *Jesus Research: An International Perspective*, ed. James H. Charlesworth and Petr Pokorný (Grand Rapids: Eerdmans, 2009), 148.

[48] Davies and Allison, *Matthew 1–7*, 450.

[49] Joel Willitts, *Matthew's Messianic Shepherd-King: In Search of "The Lost Sheep of the House of Israel"* (Berlin: De Gruyter, 2007), 157–62.

"the lost sheep of the house of Israel."[50] Similar is Scot McKnight, who argues that the inheritance refers to geographic space but that τὴν γῆν refers not to the whole earth but rather the land of Israel alone. He cites linguistic connections with the Hexateuch and Ps 37 to argue that "there is little likelihood that Jesus would have 'world' in mind." Due to the Jewish nature of Matthew's narrative, he argues that it is best to view τὴν γῆν as a reference to the land, as Israel itself is the only geographic space with which a first-century Jew would be concerned.[51]

I propose a "third way," which rejects supersessionist views of Matthew, rejects a solely spiritualized interpretation of the land and the kingdom, affirms the territorial aspect, and still argues that Matthew's Gospel views the territorial fulfillment as the whole earth, which includes Israel. The inheritance of the earth in Matt 5:5 is best viewed as a spatial/geographic aspect of the fuller kingdom, which fulfills the promise to God's people of a home consisting of geographic space. As with Isa 55–66, this territorial fulfillment extends beyond Israel alone. In my view, when one considers the trajectory of inheritance concepts throughout the Second Temple period, viewing the inheritance as the "whole earth" is actually the interpretation most consistent with the trajectory of Jewish tradition regarding inheritance.[52] In particular, the "whole earth" inheritance in Instruction and 1 Enoch and the parallels between these compositions and Matthew provide striking evidence that Jews in the Second Temple period envisioned a "whole earth" fulfillment of the inheritance. Furthermore, the heaven and earth word pairing between Matt 5:3 and 5:5 suggests that τὴν γῆν in Matt 5:5 refers not to the land of Israel alone but to the earth and the eschatological renewal of all things. This is supported within Matthew

50 Willitts, *Matthew's Messianic Shepherd-King*, 172.

51 Scot McKnight, *Sermon on the Mount*, SGBC (Grand Rapids: Zondervan, 2013), 42–43. Similar appears to be Evans, *Matthew*, 106, who argues that the Jews of the first century hoped for "national renewal" and that "the promised re-inheriting of the land would strike a hopeful chord in the hearts of his hearers." This is also the position of John Nolland, *The Gospel of Matthew: A Commentary on the Greek Text*, NIGTC (Grand Rapids: Eerdmans, 2005), 202, who argues that the land in view is "clearly the land of Israel, in the context of God's covenant promise to his people." Nolland argues this on the basis of interest in the land in Matt 4:25 and the post-exilic context of Matthew.

52 This is also the view of Charles H. Talbert, *Reading the Sermon on the Mount: Character Formation and Decision Making in Matthew 5–7* (Grand Rapids: Baker Academic, 2004), 52, who appeals to 2 En 50:2, the Pesher of Psalm 37 from Qumran, and Paul's expectation in Rom 4.

by the anticipation of cosmic renewal (Matt 19:28) and the fact that in the majority of instances in Matthew, γῆν appears to refer to the earth rather than the land of Israel (cf. Matt 5:18, 35; 6:10, 19; 9:6; 11:25; 12:42; 16:19; 18:18–19; 23:9; 24:30; 28:18).[53] Matthew 5:5 is best viewed as a functioning addition to the heaven and earth word pair (with Matt 5:3) where the inheritance of the earth is an eschatological, spatial, and this-worldly reward for present kingdom participation.

The "inherit the earth" tradition has been appropriated in a new covenantal context to describe the coming of a new creation rather than a focus on the land of Israel alone (Matt 19:28). The inheritance of the earth broadens the scope of both the covenant and the land inheritance in keeping with the way both have been appropriated into an eschatological framework; Israel is still Jesus' concern (Matt 10:5–6), but a universalistic concern for both the earth and the nations is not far behind (Matt 28:16–20), and Jesus' disciples are invited to anticipate and participate in that future in the present (Matt 5:5). The promise to inherit the earth is future tense and eschatological; as the kingdom of heaven comes to bear on the earth, those presently participating in the heavenly kingdom will inherit the earth as a result. The inheritance is guaranteed by God himself as a gift, through Jesus, who is included among Abraham's descendants. Jesus is therefore an heir to the inheritance and therefore plays a role in being a light to the nations, which highlights the universal aspect of the offer of inheritance. The inheritance is promised to those who follow God and live in an ethical way.

It is important to reiterate that inheritance in Matthew is a feature of a series of kinship metaphors found throughout the text and prolifically in several texts of the New Testament.[54] Typically, patrimonial inheritance requires the death of the father. That no father dies in Matthew's inheritance contexts might lead some to disassociate κληρονομέω in Matt 5:5 from the concept of gift or inheritance, looking instead for another translation, such as "possess" or "acquire."[55] However, this would

53 With Matt 27:45 as an exception.

54 See, for example, Paul's use of inheritance as a kinship metaphor in Gal 4:1–7 and Rom 8:17.

55 See, for example, Nathan Eubank, *Wages of Cross-Bearing and Debt of Sin: The Economy of Heaven in Matthew's Gospel*, BZNW (Berlin: De Gruyter, 2013), 70–71, who argues that Matt 5:5 refers more to recompense than inheritance. Ironically Eubank recognizes the close relationship of God's fatherhood to this verse but dismisses it as decisive for interpretation.

misunderstand the function of metaphors in discourse. As proponents of "conceptual metaphor theory" have pointed out, metaphors highlight certain aspects of any source domain that are relevant to the target domain, while hiding all aspects that are irrelevant to the metaphor.[56] In the case of Matthew and most other New Testament authors, "fatherhood" is the source domain, and God is the target domain. God is depicted as a father, but because fatherhood is a metaphor to describe God's relationship to his people, certain aspects of biological fatherhood are relevant to the depiction of God and certain aspects are not. The metaphor dispenses with all irrelevant connotations. In Matthew's theological context God does not die and Jesus rises from the dead so that the inheritance is not only something *received*, but it is also something *to be entered into* where the beneficiaries' relationship with God continues unabated. The death of God would be unthinkable to a first-century Jew, and God's Son transcends his death, but this does not negate inheritance as the proper way to understand κληρονομέω as a gift from a father to his children based on a kinship relationship. To be an heir of God's inheritance is to take on an entirely new identity, which transcends ethnic and class distinctions and which guarantees one not only reception *of* the inheritance but also entrance *into* the inheritance and eternal life therein. God's children are his heirs, and heirs enter into life through the inheritance (Matt 19:29). This kinship bond is not offered to the scribes and Pharisees, who have forsaken meekness and the love of enemies to try and take the inheritance for themselves (Matt 21:38–39), highlighting the competing path between the Jewish leaders and Jesus' *ideal disciples*.

[56] See George Lakoff and Mark Johnson, *Metaphors We Live By* (Chicago: University of Chicago Press, 1980), 10–13.

Matthew 5:6

μακάριοι οἱ πεινῶντες καὶ διψῶντες τὴν δικαιοσύνην, ὅτι αὐτοὶ χορτασθήσονται.

Flourishing are those who hunger and thirst for righteousness, because they will be filled.

Matthew's fourth beatitude corresponds to Luke's second, which reads, "Blessed are you who are hungry now, for you will be filled." Like Matthew's first beatitude, which adds "in spirit" to Luke's "poor," many interpreters have argued that Matthew turns Luke's literal "hungry" into a metaphor, therefore "spiritualizing" its meaning.[1] In antecedent Jewish traditions, hunger and thirst were used to communicate either idea: either actual physical hunger and thirst and God's provision in the face of such needs (Exod 16:1–17:7) or as a metaphor, either to describe a longing for God himself (Ps 42:2, 143:6) or a need for God's deliverance from trials or oppression (Isa 25:6, 41:17–18, 43:20, 49:10, 63:13). In some cases, both are in view; hunger and thirst describe a literal need for the purpose of highlighting a metaphorical meaning. Take, for example, Ps 107:1–9:

> 1 O give thanks to the LORD, for he is good,
> for his steadfast love endures forever.
> 2 Let the redeemed of the LORD say so,
> those he redeemed from trouble
> 3 and gathered in from the lands,
> from the east and from the west,
> from the north and from the south.

1 Whether Luke's "hungry" refers to literal hunger or hunger is used as a metaphor for a destitute economic or social condition is an open question. However, due to the corresponding woe in Luke 6:25, it is more apparent that Luke has in mind some sort of material, impoverished condition than is the case in Matthew.

[4] Some wandered in desert wastes,
  finding no way to an inhabited town;
[5] hungry and thirsty,
  their soul fainted within them.
[6] Then they cried to the LORD in their trouble,
  and he delivered them from their distress;
[7] he led them by a straight way,
  until they reached an inhabited town.
[8] Let them thank the LORD for his steadfast love,
  for his wonderful works to humankind.
[9] For he satisfies the thirsty,
  and the hungry he fills with good things.

This thanksgiving hymn refers to those in need. As Leslie C. Allen comments, this psalm describes "travelers out in the wilds, hopelessly lost, far from civilization." Allen argues that this psalm likely refers to a caravan of merchants, whose provisions have run out, but God provides to meet their material needs. These literal provisions are supplemented by a reference to the exile (vv. 2–3, which is possibly a later addition to provide an exilic context to an earlier thanksgiving hymn), which then serves as a metaphor for the repatriation of the Israelites back into their land. This hymn of thanksgiving, referring on one level to specific groups of people in need, also serves as imagery for the totality of the restored community—it gives examples of needs that have been met but uses human plight to magnify divine grace.[2]

A similar effect is found in Amos 8. In Israel, sharply contrasting economic tiers had developed among the people, and the upper class was choking out the lower. The poor were being exploited and starving, leading to God's judgment. God announces a famine on the land, "not a famine of bread, or a thirst for water, but of hearing the words of the LORD" (Amos 8:11). Bread and drink is at first used as a metaphor for God's word, but thirst is used more literally just two verses later to describe actual famine and the physical condition of those being judged (Amos 8:13).[3]

Jesus' language in the Matthean version of the beatitude appears manifestly metaphorical. Those who hunger and thirst are those longing for

[2] Leslie C. Allen, *Psalms 101–150*, WBC 21 (Grand Rapids: Thomas Nelson, 2002), 56–64. Nancy deClaissé-Walford, Rolf A. Jacobson, and Beth LaNeel Tanner, *The Book of Psalms*, NICOT (Grand Rapids: Eerdmans, 2014), 812, add the possibility that this psalm served as a liturgy of thanks offered by worshippers at a festival at the temple in Jerusalem.

[3] See Douglas Stuart, *Hosea-Jonah*, WBC 31 (Waco, Tex.: Word, 1987), 384–85.

righteousness/justice (δικαιοσύνη; *dikaiosynē*) rather than actual sustenance. However, there are interpreters who have argued that the literal meaning of hunger and thirst accompanies the metaphorical or, at least, leads into it. For example, Servais Pinckaers argues that actual hunger "is the sensation which most quickly moves us to cry out against injustice." Hunger prompts a rightful insistence for rightness to be done, and one's appetite cannot be repressed until justice is served. Pinckaers argues that in Scripture, there is no clean divide between material and spiritual needs so that what is material is carried over to the spiritual level. Because intimate relationship with God is at the center of human experience, hunger for food causes one to cry out in hunger for God. Pinckaers ties the fourth beatitude to Jesus' wilderness experience: after fasting, Jesus is physically hungry. Satan tempts Jesus to turn stones into bread, but Jesus resists and replies, "One does not live by bread alone, but by every word that comes from the mouth of God" (Matt 4:4). Echoes of Amos 8:11 abound; whereas in Amos, judgment means the loss of God's word for those who stuff themselves at the expense of those in need, in Matthew, Jesus relies on God's word to resist the temptation to stuff himself at the expense of his communion with the Father. Jesus is hungry, and yet this leads into and serves as a metaphor for Jesus' longing to honor God the Father. For Pinckaers, resistance to the fallacious attraction of earthly goods, including food and drink, among other pleasures, frees one to make room for the nobler desire to yearn after the mind and heart of God. In this sense Matthew was not changing Luke's beatitude, but rather, he was "giving expression to its integral meaning."[4]

That Jesus intended that material need would serve as a starting point for spiritual longing is possible, and Pinckaers' perspective is certainly inspiring. I think Pinckaers is right to tie the fourth beatitude to the temptation story, which appears just before the beatitudes in Matthew and which I tie to the first beatitude under the discussion on Matt 5:3. In what follows I will try to make sense of Matt 5:6 by first exploring the function of metaphor and, second, situating the term "righteousness/justice" within the overall Matthean framework.

Flourishing Are Those Who Hunger and Thirst for Righteousness

To understand Jesus' meaning, it is helpful to grasp the function of individual words in a metaphor. Metaphor does not happen at the word level

4 Servais Pinckaers, *The Pursuit of Happiness—God's Way: Living the Beatitudes* (Eugene, Ore.: Wipf & Stock, 1998), 91–95.

or even the sentence level but is entirely dependent on the overall context or "complete utterance." Rather than a "calculus of words,"[5] metaphors depend on the intention of the writer/speaker and the dynamics of the rhetorical situation.[6] When first approaching a phrase or clause, individual words are not "used metaphorically," but rather, metaphorical meaning is created when a group of words, all understood in their plain sense, are brought together into a specific context. That group of words is "interanimated" with one another to create a metaphor. Consider, for example, the clause "man is a wolf."[7] Both key terms, "man" and "wolf," must first be considered in their literal sense, and only then does the reader/hearer understand the deficiency between the two, requiring a figurative approach to the sentence. Man does not walk on all four limbs, therefore literal humans and literal wolves cannot be reconciled in a complete one-to-one comparison when one is said to "be" the other. Metaphorical meaning occurs when the words in the sentence, considered literally, are brought together and interanimated with one another in such a way that one term or idea figuratively qualifies or clarifies another. Only then is an "emergent meaning" found for one of the terms (in this case "wolf"), so only then can it be said that the term is being "used metaphorically."[8] When this happens, some possible meanings are likely eliminated immediately, and certain parts of the metaphor are hidden (again, man does not walk on all four limbs). Although the comparisons are limited, there are still several that are possible. If the speaker means that "Jerry is a wolf" because Jerry is hairier than the average person, this is very different than stating that "Jerry is a wolf" because he is a skilled hunter, or because he is ferocious, or because he is dangerous to sheep (i.e., vulnerable people). The rest of the wider context is necessary in order to decide.

This is all quite technical but still helpful in trying to understand the relationship between literal and figurative meanings in the fourth

[5] See Janet Martin Soskice, *Metaphor and Religious Language* (Oxford: Oxford University Press, 1985),

[6] See Wayne C. Booth, "Metaphor as Rhetoric: The Problem of Evaluation," in *On Metaphor*, ed. Sheldon Sacks (Chicago: University of Chicago Press, 1979), 51.

[7] An example made famous in metaphor research by Max Black, *Models and Metaphors: Studies in Language and Philosophy* (Ithaca: Cornell University Press, 1962), 25–47.

[8] See Paul Ricoeur, *Hermeneutics*, trans. David Pellauer (Cambridge: Polity Press, 2013), 47.

beatitude. Even if we can establish that Jesus was speaking metaphorically, and I think it's clear that he was, we do not need to limit ourselves to other metaphorical uses of hunger and thirst to understand Jesus' meaning. There is a sense in which, because the literal meanings of the words are never far from view, even when used in a figurative utterance, the literal uses of "hunger" and "thirst" are never truly divorced from our linguistic, emotional, psychological, and theological purview. Because associations with antecedent ideas are not made explicit, it's possible that Jesus had any number of antecedent Jewish traditions in mind or that he simply used these terms in their common, colloquial sense, without any echo or reference to previous texts, traditions, events, or ideas. Either way, metaphors function in such a way that a host of images are invoked, and whether they be literal or figurative, material or spiritual, all have potential relevance to our understanding of the terms found in the fourth beatitude.

Our understanding of the clause, then, depends on the way we understand righteousness/justice. First, we must decide on the best translation of δικαιοσύνη. "Righteousness" or "justice" are both defensible,[9] so context becomes key. Does δικαιοσύνη here refer to (a) a gift granted to the disciple by God, (b) a demand by God on the disciple's life, (c) an expectation that disciples will seek the good of the kingdom, or (d) the result of a disciple's striving or life choices? In other words, does a hunger and thirst for δικαιοσύνη refer to the justice that characterizes God's kingdom, to God's saving activity in the life of the disciple, or to ethical conduct that conforms to God's standards? Typically the position one takes depends on whether they see in the fourth beatitude a longing for God's action or the responsibility of the disciple to act.

As Eklund demonstrates, many interpretive approaches to the fourth beatitude have been largely conditioned by theological commitments and appeals to concepts of righteousness and justice from New Testament texts other than Matthew. Paul's righteousness language is often a point of discussion (especially in texts such as Rom 3),[10] and justification by faith has influenced post-Reformation readings of this verse.[11] Martin Luther, for his part, argued that the fourth beatitude referred to the good works of those who strive "to promote the general welfare and right conduct of

9 See δικαιοσύνη, *NIDNTTE*, 1:723.

10 Rebekah Eklund, *The Beatitudes through the Ages* (Grand Rapids: Eerdmans, 2021), 151.

11 Eklund, *Beatitudes*, 162–65.

every one."[12] It was later Lutheran interpreters, typified by Rudolf Bultmann, who imported a more Pauline, forensic understanding of righteousness into their reading of Matt 5:6. Based on his reading of Paul, Bultmann argues that Jesus could not have intended an ethical meaning, but instead the fourth beatitude refers to those who long to have God pronounce a verdict of "righteous" over them at the final judgment.[13]

Other interpreters have understood δικαιοσύνη in the fourth beatitude as a reference to God's justice, and hunger and thirst refers to the desire for it. The Isaianic background of the beatitudes leans in this direction. In Isa 58:6–7 God calls for a fast in the form of justice for the oppressed, where bread and shelter is supplied to the hungry. Hunger is literal, it is a need, and it also serves as an entry point into oppression more broadly. The hungry are longing for, are hungry for, both sustenance and God's justice on behalf of the captive and the brokenhearted. Similar is Isa 61:1–3, the passage that supplies vital linguistic background to Matthew's beatitudes; good news is proclaimed to the oppressed, and when justice is done, the poor are depicted as the righteous ones who display God's glory.[14] Mark Allen Powell is representative of those who read the fourth beatitude this way: hunger and thirst are metaphors not only for desire but also for deprivation, so the beatitude envisions those longing for vindication.[15] A related view extends the longing for justice to a longing for God himself—the hungry and thirsty "yearn for God above all else," which "probably includes yearning for God's justice."[16]

Chan is representative of an approach that combines a desire for God's justice with a longing to do God's will. Those who hunger and thirst for righteousness seek right conduct that accords with God's kingdom, and following the first three beatitudes, they are humble enough to know that they have not achieved it. Chan writes, "We are called actively to seek God's

12 Martin Luther, *Luther's Works*, vol. 21: *The Sermon on the Mount*, ed. Jaroslav Pelikan (St. Louis, Mo.: Concordia, 1956), 292.

13 Rudolf Bultmann, *Theology of the New Testament* (Waco, Tex.: Baylor University Press, 2007), 273.

14 See John D. W. Watts, *Isaiah 34–66*, WBC 25 (Nashville: Thomas Nelson, 2005), 843, 874. In Isa 61:3 LXX, the oppressed will be "called generations of righteousness" (κληθήσονται γενεαὶ δικαιοσύνης).

15 Mark Allan Powell, "Matthew's Beatitudes: Reversals and Rewards of the Kingdom," *CBQ* 58 (1996): 468.

16 Craig S. Keener, *A Commentary on the Gospel of Matthew* (Grand Rapids: Eerdmans, 1999), 169–70. "Thirst" as a longing for God is depicted in the Psalms. See, for example, Ps 42:2, "My soul thirsts for God, for the living God."

righteousness, which is a gift. And as we seek first God's justice, we then attain right moral conduct and relationships that have righteousness as the ethical standard."[17] The fourth beatitude is an ongoing process that does not end until the fulfillment envisioned in the eschaton, so to hunger and thirst requires a reorientation of the heart, including one's emotions, thoughts, and actions, to do what God's righteousness demands. Chan argues that humans have a natural inclination toward being lukewarm, so hungering and thirsting refer to continual striving toward faithful obedience to God.[18]

In my view, by highlighting good deeds as an aspect of righteousness, Chan is moving in the right direction. Among the Synoptic Gospels, Matthew is particularly fond of the righteousness word group,[19] and Matthew's writer(s) appear to have selected and arranged the sayings of Jesus in such a way that righteousness is highlighted throughout the narrative. Because Matthew's writer(s) is expressly interested in righteousness, Matthew is itself the best place to begin an evaluation of Jesus' meaning in Matt 5:6. As discussed in part 1, righteousness serves as an important term for bracketing the beatitudes; it appears both in Matt 5:6 and 5:10, closing out the two main stanzas of the set. The first stanza (Matt 5:3–6) is characterized by a sense of quietude—by humility, mourning, and reliance on God. The second stanza (Matt 5:7–10) is characterized by the active light that disciples bring into the lives of others—through mercy, purity, and peacemaking. Matt 5:6 indicates quietude—a desire for righteousness, which is an internal disposition that matches the heart conditions of the first stanza. Matt 5:10 indicates the willingness to sacrifice for righteousness—it is an outward manifestation of the beatitudes, which matches the outward movements of the second stanza. In the ways that the beatitudes indicate ethical internal dispositions and external outward intentions, the term "righteousness" is used by Jesus to encapsulate these ideas.

Righteousness is also vital to the immediate context of the Sermon on the Mount. In Matt 5:20, Jesus tells his disciples that if they want to

17 Yiu Sing Lúcás Chan, *The Ten Commandments and the Beatitudes: Biblical Studies and Ethics for Real Life* (Lanham, Md.: Rowman & Littlefield, 2012), 186.

18 Chan, *Ten Commandments*, 188.

19 Contrast, for example, the occurrences of the righteousness word group between Matthew (twenty-six times) and Mark (two times). See Craig A. Evans, "Fulfilling the Law and Seeking Righteousness in Matthew and in the Dead Sea Scrolls," in *Jesus, Matthew's Gospel and Early Christianity: Studies in Memory of Graham N. Stanton*, ed. Daniel M. Gurtner, Joel Willitts, and Richard A. Burridge, LNTS 435 (London: Bloomsbury T&T Clark, 2013), 102–14.

have a share in the kingdom of heaven, their righteousness (δικαιοσύνη) must exceed that of the scribes and Pharisees.[20] Jesus later clarifies that the scribes and Pharisees teach the law well, but their actions are false; they do not practice what they teach (Matt 23:3), disqualifying themselves from the kingdom and leading others down a path of hypocrisy (Matt 23:13). Greater righteousness is that which pursues matters of justice and mercy (Matt 23:23), but the scribes and Pharisees exhibit righteous behavior only when it serves to make a public show of their piety (Matt 23:5–7). These issues of justice and mercy are also described in the sermon itself: disciples are to resist retaliation (Matt 5:38–42), give alms to the poor (Matt 6:1–4), and avoid hypocrisy when judging others (Matt 7:1–5). In Matt 5:43–48 righteousness is paralleled with goodness, referring to moral behavior. God allows the sun to shine on the righteous and unrighteous alike, so the greater righteousness of the disciples requires that they follow God's lead and love their enemies. This short section ends with an injunction to be whole as God is whole (Matt 5:48), an approximation of Deut 18:13, which refers to the outward obedience to God's commands.[21]

In Matt 6:33 Jesus exhorts the disciples to "seek" (ζητέω; *zēteō*)[22] the kingdom and *God's* righteousness. Many commentators note the similarities between "seeking" and "longing" (i.e., hunger and thirst) and argue that the two verses run parallel to each other: it is not the righteousness of the disciples in view, but they are to hunger and thirst for and seek the righteousness of God. The very next clause argues that when one seeks God's righteousness, then "all these things will be given to you as well" (ταῦτα πάντα προστεθήσεται ὑμῖν). This righteousness, then, is God's gift and possibly refers to God's actions and/or God's justice. However, Matt 6:1 describes the disciples' acts of mercy as their own righteousness, which is not to be carried out in a hypocritical manner. Even as the disciples long for God's righteousness, this requires a response in

20 See John Kampen, *Matthew within Sectarian Judaism* (New Haven: Yale University Press, 2019), 78, 91, who views the Matthean community as a sectarian group. Jesus is their community spokesperson for the Mosaic tradition, and he calls his followers to join him, rather than other competing Jewish groups, if they want to "obtain life-giving wisdom." Although I do not share Kampen's optimism that we can construct a "Matthean community," Matthew does depict competing groups at the time of Jesus with opposing ideas regarding true righteousness.

21 See Evans, "Fulfilling," 106.

22 Used here in the imperative form (ζητεῖτε).

the form of outward goodness toward others and an active obedience to Jesus' ethical teachings.[23]

If righteousness in Matt 5:6 refers to the desire to obey God and exhibit a more life-giving form of mercy and service to others than is typically found among the Jewish leaders, then what exactly can be said about the *content* of this behavior? There isn't space here to develop a "theology" of righteousness in Matthew, but it isn't enough to describe righteousness simply as obedience to Torah. Jesus did say that he did not come to abolish the law (Matt 5:17), but his main concern regarding righteousness is what he calls "the weightier matters" of justice and mercy (Matt 23:23). Many of the things described in the sermon certainly qualify—Jesus envisions righteousness as that which avoids hypocrisy and actually serves those in need, the needy and broken, and enables them to see God in light of the love offered by Jesus and his followers. It is an eschatological righteousness that leads people toward the kingdom of heaven rather than away from it.[24]

Because They Will Be Filled

As with the second clauses in the other beatitudes, the passive verb χορτασθήσονται (*chortasthēsontai*) certainly implies that God is the one who will fill them—the disciples await an eschatological satisfaction at the renewal (Matt 19:28). Fill them with what? There are scholars who have argued that righteousness in this beatitude cannot refer to good works because it would not make sense for them to be "filled" with good works at the eschaton. Instead, some argue, God satisfies the disciples with himself, and if God is their satisfaction, then he must be the content of their hunger and thirst. The mistake here is the assumption that the object of the hungering and thirsting must also be the thing with which they are filled. However, those who mourn are not comforted with more mourning (Matt 5:4). Instead I read the promise of satisfaction as a reference to the fullness of the kingdom; those who strive for greater righteousness are filled with comfort, they will receive God's mercy, they will see God himself—they will be filled because theirs is the kingdom of heaven. Again the story of

23 For other considerations pointing to an ethical reading of Matt 6:33 that refers to the obedience of the disciples, see Wesley G. Olmstead, *Matthew 1–14: A Handbook on the Greek Text* (Waco, Tex.: Baylor University Press, 2019), 139.

24 What Roland Deines, "Not the Law but the Messiah: Law and Righteousness in the Gospel of Matthew—An Ongoing Debate," in *Built upon the Rock: Studies in the Gospel of Matthew*, ed. Daniel M. Gurtner and John Nolland (Grand Rapids: Eerdmans, 2008), 53–84, calls "Jesus-righteousness."

the rich young ruler is instructive. Only those who have given up everything to follow Jesus will, at the renewal, "receive a hundredfold and will inherit eternal life" (Matt 19:29).

Reflections on Matthew 5:6

It's possible that certain passages from the Hebrew Bible serve as background to the metaphor "hunger and thirst," passages such as Isa 49:10, Ps 107:9, and Amos 8:11. Ps 107 and Amos 8 are discussed above, but Isa 47:10 is also often cited by commentators. In this, the second Servant Song, the servant's mission is to restore Israel from their exile—"The prophetic word accomplishes the restoration of Israel by renewing the faith which Israel must have before it can be saved."[25] The song promises that God's people "shall not hunger or thirst," which is likely a literal promise for provision settled in the midst of a song replete with metaphors that function "as a reference to the restoration of the covenant itself."[26] Both literal and metaphorical hunger and thirst appear often in antecedent Jewish traditions to promise care and protection to God's people when they are in need.

Hunger and thirst in the fourth beatitude are metaphors for desire, and a desire for righteous living is also found in certain antecedent traditions. In the Temple Scroll, the longest scroll found among the Dead Sea Scrolls, column LI exhorts readers toward holy living. The passage speaks about the appointment of judges who are to show no partiality and take no bribes. In a passage with obvious thematic similarities to Matthew's beatitudes, God declares to the readers that they must pursue righteousness/justice in order to "take possession of the land which I give you so as an inheritance for all days." Inheritance serves as a reward for those who pursue what is right.[27]

Although many of these antecedent traditions might have played a role in the linguistic or thematic/theological development of the fourth beatitude, it's important to remember the function of metaphor described above. In order to have cultural resonance, metaphors must have cultural roots, and this cultural linguistic value is found in the common expressions

25 John L. McKenzie, *Second Isaiah*, AB (Garden City, N.Y.: Doubleday, 1968), 105.

26 Eklund, *Beatitudes*, 169.

27 See the translation in Florentino García Martínez and Eibert J. C. Tigchelaar, eds., *The Dead Sea Scrolls: Study Edition* (Leiden: Brill, 1999), 1271.

of a metaphor for a given culture. However, metaphors are most acutely affected by their immediate literary or rhetorical context, and in Matthew the context of righteousness refers most often to kingdom-oriented living. Even if the language of "hunger and thirst" in the context of a metaphor draws on its antecedent Jewish foundations in other metaphorical uses, there is enough evidence that this metaphor became somewhat ubiquitous, maybe even approaching the category of a "dead metaphor,"[28] so that through the process of polysemy, the phrase means something like "strive" or "desire" in a general sense. In other words, the object of previous metaphors for "hunger and thirst" need not be the same object of this metaphor in Matt 5:6 unless there is an explicit indication of such, and because such an explicit indication is absent from the verse, the metaphor likely serves to indicate little more than an evocative demonstration of longing.

With this in mind the fourth beatitude consists of Jesus' teaching that the disciples who flourish are those who long to do what is right, but this longing is *not* to be considered a passive longing. The rest of the beatitudes, and the whole of the sermon, demonstrate that Jesus expects that his disciples will actively pursue righteousness as a habitual course of action.[29] They long to exhibit greater righteousness and pursue a radical, counterintuitive form of kingdom-oriented living, even to the extent that they love their own enemies. Those who pursue righteousness receive the eschatological reward of being satisfied by God's promises.

[28] Dead metaphors are those that become so ubiquitous that they cease to be regarded as metaphors. They enter the lexicon as standard uses of language that can hardly be distinguished from literal speech. As Brenda B. Colijn, *Images of Salvation in the New Testament* (Downers Grove, Ill.: IVP Academic, 2010), 17, writes, dead metaphors are "victims of their own success—that is, they capture their subjects so well that they become the standard way of referring to that subject." Examples of this conventionalization include the "leg" of the race and the "foot" of the mountain.

[29] See, for example, W. D. Davies and D. C. Allison, *Matthew 1–7*, ICC (London: T&T Clark, 1988), 451, "Righteousness is to be habitually sought, as though it were meat and drink. . . . The meaning here is not passive longing but active seeking."

Matthew 5:7

μακάριοι οἱ ἐλεήμονες, ὅτι αὐτοὶ ἐλεηθήσονται.

Flourishing are those who are merciful, because they will receive mercy.

Gregory of Nyssa notes that throughout Scripture, God is called merciful. Therefore, he argues, those who observe the fifth beatitude, those who are merciful, have attained that which characterizes the divine.[1] God's mercy is certainly a prominent theme in the Hebrew Bible (e.g., Exod 33:19, 34:6), especially in the Psalms (e.g., 86:15, 103:8). For many interpreters, mercy in the fifth beatitude is a large net, sweeping the sea, catching any and all possible forms of mercy and including them in the meaning of this teaching. Gregory of Nyssa exemplifies this approach; he splits humankind into categorical opposites, such as slave/master, rich/poor, infirm/in good health, and so forth and argues that the merciful are those who seek equality by working toward the good of their neighbor.[2] Under this broad definition, mercy refers to an engagement with those in need with the aim of changing their situation.

As we shall see, mercy in Matt 5:7 likely includes a wide variety of behaviors often considered "merciful," but the best way to approach mercy in the fifth beatitude is not simply by casting the widest possible net around our definitions. Instead we should start by considering the theme of mercy presented throughout Matthew's Gospel. As it happens, Matthew shares with Luke the distinction of thematizing mercy more than maybe any other New Testament text, and Jesus in Matthew has quite a lot to say about the subject.

1 St. Gregory of Nyssa, *The Lord's Prayer, The Beatitudes*, ACW 18 (New York: Paulist, 1954), 88.

2 Gregory of Nyssa, *Beatitudes*, 88–89.

1. Mercy, Not Sacrifice

Twice in Matthew Jesus repeats a refrain that I consider to be among his central teachings. To emphasize the importance of his words, Jesus begins by stating, "Go and learn what this means," and then, in both Matt 9:13 and 12:7, Jesus states, "I desire mercy, not sacrifice." By saying this, Jesus quotes Hosea 6:6 (LXX). In Hosea, the prophet is concerned with Israel's idolatry. He points to the nation's two leadership groups, the monarchy and the priesthood (Hos 5:1), and rebukes them for drifting from God's law and for leading the people away from covenant faithfulness (Hos 6:7, 7:3). Hos 6:4 uses imagery to make the charge clear; God declares, "Your love is like a morning cloud, like the dew that goes away early." As James Limburg writes, the Israelites expected that God "would come to them just as surely as the coming of the dawn or the spring rain (Hos 6:3). Their own love for the Lord, in contrast, is as short-lived as the morning mist or the dew."[3] The capricious love of the Israelites is contrasted in Hos 6:6 with the "steadfast love" that God requires and that, by implication, he provides to his people (e.g., Hos 2:19). The "steadfast love" of Hos 6:6 is a translation of the Hebrew word חסד (*ḥesed*), a term frequently associated with God's covenant with Israel (e.g., Exod 20:6; Josh 22:5) and typically translated with glosses such as "steadfast love," "loyalty," or "mercy" (e.g., Joel 2:13).[4] According to Hos 6:6 the Israelites offer sacrifices, but they are unacceptable because of their lack of fidelity to God alone. God is uninterested in empty gestures and sacrifices disassociated from covenant commitment, and the prophet attempts to reorient the Israelites toward their allegiance to God.

The sacrifices mentioned in Hos 6:6 refer to those shared between God and his people at a fellowship meal. These sacrifices, along with the burnt offerings also mentioned, constitute liturgical worship.[5] James Luther Mays makes the important point that, for Hosea's audience in the eighth century BCE, sacrifice was an essential religious act so that religion apart from sacrifice would have been inconceivable. The declaration of Hos 6:6 "must have sounded radical and nihilistic," but the pronouncement is similar in both form and vocabulary to 1 Sam 15:22 (NRSVue), which states,

[3] James Limburg, *Hosea-Micah* (Atlanta: John Knox, 1988), 28.

[4] See Victor H. Matthews, *The Hebrew Prophets and Their Social World* (Grand Rapids: Baker Academic, 2012), 95–96.

[5] See John Goldingay, *Hosea-Micah* (Grand Rapids: Baker Academic, 2021), 108.

"Has the LORD as great delight in burnt offerings and sacrifices as in obedience to the voice of the LORD? Surely, to obey is better than sacrifice and to heed than the fat of rams."[6] For Hosea, the idea is not revolutionary; it's consistent with the revealed character of God. Sacrifices lose all meaning and potency when unfastened to covenant fealty.

Earlier in Hosea, "steadfast love" and "mercy" are brought together as companion terms to describe God's own love for his people (Hos 2:19). Love and mercy are, for God, redemptive acts, those that reach into the mire of his rebellious people to restore them from their infidelity. Medical metaphors are important to the context. In Hos 5:13, as Ephraim has been reduced to a fraction of their former selves, they appeal to their very oppressor Assyria for mercy rather than going to God. However, God declares, Assyria "is not able to cure you or heal your wound." God is the one who inflicted his people due to their infidelity (Hos 5:12, 14), and therefore only God can heal them. In their liturgical song of repentance (Hos 6:1–3), the people appear to recognize this and cry out, "Come, let us return to the LORD; for it is he who has torn, and he will heal us; he has struck down, and he will bind us up" (Hos 6:1). God is the great physician, and ultimately only he can remedy their situation. However, their actual response fails to live up to their words, as Ephraim is led poorly from within and oppressed from without.[7]

As Limburg argues, there is a contrast that comes to expression in Hos 6:6 between two fundamentally different dispositions toward God. Limburg writes, "The one thinks in terms of discharging religious obligations through the machinery of sacrifice and offering; the other speaks of loyal love and of acknowledging God as God."[8] All of the eighth-century prophets recognize this problem, but none of them speak of abolishing sacrifices and offerings; instead they call for a reformation of fidelity to God and the covenant. Limburg connects this to Jesus' use of Hos 6:6 and argues that Jesus' concern is the same. Jesus did not come to abolish the law, but he recognized, like Hosea, that his contemporaries had veered

[6] James Luther Mays, *Hosea*, OTL (Philadelphia: Westminster, 1969), 98.

[7] The exact role of the song of Hos 6:1–3 in the overall context is a matter of dispute. Rather than a cry of repentance, Goldingay, *Hosea*, 99, argues that the song consists of words that God "wants to put on people's lips." Hans Walter Wolff, *Hosea*, Hermeneia (Philadelphia: Fortress, 1974), 117, argues that the song was likely sung by the priests as a sort of self-appeasement.

[8] Limburg, *Hosea*, 29.

off course from that which concerns God most: the love of neighbor and mercy to the broken.[9]

The wider context of Hosea is important as background to Jesus' intentions and use of imagery in Matt 9:13 and 12:7. In Matt 9:10–13, Jesus and his disciples sit for a meal with tax collectors and sinners, and the Pharisees question this conduct.[10] Associating with sinners would have been, for many religious teachers, scandalous behavior, and the Pharisees would likely have considered table fellowship with sinners as a matter of ritual purity.[11] However, Matthew establishes early on that Jesus came to save his people (Matt 1:21), and just before the passage in question it is established that Jesus has the authority to forgive sins (Matt 9:2–8). As Matthias Konradt observes, Jesus' fellowship with sinners "illustrates the fact that Jesus does not keep human beings in their sinful past but with him they can receive the forgiveness of their sins."[12] Like Hosea, Jesus employs medical imagery; he stands in the place of Hosea's God and declares himself the physician who heals the sick (Matt 9:12). For the Ephraimites in Hosea, table fellowship with God was a formality abused for the purpose of religious maintenance; for Jesus, table fellowship with sinners is a restorative and transformative experience. In Hosea, God's people did not turn to him to be their great healer because they had followed their fruitless leaders into idolatry; in Matthew, Jesus rebukes the fruitless leaders for ignoring the sick and sinners and he steps in to save and heal.

In the LXX, חסד in Hos 6:6 is translated with ἔλεος (*eleos*), the same word found in Jesus' quote of Hosea in Matt 9:13. Rather than covenant loyalty, ἔλεος more specifically refers to mercy.[13] This allows Jesus to focus on the "interhuman sphere";[14] in this instance Jesus is less concerned with sinners' approach to God and more with humans' approach to one another

[9] Limburg, *Hosea*, 30. See also Matthias Konradt, *Christology, Torah, and Ethics in the Gospel of Matthew* (Waco, Tex.: Baylor University Press, 2022), 141, turning to sinners is "not a criticism of the Torah but rather precisely the fulfillment of the will of God that is expressed in the Torah and the prophets."

[10] Tax collectors were considered complicit with the oppressive economic conditions of the time. They were regarded as dishonest, greedy, and traitorous to Jewish well-being and would have been included with other disreputable groups, such as gentiles and prostitutes. See Walter T. Wilson, *The Gospel of Matthew*, vol. 1: *Matthew 1–13*, ECC (Grand Rapids: Eerdmans, 2022), 312.

[11] See Wilson, *Gospel*, 312.

[12] Konradt, *Christology*, 139.

[13] See ἔλεος, *NIDNTTE*, 2:167–68.

[14] Konradt, *Christology*, 140.

and the ways in which such an approach reflects God's own character and his desires for his people. As noted in part 1 of this study, Jesus embodies the beatitudes—he demonstrates the dispositions that he requires of his disciples. Jesus is merciful, therefore be merciful. The mercy of Jesus does not only apply to sinners, and his self-identification as the physician is not only metaphorical; it also applies to compassion for those in physical need. The infirm consistently call out to Jesus to have mercy on them and therefore heal them (Matt 9:27, 15:22, 17:15, 20:30), and when Jesus' disciples are hungry and they pluck heads of grain on the Sabbath, Jesus defends them against more accusations from the Pharisees (Matt 12:1–8). Jesus is lord of the Sabbath (Matt 12:8) and reminds the Pharisees, "If you had known what this means, 'I desire mercy and not sacrifice,' you would not have condemned the guiltless" (Matt 12:7). If observing the Sabbath causes one to neglect mercy for the hungry, then such observance is mere maintenance of law rather than an enactment of its principles.

2. Mercy as Forgiveness

Peter asks Jesus how often people must forgive those who sin against them (Matt 18:21). Essentially Jesus responds by stating that there is no limit to the number of times we must forgive (Matt 18:22). Jesus then settles into a parable about a servant who owed a king a sizable sum and could not pay, so he pleaded for mercy. Mercy was granted, and the servant was released from his debt. Immediately following, the servant ran into another who owed him a small sum and demanded his money. When the second servant could not pay, the first servant had him thrown into prison until the debt could be repaid. When the king heard this, he rebuked the first servant, saying, "Should you not have had mercy on your fellow slave, as I had mercy on you?" Several important points should be made about this story.

First, *forgiveness is radically self-inflicting*. It has become popular, in much recent preaching and in wider cultural discussions on forgiveness, to argue that forgiveness is not really about the other party—the one in need of forgiveness—but is instead about the one doing the forgiving. People should forgive for their own peace, their own benefit, to release their anger over the sin and therefore not be consumed by it—to free oneself of the burden caused by the offending party. This is, we might say, a psychological view of forgiveness. To forgive means freedom for the forgiver. I argue that this is not at all what Jesus has in mind. Instead forgiveness according to Jesus is radically self-inflicting, and it is only in this way that forgiveness is merciful. Merciful forgiveness is not about freedom for the self but the opposite—it takes the full burden of the other person's actions and absorbs their actions into oneself, releasing their penalty for their actions, for their benefit. Merciful forgiveness is the removal of the penalty for wrongdoing for the guilty party, and the cost is paid by the offended. In the parable, the king absorbs the debt at great cost to himself and receives nothing in return. The cross is a radical, selfless, self-inflicting act, which exemplifies such forgiveness. The guilty party is the one set free.

Second, *forgiveness is circular*. Compare the parable with Matt 6:12, 14.[15] The Lord's prayer asks God to forgive those who have already forgiven others and states that "if you do not forgive others, neither will your Father forgive your trespasses." In the prayer, interhuman forgiveness precedes the request for God's, but in the parable God's forgiveness precedes and generates human forgiveness. Konradt calls this a "multidimensional connection" between divine forgiveness and forgiveness between human beings[16]—God's forgiveness surpasses that which his people will ever be asked to offer, but all human forgiveness must reflect on God's own mercy and be extended in light of the forgiveness that each person has received. The parable ends the same way as the prayer; the first servant ends up in prison, and Jesus declares, "So my heavenly Father will also do to every one of you, if you do not forgive your brother or sister from your heart" (Matt 18:35). Forgiveness is unlimited but requires the development of an imitating heart, seeking to be molded by God's forgiveness so as to therefore model it. God's mercy is bountiful, but to presume on it leads to ruin. Failing to forgive cuts off the circle of mercy and causes one to forfeit the remission of debt that was granted.[17]

Third, *Jesus embodies forgiveness*. The merciful forgiveness of Jesus is presented practically within the Gospel. Peter later denies Jesus (Matt 26:69–75) but is still thereafter counted among his disciples at the great commission (Matt 28:16–20). The chance for imitation is given proper expression so that the very same disciple that asked how often we must forgive is the one who benefits from Jesus' embodiment of his own teaching.

3. Mercy as a Weightier Matter of Law

As I've argued consistently throughout this study, the expectations of ideal discipleship described by the beatitudes are sharply contrasted with the

15 See also the strikingly similar passage in Sir 28:1–7.
16 Konradt, *Christology*, 136.
17 Konradt, *Christology*, 138.

failure of the Jewish leaders to exhibit such dispositions, and this is as strikingly apparent regarding the fifth beatitude as it is anywhere else. In a contrasting woe, Jesus rebukes the scribes and Pharisees for being consumed by minor issues, such as the tithe of herbs and spices, while neglecting justice, mercy, and faithfulness (Matt 23:23). Jesus does not want them to neglect the former, but the latter are certainly far closer to God's heart. Hosea 6:6 is presumably still hovering in the background here and is a passage that likely informed Jesus' entire approach to mercy and the will of God regarding interhuman relationships.

Flourishing Are Those Who Are Merciful

As we have seen, mercy is an important theme for Jesus. Jesus embodied mercy through his healings and through his approach to the lost, extending reconciliation, acceptance, and forgiveness. In one of Jesus' central teachings—that he desires mercy and not sacrifice—he prefaces this with the rejoinder, "Go and learn what this means" (Matt 9:13). There is a distinctive emphasis placed here through these words on the importance of this teaching, both to Jesus' mission and to God's will. Habit-forming practices of devotion are a good thing until they become markers of religious maintenance, and when they replace fellowship and interpersonal feats of compassion, they fail to mirror God's own conduct. God is merciful, and those who flourish are those who imitate God. Jesus is merciful, and those who flourish are those who imitate Jesus.

Matthew's fifth beatitude has no parallel in Luke. However, as in Matthew, Luke follows the beatitudes with Jesus' teaching concerning the love of enemies. Luke 6:36 states, "Be merciful, just as your Father is merciful," and in Matthew, this runs parallel with "Be perfect, therefore, as your heavenly Father is perfect" (Matt 5:48). In other words, the Lukan exhortation to love enemies by showing mercy, even to them, is replaced in Matthew by a reference to general wholeness and flourishing in acts of love toward enemies, but the Matthean beatitudes cover the same concept of mercy and surely imply that enemies are to be included in the disciples' merciful behavior. Again this is illustrated in the immediate context by God's own actions. Jesus tells his disciples, love your enemies "so that you may be children of your Father in heaven; for he makes his sun rise on the evil and on the good, and sends rain on the righteous and on the unrighteous" (Matt 5:45). Extending mercy to enemies is counterintuitive, but to do so reflects divine mercy.

Because They Will Receive Mercy

The fifth beatitude is the only one that is balanced between the first and second half. For example, those who mourn do not receive mourning but the opposite—they receive comfort. Here in Matt 5:7, the merciful receive mercy. As Eklund states, "The beatitude is set on a kind of continual loop, from mercy to mercy."[18]

There is a difficulty regarding this beatitude and the implications of its associated passages regarding mercy throughout Matthew. The question arises, does God withhold mercy from those who fail to extend it to others? The book of James appears to echo this beatitude when it states, "For judgment will be without mercy to anyone who has shown no mercy; mercy triumphs over judgment" (Jas 2:13). Similarly, Jesus' teaching regarding mercy was taken up as vital among the first Christian interpreters. 1 Clement, one of the earliest extant Christian writings, includes a long passage that echoes not only Matt 5:7 but also possibly other beatitudinal ideas:

> Let us therefore be humble, brothers, laying aside all arrogance and conceit and foolishness and anger, and let us do what is written. For the Holy Spirit says: "Let not the wise man boast about his wisdom, nor the strong about his strength, nor the rich about his wealth; but let the one who boasts boast in the Lord, to seek him out and do justice and righteousness." Most of all, let us remember the words of the Lord Jesus, which he spoke as he taught gentleness and patience. For he said this: "Show mercy so that you may receive mercy, forgive, so that you may be forgiven. As you do, so shall it be done to you. As you give, so shall it be given to you. As you judge, so shall you be judged. As you show kindness, so shall kindness be shown to you. With the measure you use it will be measured to you." (1 Clem 13:1–2)[19]

In wording that takes up the intent of Jesus' language in Matthew, 1 Clement understands that only the merciful will receive mercy, and only those

[18] Rebekah Eklund, *The Beatitudes through the Ages* (Grand Rapids: Eerdmans, 2021), 172.

[19] Michael W. Holmes, *The Apostolic Fathers: Greek Texts and English Translations*, 3rd ed. (Grand Rapids: Baker Academic, 2007), 61–63. A portion of these lines are also found in Polycarp, *The Letter to the Philippians* 2.3. See Paul Foster, "The Text of the New Testament in the Apostolic Fathers," in *The Early Text of the New Testament*, ed. Charles E. Hill and Michael J. Kruger (Oxford: Oxford University Press, 2012), 288–89, who argues that it is not possible to be sure which Gospel Clement was following, as his citations are free form, but his words are closest to Matthew's.

who forgive will be forgiven. Eklund explains elegantly that a possible solution to this problem is to take mercy to its logical end: God shows mercy to the undeserving; therefore, when disciples of Jesus fail to show mercy, they are then undeserving to receive it, making them candidates for God's mercy.[20] Although this suggestion is both reasonable and possible, it does extend Jesus' teaching beyond his specific language in Matthew. If we want to grant the appropriate gravity to Jesus' actual words, he states clearly enough that those who do not forgive will not be forgiven, and those who fail to show mercy will not receive it. This is similarly embedded into a judgment scene at the end of Matthew (25:31–46). Although specific terms for mercy are missing from the passage, mercy is the dominant theme of the entire scene, where Jesus makes clear that those who fail to show mercy will be disqualified from the inheritance of eternal life.[21] We do not want to limit the confines of God's grace, but neither do we want to presume on it or fail to appreciate the weight of Jesus' expectations.

It might be enough to suggest that those who lack mercy and fail to forgive never had a share in God in the first place, but the result is largely the same: the scribes and Pharisees, as those who would have expected to have a share in God's kingdom, are said to have forfeited this (Matt 23:13), and their lack of mercy is stated explicitly as one of the reasons this is so (Matt 23:23). The language of the fifth beatitude is perfectly consistent with this approach to mercy found throughout Matthew's Gospel. The disciples receive mercy from God, and this experience fuels their Christ-like existence. Mercy is "a fundamental expression of the discipleship of Christ" and "an essential manifestation of Christian identity."[22]

Reflections on Matthew 5:7

One of my favorite scenes in all of literature is from Leo Tolstoy's great novel *War and Peace*. Pierre, one of the novel's protagonists and a lavishly wealthy man, finds himself a prisoner of war, confined to the barracks, and surrounded by strangers in the dark. He was starving, a new condition for him, when a man named Platon Karataev, who was poor in life but wealthy in virtue, reveals potatoes that he had hidden and shares

20 Eklund, *Beatitudes*, 193.

21 For details regarding Matt 25:31–46, see my *God's Will and Testament: Inheritance in the Gospel of Matthew and Jewish Tradition* (Waco, Tex.: Baylor University Press, 2021), 337–53.

22 Konradt, *Christology*, 157.

them with Pierre.[23] Karataev's great mercy and saintly disposition has an immense and lasting impact on Pierre that could be felt until the final pages of the story. Although fiction, it is true to Jesus' approach—mercy is not bound by power structures but is instead best understood through resonance. If those in a privileged position have a harder time expressing mercy than those in need of it, this is not because it is impossible for the affluent to understand mercy but because it's often harder for them to enter into the position of the lowly and therefore identify with mercy's power. As Thomas Merton writes,

> Such compassion is not learned without suffering. It is not to be found in a complacent life, in which we platonically forgive the sins of others without any sense that we ourselves are involved in a world of sin. If we want to know God, we must learn to understand the weaknesses and sins and imperfections of other men as if they were our own. We must feel their poverty as Christ experienced our own.[24]

Mercy is aided by synchronicity with the other, by solidarity with another's plight and a willingness to enter into their chaos.[25] To be a disciple of Jesus is to willingly take on oneself the path of lowliness and therefore identify with those who are lost, those who are sick, those in need of forgiveness;[26] it is to live with the constant remembrance of all the mercy that one has themselves received and the forgiveness granted to them when they were among the undeserving.

Identifying with those who suffer, of course, is not enough—an ideal disciple must seek to relieve the plight of the sufferer. This is the example Jesus provides and the ministry he passes on to his disciples (Matt 10:5–10). Such activity requires that the disciple possess a loving disposition toward others and that they not be prejudiced against others, neither their person nor their needs. The mercy and forgiveness of Jesus extended precisely toward those whom the culture at large would have considered the least qualified to receive it. Mercy can be costly, but to the one who understands Jesus' heart, they'll come to know that he desires it more than sacrifice. Ideal disciples imitate Jesus by caring for those in need, even

23 See Leo Tolstoy, *War and Peace*, vol. 4, pt. 1, chap. 7.

24 Thomas Merton, *No Man Is an Island* (New York: Harcourt, 1955), 212.

25 See Yiu Sing Lúcás Chan, *The Ten Commandments and the Beatitudes: Biblical Studies and Ethics for Real Life* (Lanham, Md.: Rowman & Littlefield, 2012), 196.

26 See Gregory of Nyssa, *Beatitudes*, 89, "Mercy is a voluntary sorrow that joins itself to the sufferings of others."

to the extent that they love their enemies and withhold from others the punishment that they deserve. As Metropolitan Hilarion Alfeyev writes, the merciful heart envisioned in the fifth beatitude "is the image of divine mercy that extends over all creation. . . . What is spoken of here is not only a pattern of behavior, but an inner quality as well."[27] In other words, mercy is not only a form of outward behavior but also an inner disposition that does not show prejudice. Those who extend mercy receive it as an eschatological reward. Mercy knows no limits, and a fellowship of mercy can transform lives.

27 Metropolitan Hilarion Alfeyev, *Jesus Christ, His Life and Teaching*, vol. 2: *The Sermon on the Mount* (Yonkers, N.Y.: St. Vladimir's Seminary Press, 2019), 78.

Matthew 5:8

μακάριοι οἱ καθαροὶ τῇ καρδίᾳ, ὅτι αὐτοὶ τὸν θεὸν ὄψονται.

Flourishing are those who are pure in heart, because they will see God.

The sixth beatitude has no parallel in Luke. It follows the first beatitude as the only other with a dative qualifier; the poor are poor *in spirit*, and the pure are the pure *in heart*. This appears to entirely internalize the kind of purity that Jesus has in mind, though as we'll see, this is not necessarily the case. One might expect that qualifying a subject describes something about it, therefore adding clarity, but in the case of this beatitude, the qualifier has potentially complicated the matter in its own way, as interpreters have separated out "pure" and "heart" as distinct ideas, looking to analyze them individually and then tie them together to better understand the full phrase. As problematic as this approach might be, there is a wisdom in it, as there are few plain antecedents that supply lucid parallels to the full phrase.

Most commentators highlight one specific psalm as the most likely background, if not to the words Jesus uses, then at least to the ideas he has in mind. Psalm 24:3–6 states,

> 3 Who shall ascend the hill of the Lord?
> And who shall stand in his holy place?
> 4 Those who have clean hands and pure hearts,
> who do not lift up their souls to what is false,
> and do not swear deceitfully.
> 5 They will receive blessing from the Lord,
> and vindication from the God of their salvation.
> 6 Such is the company of those who seek him,
> who seek the face of the God of Jacob.

The affinities are clear: the psalm refers to the pure in heart as those who seek the face of God. A liturgical psalm, the exact background is a matter of debate, but there is agreement that the psalm refers to God and people entering into each other's spheres. There is a contrast between the natures of God and humans, and the contrast is such that humans, in their fundamental condition, are unqualified to access God's presence. As humans attempt to ascend from a profane world into the holy presence of God, their access is granted not by ritual purity but moral purity—by clean hands and pure hearts.[1] "Clean hands" is an ethical phrase and is followed by a description of those who deal in truth.[2] Gordon J. Wenham argues that the phrase "what is false" in Ps 24:4 refers to idolatry[3] so that this verse applies both to faithlessness and falseness. To enter God's presence is to be blessed by him and to represent his name, and the duplicitous and hypocritical have no place there.[4]

Although the language and themes of the Psalms likely influenced Jesus' language regarding pure in heart, it is also possible that other ideas regarding purity are germane to the overall story of Matthew. Purity within Matthew's narrative must be understood in order to interpret the phrase "pure in heart."

Flourishing Are Those Who Are Pure in Heart

Purity is a matter of central importance in the Hebrew Bible. It relates to sacred objects, divine service, liturgical worship, sacrifices, the tabernacle, and the temple. That which is impure cannot mix with that which is sacred. Impurity can be ritual or moral; it can refer to physical injury or disease (Lev 21:17–23). And although impurity can exist in the realms of the profane, it is incapable of entering into God's presence. Entering into a sacred space with impurities would cause one to be cut off from God and his people (Lev 22:3). As Matthew Thiessen writes, the boundaries between the holy and the profane "were meant not only to safeguard

1 See Nancy deClaissé-Walford, Rolf A. Jacobson, and Beth LaNeel Tanner, *The Book of Psalms*, NICOT (Grand Rapids: Eerdmans, 2014), 247–53.

2 Cf. Psalm 51. The psalm deals with sins and the corruption of the inward self, and the psalmist asks God, "Create in me a clean heart, O God, and put a new and right spirit within me. Do not cast me away from your presence, and do not take your holy spirit from me."

3 Gordon J. Wenham, *Psalms as Torah: Reading Biblical Song Ethically* (Grand Rapids: Baker Academic, 2012), 102.

4 See also Psalm 73:1–3, which contrasts those who are pure in heart with those who are arrogant.

The term occurs often in Matthew (e.g., Matt 5:28; 6:21; 9:4; 11:29; 12:34, 40; 13:15, 19; 15:18; 18:35; 22:37; 24:48) and is often consistent with this meaning. Those who lust commit adultery in the heart (Matt 5:28), Jesus is "humble in heart" (Matt 11:29), knowledge of the kingdom is internalized when it is "sown in the heart" (Matt 13:19), and the desire to do external acts of evil comes from within the heart, or the internal self (Matt 15:18–19). The heart has a profound impact on outward activity but does so as a source from within.

Not only does Jesus have internal purity in mind, but we can be even still more specific by once again (as we've done with the other beatitudes) comparing Jesus' words with the behavior of the Jewish leaders. In Matt 12:22–37 when Jesus cures a demon-possessed man, the Pharisees accuse him of doing so through demonic powers. Jesus points out the poverty of their logic and rebukes them for attributing God's good works to evil forces. They do so, Jesus says, because there is evil in their hearts. The rising conflict between them escalates in Matt 23, when Jesus repeatedly accuses the scribes and Pharisees of hypocrisy. In modern usage, hypocrisy refers to those who do not behave in a way that is consistent with their words. Although the scribes and Pharisees are guilty of this too (cf. Matt 23:3), this is not the meaning of the term "hypocrite" (ὑποκριτής; *hypokritēs*) used by Jesus to describe the Jewish leaders throughout Matthew (cf. 6:2, 5, 16; 23:13, 15, 25, 27, 29). Instead hypocrisy refers to a form of playacting, a posturing for the public where they perform outward signs of piety while their inner selves remain impure.[12] The hypocrite judges others without considering their own faults (Matt 7:5). The issue of purity is addressed by Jesus in Matt 23:25–28, as he states that the scribes and Pharisees clean the outside of the cup and the plate while the inside is full of greed; they are like whitewashed tombs, clean on the outside, but on the inside, they are full of death and filth. These images, carefully chosen by Jesus, refer to ritual contamination in a clever mixing of the literal with the figurative. The scribes and Pharisees, according to Jesus, are actually concerned, in a literal sense, with ritual cleanness and purification—with the literal cleansing of dishes and utensils—but they are unconcerned with the inner state of their own personal purity. Similarly, tombs epitomized ritual impurity, and the scribes and Pharisees resemble such tombs—clean on the outside but impure within.[13] These woes extend the argument of

12 See ὑποκρίνομαι, *NIDNTTE*, 4:563.

13 See Craig L. Blomberg, *Matthew*, NAC 22 (Nashville: B&H Publishing, 1992), 347.

the woe just before (Matt 23:23), described in the previous section of this study, in which Jesus accuses the scribes and Pharisees of caring about lesser matters of the law while ignoring the weightier matters, such as justice and mercy.

This contrast with the Jewish leaders helps to explain what Jesus means by purity in heart. The contexts of ritual and moral impurity are clearly important to the background of the phrase, but in the sixth beatitude Jesus refers to internal purity, or "integrity of the whole being," where "the inner self finds parallel expressions in outward actions."[14] Piety should not simply be theater for public consumption but rather a condition of the heart where the actions of the disciple reflect the character of the teacher. Ceremonial purity is not enough to deal with one's inward being.[15] Instead purity of heart has a Godward orientation, what Allison calls "a heart undivided in allegiance and so rightly directed."[16] There is a way in which this beatitude can be viewed as an extension of the previous one: Jesus is merciful and provides forgiveness, which then motivates and empowers the mercy and forgiveness offered by his disciples to others. This forgiven state generates in the ideal disciple an inward state of gratitude and a humility in heart that mirrors that of Jesus' own heart (Matt 11:29), and this inward purity is of more consequence than ceremonial cleansing. Jesus does not abrogate the need for purity and, by use of the metaphor, confirms that ritual impurity is still in force.[17] Instead Jesus creates the conditions by which purity becomes total and permanent.

Because They Will See God

Considerable attention has been given to what it means to "see" (ὁράω; *horaō*) God. The focus has largely been on one's ability to physically "see" God, noting the two potentially contrasting traditions pertaining to this possibility. On the one hand there are assertions in biblical texts that it is impossible to see God (Exod 33:19–20; John 1:18; 1 Tim 6:16). On the other hand there are passages that speak of this possibility (Gen 32:30; Job 19:25–27). Various solutions have been proposed, such as that (a) God can

[14] Yiu Sing Lúcás Chan, *The Ten Commandments and the Beatitudes: Biblical Studies and Ethics for Real Life* (Lanham, Md.: Rowman & Littlefield, 2012), 203.

[15] Timothy D. Howell, *The Matthean Beatitudes in Their Jewish Setting: A Literary Speech Act Analysis*, SBL 144 (New York: Peter Lang, 2011), 145.

[16] Dale C. Allison, *The Sermon on the Mount: Inspiring the Moral Imagination* (New York: Crossroad, 1999), 51.

[17] Thiessen, *Jesus*, 111–12.

be "seen" through his good actions, (b) God can be seen through Jesus, his son, or (c) God cannot be seen in this present life, but the pure in heart will see him after death.[18] The first two options fit the discipleship orientation of the beatitudes and the third option fits the eschatological orientation of the beatitudes, but I argue that none of these makes the best sense of what Jesus had in mind.

We will remember that Matt 5:8 appears to allude to Ps 24:3–6. The psalmist declares that only those with clean hands and pure hearts, who avoid duplicity and idolatry, can ascend to the presence of God. Purity was all about access and impurity, the denial of it. The relative "visibility" of God is irrelevant to the particular issue of purity in Matt 5:8. To "see God," in its relationship to purity, is about ingress, the right to enter God's presence and the grant of access to direct fellowship. In this sense, to "see" God is a metaphor for "being with" him.[19] Solving the degree to which God is "visible" to the pure in heart is, in a theological sense, an interesting question but is not directly relevant to Jesus' meaning in this beatitude. Instead those who "see" God are those granted fellowship with God because their hearts are pure. In a way that is consistent with the other beatitudes, this is primarily granted in the future, but there is a sense in which Jesus, both through his presence and his purifying mission, provides fellowship with God to his disciples in their present earthly lives.

Reflections on Matthew 5:8

Regarding the sixth beatitude, Gregory of Nyssa notes the obvious difficulties for the life of the disciple when he writes, "The seeing has been made dependent upon purity of heart, my mind once more grows dizzy, lest perhaps purity of heart should be impossible to achieve because it surpasses our nature." This lament thankfully does not last long because,

[18] See the descriptions of these options by Metropolitan Hilarion Alfeyev, *Jesus Christ, His Life and Teaching*, vol. 2: *The Sermon on the Mount* (Yonkers, N.Y.: St. Vladimir's Seminary Press, 2019), 82–83. For a description of how these options as well as others have been expressed throughout the history of interpretation, see Rebekah Eklund, *The Beatitudes through the Ages* (Grand Rapids: Eerdmans, 2021), 215–34.

[19] Similar is Dale C. Allison Jr., *Studies in Matthew: Interpretation Past and Present* (Grand Rapids: Baker Academic, 2005), 43–63, who provides a helpful summary of at least seven interpretive options but argues that "to experience God" is an option that has the possibility of including several of the others. Allison argues that seeing God in the psalms refers to experiencing God but that the total experience can include many other possible ideas; "multiple meanings need not always be contradictory meanings."

on reflection, Gregory notes that birds are not asked to fly without wings, and creatures of the land are not asked to survive in the water; therefore "nothing is enforced that is beyond nature. Hence, we shall realize that neither does the beatitude set forth what outstrips hope."[20] God, through Jesus, both as exemplar and as the one who purifies, provides his disciples with everything that they need to become pure in heart and therefore know God.

Bruner notes yet another difficulty. Typically in the first-century Jewish world, there were outward disciplines that would demonstrate one's fidelity to God, such as Sabbath observance, Scripture study, and purification rites. Conversely, Jesus uses the beatitudes to describe thriving through entirely different, inward dispositions. To be sure, these dispositions manifest themselves in observable outward behaviors, but the internal condition bears the weight of emphasis in the beatitudes, which precedes all subsequent instructions regarding outward conduct. Jesus is concerned with the center of the whole person, with those who are poor in spirit, and those who are pure in heart.[21] The difficulty here is in the absence of concrete specificity: whereas performative purity has clear guidelines, the beatitudes require the interpreter to engage detailed exegesis of themes and terms, and they require of the disciple a considerable exegesis of the inner self.

Scot McKnight is helpful here. He argues that because "pure in heart" refers to those who pursue God's will and to those who understand that this has greater value than one's public reputation, then Matt 6:1–18 can be understood as an extended commentary on the sixth beatitude.[22] The disciple desires not possessions, wealth, or public adoration but instead seeks God, God's kingdom, and a future characterized by God's goodness. Following Jesus' lead in living for God's purposes ensures one's own fellowship with God.

20 St. Gregory of Nyssa, *The Lord's Prayer, The Beatitudes*, ACW 18 (New York: Paulist, 1954), 96–97.

21 Frederick Dale Bruner, *Matthew: A Commentary*, vol. 1: *The Christbook, Matthew 1–12* (Grand Rapids: Eerdmans, 2004), 175.

22 Scot McKnight, *Sermon on the Mount*, SGBC (Grand Rapids: Zondervan, 2013), 45.

Matthew 5:9

μακάριοι οἱ εἰρηνοποιοί, ὅτι αὐτοὶ υἱοὶ θεοῦ κληθήσονται.

Flourishing are the peacemakers, because they will be called children of God.

Although I've argued throughout this book that all of Jesus' beatitudes in Matthew are virtuous dispositions, this seventh beatitude is the most obviously so. Even those scholars who argue that the beatitudes are best viewed as unfortunate circumstances to be avoided agree that Matt 5:9 is an exception, as peacemaking is an obvious good, not only as a disposition but also as an active outward behavior. Peacemaking is an important concept in certain parts of the Hebrew Bible (e.g., Prov 10:10, 12:20); however, the adjective Jesus uses here for "peacemakers," εἰρηνοποιός (*eirēnopoios*), is found nowhere else in the LXX or the New Testament. It is important to remember that words, though often used to label or refer to concepts, cannot be *equated* with them. Words for peace in both Hebrew (שלום; *šālom*; often transliterated as *shalom*) and Greek (εἰρήνη; *eirēnē*) are common in the biblical literature,[1] and the concept of peacemaking is recurrent even in texts and passages where the term εἰρηνοποιός is not found. In other words, peacemaking is important in biblical texts even if Jesus' word for peacemaking in Matt 5:9 is rare.

The Hebrew term *shalom* has a wide range of meaning so that it's typically wisest to discuss its meaning specifically within a given context rather than offering sweeping descriptions of the theological "content" of the term. In other words, *shalom* does not mean everything that *shalom can* mean in every given instance of the term. Having said that, it can safely be argued that the word often connotes not only the absence of

[1] In the LXX, εἰρήνη typically translates שלום, and εἰρήνη is found over ninety times in the New Testament, including in every book except 1 John. See εἰρήνη, *NIDNTTE*, 2:114.

conflict but also a sense of wholeness, justice, welfare, reconciliation, and the rectification of that which is unsettled or wrong.[2] Because the LXX often features εἰρήνη as the translation of *shalom*, εἰρήνη has in many places picked up the same connotative meanings. These ideas serve as the starting points to understanding the seventh beatitude, but because the full theological background of *shalom* is quite broad and should not be imported into every passage where the ideas of peace are found, the particular Matthean context is essential for interpreting Matt 5:9.

Flourishing Are the Peacemakers

Although the term εἰρηνοποιός is found nowhere else in the New Testament, it is used in antecedent Greek literature, typically to refer to peacemaking in a time of war.[3] Even though this important background has been introduced into interpretations on the seventh beatitude, especially recently in the wake of the wars of the twentieth century,[4] most exegetes agree that peacemaking in times of war (or in an effort to avoid wars in the future) is a matter of subsequent theological reflection on peacemaking rather than a feature germane to Jesus' intent in the passage.[5] This conclusion certainly does not diminish the important role of the beatitude in encouraging peace in the face of war, but those seeking to understand how the seventh beatitude fits into the Matthean context will need to look for other possible referents.

Eklund helpfully organizes the possibilities into four primary categories: making peace with God, making peace within oneself, making peace with those who are near (such as neighbors, family, and friends), and

2 See Philip J. Nel, שָׁלֵם, *NIDOTTE*, 4:130.

3 Cf. Xenophon, *Hellenica* 6.3.4.

4 See Rebekah Eklund, *The Beatitudes through the Ages* (Grand Rapids: Eerdmans, 2021), 245–48.

5 See, for example, Yiu Sing Lúcás Chan, *The Ten Commandments and the Beatitudes: Biblical Studies and Ethics for Real Life* (Lanham, Md.: Rowman & Littlefield, 2012), 211–12, who suggests other referents but extends the goals of peace to political and social agendas as the product of the development of peacemaking as a virtue. See also the interesting qualifier by W. D. Davies and D. C. Allison, *Matthew 1–7*, ICC (London: T&T Clark, 1988), 458, who offer the possibility that the beatitude reflects not on war generally but as a response to the Jewish war with Rome. In this case the beatitude would not directly be attributable to Jesus but would rather be a product of the postwar community reflecting on Jesus' role as a peacemaker and suggesting that war with Rome was the wrong course of action.

making peace with those who are far (such as between nations).[6] The first category, peace with God, is a central theme regarding the pursuit of *shalom* in the Hebrew Bible and can be found in many passages concerned with reconciliation between God and his people. Recognizing that Matt 5:9 connects peace with the right to be called children of God, several of these passages have been suggested as possible background to the seventh beatitude. For example, Ps 85:8–10 states,

> 8 Let me hear what God the LORD will speak,
> for he will speak peace to his people,
> to his faithful, to those who turn to him in their hearts.
> 9 Surely his salvation is at hand for those who fear him,
> that his glory may dwell in our land.
> 10 Steadfast love and faithfulness will meet;
> righteousness and peace will kiss each other.

The psalmist reflects a time of estrangement and, remembering God's faithfulness, calls out for peace, which, in this context, refers to a restored relationship with God. God's *shalom* is about salvation and steadfast love.[7] Similar is Isa 52:7, where peace is announced as good news: "How beautiful upon the mountains are the feet of the messenger who announces peace, who brings good news, who announces salvation, who says to Zion, 'Your God reigns.'" Israel, in its estrangement, sees the end of its tribulation and, in jubilation, announces reconciliation with God as their king.[8]

Although a compelling argument can be made that peace with God serves as the biblical foundation for all other forms of peacemaking, the immediate context in Matthew suggests a different referent for Matt 5:9. The expectation of peacemaking directly precedes the final two beatitudes,

6 Eklund, *Beatitudes*, 236.

7 Beth Tanner, in Nancy deClaissé-Walford, Rolf A. Jacobson, and Beth LaNeel Tanner, *The Book of Psalms*, NICOT (Grand Rapids: Eerdmans, 2014), 655, points out that scholars often attempt to provide the precise historical moment of estrangement that occasioned this psalm but that enough possibilities exist that the psalm is best widely applied to many such moments. Tanner writes, "The issue in the psalm is the breach that needs to be healed, not the exact event that caused the breach."

8 See Claus Westermann, *Isaiah 40–66*, OTL (Philadelphia: Westminster, 1969), 251. Timothy D. Howell, *The Matthean Beatitudes in Their Jewish Setting: A Literary Speech Act Analysis*, SBL 144 (New York: Peter Lang, 2011), 146, argues that based on Matthew's prolific use of Isaiah, this passage lies in the background of the Matthean beatitude.

both of which deal with persecution. Persecution, at least the sort of which Jesus speaks, is something to be endured and is never a cause for retaliation, schism, or violent response. However, in the direct context of the Sermon on the Mount, Jesus goes even further: it is not enough simply to avoid reprisal and violence—the goal is not static forbearance or the tolerance of one's circumstances; instead the goal is active love toward one's enemies. Metropolitan Alfeyev calls Matt 5:44–45 a "direct continuation" of the seventh beatitude: "Making peace is conceived not as the passive expectation of the development of events, but as a person's intervention in events that are not developing in the way they ought to from a religious point of view."[9] Jesus does not teach his disciples to "put up with" their enemies but to love them; he does not teach his disciples merely to *live* at peace with others but to *make* peace with others. Peacemaking is about avoiding hatred and also about actively seeking reconciliation.

Once the disciple grapples with the difficult task of actively loving enemies and internalizes this path as their own, the other forms of peacemaking described in the Sermon on the Mount become more manageable. Disciples are not to get angry with another, and if they do, they are to seek reconciliation (Matt 5:21–26). If someone sins against the disciple, they are to avoid retaliation and instead actively bless the offending party (Matt 5:38–42). Other behaviors described by the sermon can also be viewed as those that facilitate peacemaking, such as giving alms (Matt 6:1–4), avoiding hypocritical judgments of others (Matt 7:1–5), and treating others as one wants to be treated (Matt 7:12). The previous beatitudes can also be viewed as modes of peacemaking, such as showing mercy and offering forgiveness to others, even if they are considered undeserving based on their social or sinful circumstances (see above the discussion on Matt 5:7).

The observant reader of Matthew's Gospel runs into an apparent contradiction at Matt 10:34: "Do not think that I have come to bring peace to the earth; I have not come to bring peace, but a sword." The apparent discrepancy is settled by the immediate context of Matt 10 and the apocalyptic imagery of the sword. Jesus sends his disciples to the lost sheep of the house of Israel, and he predicts that his disciples will face rejection and persecution due to their alliance with Jesus and to the nature of their message. This rejection will engender division, even among families, but the disciples are called to remain true to Jesus and his mission and steadfast

9 Metropolitan Hilarion Alfeyev, *Jesus Christ, His Life and Teaching*, vol. 2: *The Sermon on the Mount* (Yonkers, N.Y.: St. Vladimir's Seminary Press, 2019), 86.

in the face of conflict (Matt 10:16–25). It is important to recognize what is likely implied; the conflict originates with the nondisciple who rejects the disciple, rather than the other way around (Matt 10:40–42).[10] Those who welcome the disciples are not destined for the sword but are in line to be rewarded. The sword is an eschatological image (e.g., Ezek 38:21), and Jesus' anticipation of conflict matches with traditional eschatological expectation. Interestingly, in the only other mention of swords in Matthew, it is Jesus' opponents who arrive to arrest him while bearing swords. When one of the disciples draws his own sword in defense of his Lord, Jesus rebukes him and demands that he resheath his weapon (Matt 26:47–56). The disciples are called to be active agents of peace, and in this, there are no exceptions. Even enemies are to be loved. However, the messianic ministry of Jesus is sure to bring conflict, and Jesus presents this not only as an inevitability but also as an aspect of his very coming.[11]

Because They Will Be Called Children of God

That peacemakers are children of God implies that God is their father. Explicit references to God as father are not common in the Hebrew Bible (cf. Deut 32:4–6; Isa 63:16, 64:8; Jer 31:9). When such references appear, they primarily refer to God's fatherhood over corporate Israel. Other passages imply God's fatherhood by referring to Israel as God's son (cf. Exod 4:22–23; Jer 3:19; 1 Kgs 8:36; Isa 61:7–9). Less frequently God is also referred to as a father to the king of Israel (2 Sam 7:12–14). Despite the infrequency of references, Thompson has argued persuasively that God as father was an important concept to the ancient Israelites and that the idea of God's fatherhood was much more common than the words used to describe him as such. The God-as-father designation served to highlight three key activities of God in relation to his people. First, God as father is the head of the clan or family of Israel and therefore Israel's chief ancestor. As such, it is God who is responsible to provide an inheritance to his heirs. This inheritance was important to the discussion above concerning Matt 5:5. Second, God the Father is one who cares for his children and provides for their protection and security. Third, God the Father is a figure of authority

10 See Craig L. Blomberg, *Matthew*, NAC 22 (Nashville: B&H Publishing, 1992), 180.

11 See Walter T. Wilson, *The Gospel of Matthew*, vol. 1: *Matthew 1–13*, ECC (Grand Rapids: Eerdmans, 2022), 370–71. See also Rudolf Schnackenburg, *The Gospel of Matthew* (Grand Rapids: Eerdmans, 2002), 101, the gospel message is one of peace but has the power to divide.

who must be honored and obeyed.[12] Although God is described as a father to Israel's king, Thompson argues that the concept of God as father is primarily corporate, referring to his actions toward a people whom he creates and treats in a special way among the whole of humanity.[13]

Although the corporate dimensions of God's fatherhood are important, Matthew leads with God's fatherhood over Jesus as his unique son. The infancy narrative quotes Hos 11:1, which states, "When Israel was a child, I loved him, and out of Egypt I called my son." In Hosea this referred to all of Israel as God's son; the passage refers to the Exodus as an analogy for the situation with the Ephraimites described by the book.[14] Matt 2:15 applies Hosea's reference of the Exodus to Jesus as the Son of God, which fits with the prominent Exodus typologies embedded throughout the first Gospel.[15] God's sons Israel have pointed to God's unique son Jesus. Shortly thereafter in Matthew's narrative, when Jesus is baptized, a voice from heaven refers to Jesus as "my Son, the Beloved, with whom I am well pleased" (Matt 3:17). Jesus is then consistently depicted as referring to God as "my father," by far his most common way of addressing God. Although God is a father to many, Jesus' address to God signals a uniqueness of the nature of the relationship between father and son, and this relationship is in many ways extended to Jesus' disciples.[16]

Although it is important to understand God's fatherhood from within Matthew's Gospel, the way in which this important idea was received across early Christian tradition is instructive for understanding the earliest applications of the idea. For example, Mark's Gospel preserves a version of Jesus' prayer in Gethsemane in which he prays to God as "*Abba*, Father" (αββα ὁ πατήρ; *abba ho patér*; Mark 14:36). "*Abba*" is a Semitic form of address, paired here with the typical Greek word for "father." There is a pervasive notion in popular teachings about this address that *abba* was a childlike way of addressing a father and that the term means something like "daddy." However, scholars have argued for decades that

12 Marianne Meye Thompson, *The Promise of the Father: Jesus and God in the New Testament* (Louisville: Westminster John Knox, 2000), 18.

13 Thompson, *Promise*, 20.

14 See John Goldingay, *Hosea-Micah* (Grand Rapids: Baker Academic, 2021), 156–57.

15 On Exodus typologies in Matthew, see Dale C. Allison Jr., *The New Moses: A Matthean Typology* (Eugene, Ore.: Wipf & Stock, 1993).

16 See Stephen Westerholm, *Understanding Matthew: The Early Christian Worldview of the First Gospel* (Grand Rapids: Baker Academic, 2006), 113–17.

this is a later trajectory of the term's usage and is not a connotation of the term at the time Jesus used it.[17] Instead *abba* was a respectful way that adults would address their own fathers within the everyday rhythms of family life. Having said that, the term does imply intimacy in a personal relationship, and there is no evidence that anyone prior to Jesus used the word *abba* in prayer as an address to God.[18] This address, αββα ὁ πατήρ, appears to imply a unique and intimate relationship between God the Father and Jesus as Son. The address is found just two other times in the New Testament, both in letters of Paul (Gal 4:6; Rom 8:15). In both of these passages, it is God's people, as his children, who are allowed to cry out, "Abba! Father!" Importantly, these two addresses are found in two of the only places in the New Testament where a child of God becomes such through "adoption" (υἱοθεσία; *huiothesia*; cf. Rom 8:15, 23; 9:4; Gal 4:5; Eph 1:5). The adopted children of God, those who are brought into God's family through Christ, are encouraged to embrace Jesus' own personal address to the Father and make it their own—the intimacy between *the* Father and *the* Son is extended through the Son to those who enter the family as co-siblings and coheirs with Jesus (cf. Rom 8:15).

The address "abba, father" is not found in Matthew, nor are specific words for the "adoptive" nature of the relationship between God and his people that we find in Paul's letters. However, these passages in Mark and Paul are analogous and instructive for the way this relationship is described in Matthew. Jesus is already, in infancy, God's unique son (Matt 2:15), and through the unique son, his disciples *become* children of God in an adoptive sense. Although there is a popular notion that all humans are "God's children," this is not a biblical concept. Instead God's own people are God's children, and this relationship is gained only through association with Jesus (cf. John 1:12–13). This relationship brings one into intimacy with God and this intimacy fuels one's imitation of God and his son.

Thompson's third category mentioned above, that God is a father who must be honored and obeyed, stands out in relationship to the seventh beatitude. Those who are God's children are those who imitate God—by living as peacemakers they *will be* called his children. This verse is connected to Matt 5:45; disciples must love their enemies "*so that you may be children of your Father in heaven*." Being God's children is a matter of *becoming*, and in Matthew obedience to God's will and ways is a central

17 See James Barr, "'Abbā Isn't 'Daddy,'" *JTS* 39 (1988): 28–47.

18 See ἀββά, *NIDNTTE*, 1:85.

motif. Jesus prays, in the garden of Gethsemane, "My Father, if it is possible, let this cup pass from me; yet not what I want but what you want" (Matt 26:39). Jesus models obedience to the will of God, and this theme is prominent throughout the narrative—ideal disciples are expected to follow Jesus in their obedience to the Father by living in light of his will and extending God's character to others. Those who are unwilling to do God's will have no part with Jesus and his followers (cf. Matt 7:21; 12:48–50). To those who are Jesus' followers, his father becomes "your Father" (Matt 10:20, 18:14).[19]

Reflections on Matthew 5:9

Liu Xiaobo, winner of the 2010 Nobel Peace Prize, was persecuted and imprisoned precisely due to his efforts in peacemaking. Liu is known for his "final statement," delivered at his trial in 2009, in which he stated, "I have no enemies, and no hatred. None of the police who have watched, arrested, or interrogated me, none of the prosecutors who have indicted me, and none of the judges who will judge me are my enemies."[20] Liu, whose untimely passing in 2017 came shortly after being granted medical parole from a Chinese prison, argued that hatred was corrosive to an entire society, and he sought peacemaking as an antidote. Although I'm not aware of any evidence that Liu became a follower of Jesus before he died, he maintained close friendships with Christians, and he stated in print on several occasions that Jesus' peacemaking activities were a considerable influence on his own approach to peacemaking in his Chinese context. In a short piece written during Liu's third incarceration, he wrote,

> Jesus exemplified opposition without hatred or the desire for retaliation; his heart was filled with boundless love and forgiveness. Completely eschewing violence, he epitomized passive resistance, serenely defiant even as he meekly carried his own cross. No matter how profane and pragmatic our world is, we will have passion, miracles, and beauty as long as we have the example of Jesus Christ.[21]

[19] See William M. Wright IV, *The Lord's Prayer: Matthew 6 and Luke 11 for the Life of the Church* (Grand Rapids: Baker Academic, 2023), 59–60, "Jesus opens up his relationship with the Father and incorporates his disciples into it."

[20] Liu Xiaobo, *No Enemies, No Hatred: Selected Essays and Poems*, ed. Perry Link, Tienchi Martin-Liao, and Liu Xia (Cambridge, Mass.: Belknap, 2012), 322.

[21] Liu, *No Enemies*, 130. For other examples of Liu's reflections on Jesus, see the poem "Looking up at Jesus" in *No Enemies*, 131–33, and the poem

This boundless love and forgiveness has inspired other famous peacemakers. Bonhoeffer wrote on this passage, arguing that Jesus' ideal disciples endure suffering and choose not to inflict it on others, even their enemies. They do everything in their power "to overcome evil with Good." Disciples carry the cross of their Lord because the cross, more than any other place, is where peace was made.[22] Nouwen, in a short book on peacemaking, argues that if disciples follow Jesus' lead, then peacemaking "is unconditional, unlimited, and uncompromising."[23] Martin Luther King Jr., in a sermon on Matt 5, argued that the love of enemies is "a profound and ultimately inescapable admonition," which breaks the chain of evil and hate and is therefore the only way "to realize a unique relationship with God."[24]

One could argue, of course, that even if Jesus did not have enemies, he did have opponents. Like the other beatitudes, it's important to note that Matt 5:9 is contrasted with a woe against the scribes and Pharisees. In Matt 23:15 Jesus states, "Woe to you, scribes and Pharisees, hypocrites! For you cross sea and land to make a single convert, and you make the new convert twice as much a child of hell as yourselves." Of course context here is important. As I argue in the introduction to this study, the Jewish leaders are supposed to lead God's people into alignment with God's will, and Jesus' argument is that they've led God's people directly into the opposite direction. Jesus seeks ideal disciples for the purpose of peacemaking, where peacemakers can be declared *children of God*. In Matt 23:15 Jesus condemns the scribes and Pharisees for instead discipling *children of hell*. The connection between these verses is apparent enough when we consider the fate of the disciples of both groups, those following Jesus and those following his opponents. Jesus highlights the dereliction of responsibility to God and the repercussions of false discipleship so that those choosing between ideal and false discipleship are clear on the differences. Seen in this light an argument can be made that Jesus' prophetic rebuke is warranted. The reproach is rooted in Jesus' desire to see people find their way to God and to seek and do his will.

"Experiencing Death" in Liu Xiaobo, *June Fourth Elegies*, trans. Jeffrey Yang (Minneapolis: Graywolf Press, 2012), 3–15.

22 Dietrich Bonhoeffer, *The Cost of Discipleship* (New York: Touchstone, 2018), 112–13.

23 Henri Nouwen, *Peacework: Prayer, Resistance, Community* (Maryknoll, N.Y.: Orbis, 2005), 17.

24 Martin Luther King Jr., *Strength to Love* (Minneapolis: Fortress, 2010), 43–52.

And this is what it means to be a child of God—to seek and do his will. As Eklund writes, "To be a 'son of X' means to display the qualities of X."[25] When do peacemakers become children of God? Although, like the other verbs in the second clauses of the beatitudes in Matt 5:4–9, κληθήσονται (*klēthēsontai*; will be called) is in the future tense, there is a compelling case to be made that the realization of this designation does not only anticipate an eschatological fulfillment. This beatitude, maybe more than any other save for Matt 5:7, extends an inner disposition toward a clear directive for outward engagement. Those who are peaceable must strive to make peace, and when this is accomplished, the peacemaker is called God's child. Peaceability is an inner disposition that anticipates outward peacemaking actions. The eschatological promise is still relevant, and maybe even primary, because the child of God can never bring about peace perfectly in this life. But eschatological *shalom* is echoed in the present by God's children, who take on this role as followers of Jesus.[26] As Howell argues, "Jesus was pointing to the reality that peacemakers were reflective of being in the family of God since God promised to bring ultimate *shalom* on the earth. Peace differentiated the children of God because it was in the nature of God to make peace."[27]

25 Eklund, *Beatitudes*, 254.
26 Eklund, *Beatitudes*, 254.
27 Howell, *Matthean*, 152.

Matthew 5:10–12

μακάριοι οἱ δεδιωγμένοι ἕνεκεν δικαιοσύνης, ὅτι αὐτῶν ἐστιν ἡ βασιλεία τῶν οὐρανῶν.
μακάριοί ἐστε ὅταν ὀνειδίσωσιν ὑμᾶς καὶ διώξωσιν καὶ εἴπωσιν πᾶν πονηρὸν καθ' ὑμῶν ψευδόμενοι ἕνεκεν ἐμοῦ.
χαίρετε καὶ ἀγαλλιᾶσθε, ὅτι ὁ μισθὸς ὑμῶν πολὺς ἐν τοῖς οὐρανοῖς· οὕτως γὰρ ἐδίωξαν τοὺς προφήτας τοὺς πρὸ ὑμῶν.

> Flourishing are those who are persecuted for the sake of righteousness, because theirs is the kingdom of heaven.
> Flourishing are you when others reproach and persecute you and speak all kinds of evil against you falsely on account of me.
> Rejoice and be glad, because your reward is great in heaven. For in this way they persecuted the prophets who were before you.

These three verses contain two beatitudes, the eighth and the ninth. However, they are often studied together for their obvious thematic similarities. Indeed the connection between these verses is so clear that Matt 5:10 is often viewed as a single, eighth beatitude, with Matt 5:11–12 serving not as a ninth beatitude but rather as a long commentary on the eighth.[1] As discussed in part 1, it is better to see two beatitudes here rather than one: one beginning in verse 10 and another in verse 11. However, due to their thematic link they will be discussed together in this section.

Flourishing Are Those Who Are Persecuted for the Sake of Righteousness

Persecuted hardly seems like a condition for those who flourish. It is, most would say, a circumstance to be avoided. Conversely, there are those

[1] For example, see Yiu Sing Lúcás Chan, *The Ten Commandments and the Beatitudes: Biblical Studies and Ethics for Real Life* (Lanham, Md.: Rowman & Littlefield, 2012), 220.

who believe that persecution is the mark of discipleship, and therefore a sort of persecution complex is developed where the disciple embraces and almost craves it. It is important to note here that persecution is not the thing to be sought. Instead righteousness is that which the disciple seeks (Matt 5:6), and persecution is often the result of those who live out Jesus' designs for righteousness. I do not think Jesus intends for his disciples to *pursue* persecution, and at least at this early point in the narrative, he does not go so far as to declare it inevitable. However, he does appear to predict it, or at least anticipate it as a norm, and later in the story, after conflicts unfold, Jesus declares persecution unavoidable (Matt 24:9–14). Such an anticipation is rooted in Israel's heritage and Jesus' earliest experiences. Later in Matthew Jesus would make much of the poor treatment that the prophets of old received. They were God's messengers and yet were killed by their own people (Matt 23:35). This tradition is prominent in Jesus' own thinking and informs his sense of rejection (cf. Matt 13:57–58). One might suggest that an underlying inference of Jesus' teaching is that persecution can only be done to the righteous; trials brought on the wicked are not forms of persecution but punishment. In other words, persecution is typically undue treatment of the innocent or, at the very least, a strong overreaction to one's sins. If the righteous are pursued with abuse, reproach, slander, or violence, then this amounts to persecution or punishment meted out unjustly. Because the righteous are persecuted precisely *because of* their righteousness, then it stands to reason that their persecution is inflicted by the wicked.

Jesus explicitly refers to the prophets of old as examples of persecution, but he might also have been alluding to the Wisdom of Solomon, a deuterocanonical text likely written sometime in the first century BCE.[2] Although the extent of Wisdom's influence is disputed, it was known widely at the time of Jesus, and several compelling studies have entertained (or argued in favor of) an awareness and interaction with the text by New Testament authors.[3] David deSilva argues for a possible echo of Wis 2:16–20 in Matthew's crucifixion narrative in which the reference to Jesus as God's Son in Matt 27:43 would become a composite citation with

2 For a standard critical edition, see Joseph Ziegler, *Sapientia Salomonis*, Septuaginta 12.1 (Göttingen: Vandenhoeck & Ruprecht, 1980).

3 However, the possible interaction with Wisdom of Solomon is more pronounced in Paul's letters, particularly Romans, than it is in the Gospels. For a recent engagement, see Jonathan A. Linebaugh, *The Word of the Cross: Reading Paul* (Grand Rapids: Eerdmans, 2022), 97–122.

Ps 22:8. In Wisdom the wicked seek to test the righteous man who claims that God is his father. In Matthew the onlookers test the claim that Jesus is God's Son by mocking him in his death (Matt 27:38–44).[4]

After extolling righteousness as a way to seek the heart of God (Wis 1:1–15), the writer of Wisdom turns his pen toward the wicked, who see in life a meaninglessness that generates nothing more than hedonism. The wicked, viewing the righteous through their own sense of futility, seek to persecute them. "Let us oppress the righteous poor man" (Wis 2:10), say the wicked:

> 12 "Let us lie in wait for the righteous man,
> because he is inconvenient to us and opposes our actions;
> he reproaches us for sins against the law
> and accuses us of sins against our training.
> 13 He professes to have knowledge of God
> and calls himself a child of the Lord.
> 14 He became to us a reproof of our thoughts;
> the very sight of him is a burden to us,
> 15 because his manner of life is unlike that of others,
> and his ways are strange.
> 16 We are considered by him as something base,
> and he avoids our ways as unclean;
> he calls the last end of the righteous happy
> and boasts that God is his father.
> 17 Let us see if his words are true,
> and let us test what will happen at the end of his life,
> 18 for if the righteous man is God's child, he will help him
> and will deliver him from the hand of his adversaries.
> 19 Let us test him with insult and torture,
> so that we may find out how reasonable he is
> and make trial of his forbearance.
> 20 Let us condemn him to a shameful death,
> for, according to what he says, he will be protected."

The affinities between this passage and the crucifixion scene are evident. In Wis 2:12–20 the righteous man is persecuted precisely because of his righteousness—precisely because his ways are contrasted with the wicked. His ways are not like theirs; they have different understandings of the law,

4 David A. deSilva, *Introducing the Apocrypha: Message, Context, and Significance* (Grand Rapids: Baker Academic, 2018), 157. DeSilva demonstrates that the Wisdom of Solomon remained popular into the early church and was cited by early Christian writers, such as Origen and Augustine.

different ways to apply the law. The righteous man rebukes the wicked, and this conflict leads to violence and death. In Matthew these same themes dominate the conflicts between Jesus and his opponents. Jesus places his trust in the Father, and the mocking he receives is closely paralleled by that depicted in Wisdom—he is mocked because he is God's Son, and his adversaries dare him to prove it. The only proof they will accept is proof on their own terms.

This same passage in Wisdom might also have influenced Jesus' words in Matt 5:10–12. Jesus prepares his disciples for persecution and warns them that it will befall them precisely because of their righteousness. Because Jesus claims in the beatitudes that his disciples are pure—that they have sought righteousness, that they have intimacy with God, that they are children of God—his adversaries will persecute them as they will persecute him. It is important to make a careful distinction here: many interpreters have argued that Jesus' disciples face persecution expressly because they exhibit the beatitudes.[5] I do not think this is the case. Relying on God, being humble, peacemaking—these dispositions are not in themselves offensive, and most Jews at the time would have agreed that they were God-honoring traits. No, the problem the disciples face is not that they exhibit these dispositions but that Jesus declares that the current Jewish leaders do not. The dispositions of the beatitudes, and Jesus' other teachings, have prepared the disciples for a greater righteousness that is explicitly contrasted with certain Jewish leaders (Matt 5:20), and the disciples have been prepared for a mission to reach God's people that the current leaders have failed to reach (Matt 9:36–38). Jesus declares that his disciples exhibit these God-honoring dispositions while performing activities that many Jewish leaders found condemnable. The expression of the beatitudes become matters of conflict because of the particular way in which they are manifested in the outward behavior of Jesus and his followers—behaviors such as dining with sinners and healing on the Sabbath. The contrast of their approach both to God and to God's people laid the foundations over time for the climactic events described at the end of the Gospel.

The conflict begins early, when John the Baptist accosts the Sadducees and Pharisees for their ineptitude (Matt 3:7). Jesus might have had John's arrest in mind as a form of persecution since it was the result of righteous

[5] There is a rich history of this interpretation. See Rebekah Eklund, *The Beatitudes through the Ages* (Grand Rapids: Eerdmans, 2021), 262.

pronouncements (Matt 14:1–12). That Jesus thought about persecution not as a general, scopic, or nebulous concept but instead as one with a specific and foreseeable referent to the disciples' own circumstances is indicated by Matt 23:34 (NRSVue) in which Jesus declares to the scribes and Pharisees, "For this reason I send you prophets, sages, and scribes, some of whom you will kill and crucify, and some you will flog in your synagogues and pursue from town to town." Many scholars argue, rightly in my view, that Jesus here refers to his disciples as those who have been sent out by Jesus to serve the people and have faced persecution at the hands of the Jewish leaders.[6] This Jesus predicted when he sent his disciples to the lost sheep of Israel in Matt 10:16–18, warning them that they are being sent out as sheep among wolves and that they can expect resistance specifically because they are aligned with him and his mission. With all of this said, three important points can be made about the features of these beatitudes.

First, by telling the disciples that they will be persecuted "for the sake of righteousness," Jesus recalls the fourth beatitude. Righteousness refers to their outward participation in Jesus' mission and their obedience to God.[7] The disciples are not persecuted because they exhibit moral precepts but because they exhibit them in the context of Jesus' ministry and by following his lead in the fulfillment of the law (Matt 5:17) and in his particular expression of demonstrating the weightier matters of the law through acts of mercy and justice.[8]

Second, by telling the disciples that they will be persecuted "on account of me," Jesus seeks to confirm the disciples in their ministry and comfort them in the idea that they share his fate. Once again Jesus models the beatitudes. As an aspect of persecution, people will speak falsely against the disciples. In Jesus' trial the Jewish leaders seek those who will swear falsely against Jesus (Matt 26:57). The disciples will be reproached, and so will Jesus (Matt 27:27–44).[9] The disciples are not being persecuted because of

6 See, for example, Craig L. Blomberg, *Matthew*, NAC 22 (Nashville: B&H Publishing, 1992), 271; Douglas R. A. Hare, *Matthew* (Louisville: John Knox, 1993), 348–49; Charles H. Talbert, *Matthew*, Paideia (Grand Rapids: Baker Academic, 2010), 259; Curtis Mitch and Edward Sri, *The Gospel of Matthew*, CCSS (Grand Rapids: Baker Academic, 2010), 297–98.

7 See W. D. Davies and D. C. Allison, *Matthew 1–7*, ICC (London: T&T Clark, 1988), 459–60.

8 See Metropolitan Hilarion Alfeyev, *Jesus Christ, His Life and Teaching*, vol. 2: *The Sermon on the Mount* (Yonkers, N.Y.: St. Vladimir's Seminary Press, 2019), 95.

9 See Nathan Eubank, *Wages of Cross-Bearing and Debt of Sin: The Economy of Heaven in Matthew's Gospel*, BZNW (Berlin: De Gruyter, 2013), 181–83.

anything wrong with them or with their actions but because they share in the mission of their Lord.[10]

Third, the first eight beatitudes all appear in the third-person plural, "they." In Matt 5:11–12 the ninth beatitude shifts to the second-person plural, "you." The "whosoever" declarations are, with the ninth beatitude, changed to a specific declaration to Jesus' disciples. This might indicate a stylistic change so that the beatitudes can shift smoothly into the second-person construction of Matt 5:13–16,[11] but the most important reason is to contextualize persecution for the disciples. Gone are the invitations for all who want to follow. They are replaced with the somber reality of commitment—persecution is coming to "you," Jesus' disciples, but do not worry, for you are in great company. Rejoice and be glad because your reward surpasses the sorrow of your trials.

Because Theirs Is the Kingdom of Heaven

As discussed under Matt 5:3 above, the kingdom of heaven forms an *inclusio* around the first eight beatitudes.[12] This means that all of the eschatological blessings described between beatitudes two through seven are aspects of the fuller kingdom blessing. Jesus, in his inauguration of the kingdom, has come to fulfill Israel's story and invite his followers into full participation. To receive the kingdom is to be comforted, to inherit the earth, to be filled, to receive mercy, to see God, to be called children of God. Jesus raises up disciples, instills in them these insights, and then sends them into the world to proclaim and to heal, both among the house of Israel and to the ends of the earth. The kingdom mentioned in Matt 5:10 also then extends to the ninth beatitude and connects to its unique features. In all of the beatitudes, only the ninth contains imperatives, and only the ninth refers to rewards. When the disciples are persecuted, they are commanded to "rejoice and be glad," for their reward is great in heaven. So what sort of reward can the disciples expect? The simple answer is that the reward that awaits them in heaven is the fullest accomplishment of the kingdom. Therefore although the kingdom forms an *inclusio* around beatitudes one through eight, it is envisioned in the ninth beatitude as the consummation of the Christlike life. This is the simple answer, but it is full of complexities.

10 See Timothy D. Howell, *The Matthean Beatitudes in Their Jewish Setting: A Literary Speech Act Analysis*, SBL 144 (New York: Peter Lang, 2011), 148.

11 Davies and Allison, *Matthew 1–7*, 461.

12 For a brief description of the nature of the kingdom of heaven, see the discussion of Matt 5:3.

Nathan Eubank has made a compelling case that rewards are an important feature in the whole of the Matthean narrative. Throughout the Gospel Jesus not only invites people to follow him; he requires considerable commitment. In Matt 16:13–28 (NRSVue) Jesus predicts his own persecution and death and tells his disciples, "If any wish to come after me, let them deny themselves and take up their cross and follow me. For those who want to save their life will lose it, and those who lose their life for my sake will find it" (Matt 16:24–25). Those who bear their cross, those who abandon earthly treasure for kingdom commitment, those who follow Jesus into his persecution will be repaid with eternal life. In Matt 19:16–29, when the rich young ruler declines to abandon his earthly treasures for kingdom commitment, Jesus tells the disciples that because they've left everything to follow him, they will be rewarded at the eschatological renewal by reigning with him in his glory. Furthermore, anyone else who surrenders all for Jesus' sake will inherit eternal life. In Matt 20:17–28 Jesus again predicts his persecution and death, and the mother of the sons of Zebedee asks Jesus to give her sons privilege in the coming kingdom. Jesus replies that anyone willing to serve and to face persecution for his sake will be rewarded by Jesus' father. Eubank connects these passages to the beatitudes, arguing that a willingness to give one's life for Jesus' sake leads to eschatological reward.[13]

Eubank connects this call to commitment to the scribes and Pharisees, who will be denied heavenly treasures. As the sons of those who murdered the prophets, Jesus tells the scribes and Pharisees that they have filled up the "measure" of their ancestors (Matt 23:32). Eubank convincingly explains the meaning of this phrase, "the measure of your ancestors," by comparing it to Jesus' teaching on judgment in the Sermon on the Mount (Matt 7:1–5). In Matt 7 "the harshness or leniency with which one judges others will determine the harshness or leniency by which one will be judged by God."[14] Matthew 7:2 states, "The measure you give will be the measure you get." Jesus' point here is not that everyone receives a punishment fitting their crimes because we know that God forgives beyond what one deserves, if only they ask for his forgiveness (Matt 18:21–35). The point, rather, is that "God will judge a person using the same standard

13 Eubank, *Wages*, 147. See also Klyne R. Snodgrass, *You Need a Better Gospel: Reclaiming the Good News of Participation with Christ* (Grand Rapids: Baker Academic, 2022), 83, "The demands of self-denial, of cross-bearing in imitation of Jesus, of following him, of dying and rising are nonnegotiable."

14 Eubank, *Wages*, 65.

of judgment that that person used in judging others."[15] Because God uses the same measure to assess one's sins used by that person to assess another's, it is unwise to exaggerate another's sins or stubbornly hold their sins against them. Rather than keeping careful records of others' sins, the wise move is to abundantly and unreservedly offer forgiveness. The contexts of Matt 7:2 and 23:32 do not provide an exact parallel because 23:32 does not describe judgment and forgiveness, but the nature of the "measure" is the same. Eubank argues that according to Jesus, the sins of the scribes and Pharisees have piled up to a breaking point because rather than leading with mercy, they have persecuted God's servants. The measure is full against them, and their creditor has come to settle accounts. The scribes and Pharisees have stored up punishment rather than reward.[16]

A similar contrast between storing up earthly versus heavenly rewards is found in the Sermon on the Mount. In Matt 6:1–21 those who practice their righteousness for the praise of others, concerning almsgiving, prayer, and fasting, have stored up their treasures on earth and have received their reward. Conversely, those who do such things not for public applause but instead to honor God will be rewarded with treasures in heaven, the only place that treasures cannot be eroded or stolen (Matt 6:19–21). To revisit the Wisdom of Solomon passage discussed above, this concept is also found in that passage. The wicked seek earthly pleasures, while the righteous obtain "wages of holiness" (Wis 2:22).

This far-reaching Matthean concept of "wages" as rewards finds its earliest expression in the beatitudes. It is only those who surrender themselves to Jesus and his kingdom that receive the kingdom as their reward. As with the other beatitudes, Jesus models and embodies his own beatitudinal teachings because he suffers reproaches and violence for the sake of the kingdom. The reward is an eschatological promise, but it is an assured one. The reward of the kingdom far outweighs the pains of the coming persecution, so the disciples can "rejoice and be glad."

Reflections on Matthew 5:10–12

Once, many years ago, I went for a job interview at a Christian nonprofit focused on fundraising. During the interview the founder of the organization asked me if I had any enemies. "No," I replied, "not that I'm aware of." He reproached me and said, "Well, if there isn't someone out there

[15] Eubank, *Wages*, 65.
[16] Eubank, *Wages*, 63–67.

persecuting you, you aren't really being effective. All good work creates resistance." I disagreed with his premise, was offered the job anyway, and declined, only to find out that a few years later, that same interviewer was arrested for misappropriating funds. I can't help but wonder if he thought his arrest was an unjust form of persecution for all of his good work.

This is a popular notion, the idea that persecution is actually a mark of the ideal disciple. I do not think this is what Jesus had in mind. As the seventh beatitude states explicitly, those who flourish are peacemakers, and I would argue that the other beatitudes facilitate peacemaking through virtuous dispositions—they generate in the disciple a humble peaceability that leads to goodwill. To assume that one must be persecuted, that one must have enemies to be a good disciple, is a presumption on Jesus' aim to prepare his disciples for coming trials. Persecution is possible for all and inevitable for some, but it is not to be sought or assumed and certainly not to be arrogantly celebrated regardless of the circumstances. Yes, often disciples are persecuted precisely because they are in good company—in the company of Jesus and God's faithful servants. On this point Jesus was clear. When a disciple is reproached or persecuted for the sake of righteousness, then the disciple can rejoice because God sees their faithfulness and they will be rewarded in heaven. To test one's faithfulness only by the presence of persecution is to misunderstand Jesus' desire for peacemaking and often serves as little more than an excuse for one's own contentiousness and poor behavior toward others. Rather than justifying one's own worthiness as a disciple by the presence of persecution, the beatitudes suggest that a better guide is similar to Paul's words in Rom 12:18, "If it is possible, so far as it depends on you, live peaceably with all." Persecution often comes for the faithful but does not in itself demonstrate fidelity.

Peaceability is the goal, but Jesus had a very sagacious grasp of the conditions under which he was announcing the kingdom. He knew that when declaring that greater righteousness was something other than that which was demonstrated by the Jewish leaders, resistance was certain. It just so happens that the very dispositions Jesus taught are the same ones that best prepared the disciples to endure the coming storms. The reward of the kingdom might have served as a motivator to sustain discipleship in the face of struggle, but the beatitudes prepared them to flourish in the midst of these circumstances. They could endure persecution because they relied on God, because they were meek, because they joined Jesus in mourning the state of things and in aiming to rescue the world from its brokenness. Their desire for righteousness would prepare them to remain steadfast in the midst of risky work where they were exposed to questioning and open judgments and eventually to threats for declaring the reprehensible conditions of the status quo. This is what dispositions do: they predict the ways a person or thing might react when forces or circumstances are enacted on them. When a glass is dropped, it breaks; when a rubber band is pulled, it stretches; and when a disciple is persecuted, their virtuous dispositions predict the ways in which they'll respond. The beatitudes do not in themselves lead one into persecution, but they do prepare one to endure it well, and because they endure it in a Christlike manner, they are shown to belong to God's kingdom.

CONCLUSION

In this book, I have attempted to explain the meaning of Jesus' beatitudes, as they are found in Matthew's Gospel, with the following emphases of approach:

(1) By comparing each beatitude to similar language and themes within Matthew's Gospel
(2) By analyzing each beatitude through the contrast between ideal disciples and the failed Jewish leaders
(3) By viewing each beatitude in light of the antecedent Jewish traditions that likely had the greatest influence on Jesus' ideas and word choices

There is no claim here that this approach is novel, though there are some comparisons made and parallels explored that I have not found elsewhere. My approach in this book has been to conduct a *narrative* analysis of the ways that Matthew's writer(s) describes the historical setting of Jesus and his first followers without trying to justify Matthew's story or word choices through historical or sociocritical reconstructions. Often in studies on the beatitudes, the various major themes have been analyzed using broad cultural or religious categories, especially as it pertains to applying the beatitudes to various life settings. Although some of these reflections are present in this book, the goal here has been to understand the beatitudes only through Matthew's own presentation. Why did Matthew's writer(s) choose *these* specific beatitudes? Some scholars have argued that these nine were chosen to establish specific structures, either poetic or based on patterns of numbers.[1] Although I agree that these things factor into Matthew's layout and such reflections are fruitful, I have instead chosen to focus on the way these beatitudes develop important themes across

1 See, for example, W. D. Davies and D. C. Allison, *Matthew 1–7*, ICC (London: T&T Clark, 1988), 459, who argue that the ninth beatitude was added not for thematic reasons but to assist in the triadic structures of the Sermon in the Mount. Matthew's writer(s) received eight beatitudes and created a ninth to have three sets of three.

the whole story. My conviction is that Matthew's own Gospel narrative best explains the beatitudes he used to construct his list and the meanings of the features found within each beatitude. This also suggests that Matthew's beatitudes are closely linked with Matthew's entire structure and story. They serve not only as an introduction to the Sermon on the Mount, but their themes permeate the whole book and anticipate much of what comes next.

The goal of this book has not been to understand the full breadth of Matthew's depiction of Jesus' first disciples, nor has it been to develop a theory of discipleship. Many helpful studies engage in these discussions.[2] Instead the goal here has been to understand the role that the beatitudes play in describing the ethical dispositions of ideal disciples—meaning, not any of Jesus' specific earliest disciples (although they factor prominently both in Matthew's narrative and in the discussions of this book) but rather in the ways that the beatitudes help to detail what Jesus expects of *any* disciples. In Matthew's depiction these beatitudes are "whosoever" beatitudes—they are invitations to all who seek to participate in God's kingdom and introductions to kingdom-oriented habits that prepare ideal disciples for kingdom righteousness and kingdom-oriented mission. Although the beatitudes fit within Matthew's narrative framework, they are open-ended invitations first to the crowds that were interested in Jesus' teachings and subsequently to any and all who now find within them a pathway toward greater kingdom righteousness.

The beatitudes necessarily include a vision toward particular behaviors, but the subjects of the beatitudes are not behaviors; they are people—they are *those who* . . . exhibit the inner dispositions described therein. These people—these *ideal disciples*—flourish because they have followed Jesus, they have sought to replicate his own words and deeds of love and service, and they have sought to display God's character in their own involvement in God's kingdom-oriented mission toward the lost sheep of the house of Israel and to the nations. The disciples are marked by an interior

[2] See, for example, Günther Bornkamm, Gerhard Barth, and Heinz Joachim Held, *Tradition and Interpretation in Matthew* (Philadelphia: Westminster, 1963); Ulrich Luz, "The Disciples in the Gospel according to Matthew," in *The Interpretation of Matthew*, ed. Graham Stanton (Edinburgh: T&T Clark, 1995), 115–48; Jeannine K. Brown, *The Disciples in Narrative Perspective: The Portrayal and Function of the Matthean Disciples*, AB 9 (Atlanta: SBL, 2002); Michael J. Wilkins, *Discipleship in the Ancient World and Matthew's Gospel* (Eugene, Ore.: Wipf & Stock, 2015).

transformation and therefore display the virtues that demonstrate the nature of God's kingdom.[3] It is important to understand that these virtues are not in themselves salvific—they are not about how one "gets in." They are about proximity and fellowship with the Father and imitating the Son, and they describe those who flourish in Jesus' kingdom and join him in his mission to save the lost.

It is important to recognize that Jesus' vision of flourishing, although oriented toward demonstrating the character of God, is in many ways countercultural. Philosophers in the ancient world were all preoccupied with the concepts of flourishing and living a fulfilled life. They pursued "teleiotation" (meaning humanity's "ultimate end") as well as eudaimonia, a word used to describe the flourishing life that leads one there.[4] Different philosophical systems had different approaches to identifying humanity's supreme good, but all were concerned with wisdom and the practical matters of living a flourishing life. Some systems were built around pursuing pleasure and avoiding pain; others were built around the cultivation of ethics. But ultimately the goal was to consider one's supreme value and actively orient the whole of one's life toward serving that ultimate end.[5]

Although there are laudable elements of these various approaches and we can celebrate many of the virtues used by philosophers to describe the flourishing life (such as courage, moderation, gentleness, truthfulness, and justice), there are many ways in which Jesus describes a flourishing

3 See William C. Mattison III, *Introducing Moral Theology: True Happiness and the Virtues* (Grand Rapids: Brazos, 2008), 65.

4 See the description by Joshua W. Jipp, *Pauline Theology as a Way of Life: A Vision of Human Flourishing in Christ* (Grand Rapids: Baker Academic, 2023), 21–54.

5 Aristotle opens his *Nicomachean Ethics* with an evaluation of this topic. See Aristotle, *Aristotle's Nicomachean Ethics*, trans. Robert C. Bartlett and Susan D. Collins (Chicago: University of Chicago Press, 2011), 1–25. For an introduction to Aristotle's understanding of eudaimonia, see C. D. C. Reeve, "Beginning and Ending with *Eudaimonia*," in *The Cambridge Companion to Aristotle's "Nicomachean Ethics,"* ed. Ronald Polansky (Cambridge: Cambridge University Press, 2014), 14–33. Aristotle argued that virtue was the starting point for flourishing but that some external goods were also necessary. Subsequent philosophers were in large part responding to these criteria. For example, Stoic philosophers argued that material circumstances were irrelevant to a flourishing life and that one needed only to achieve a moral character. See the opening comments by William O. Stephens, *Stoic Ethics: Epictetus and Happiness as Freedom* (London: Bloomsbury, 2018), 1–5.

life that are foreign to other philosophical systems. The life of an ideal disciple is a difficult one. The beatitudes do not lead one directly into suffering, but neither do they help one to avoid it. In fact, they assist one in enduring suffering as a probable reverberation of profitably pursuing God and his righteousness.

The truth is, Jesus' actual first disciples sometimes fail to follow Jesus according to his teachings and his needs. They are often depicted as those with little faith (Matt 8:26, 14:31, 16:8, 17:20), little understanding (Matt 16:21–23), and little energy (Matt 26:36–46), and their resolve is not always steadfast (Matt 26:69–75). However, despite their failures, there is grace, and at the end of Matthew they are all entrusted with the extension of Jesus' mission, not only to proclaim the kingdom and its values but also to make disciples themselves (Matt 28:16–20). There is something ironic and beautiful about the often-failing followers being found ideal enough to further the mission of their Lord, and despite any imposter syndrome they might have faced, go they did, with the conviction that their crucified Lord was now their resurrected Lord and that he would be with them always, to the end of the age (Matt 28:20).

The end of the age promised to be a glorious time. If the end of the age has anything to do with the time of renewal (Matt 19:28), then the disciples are promised a leadership role, to go along with all that they were promised in the second clauses of the beatitudes. The first clauses were both ethically driven and *immanency* driven—they detailed a flourishing life of virtuous dispositions and they described dispositions marinated in urgency for the lost. This urgency is motivated by love and by an evaluation of the brokenness of the world; the disciples are not enrolled in a long-game form of slow cultivation but are recruited into a pressing vocation with immediate significance. God's people are lost and without a shepherd and the laborers are few, and Jesus will not let them wander any longer without mercy prevailing on their lives.

The beatitudes do not describe the summation of virtue but a starting point. They are the initial dispositions that lead one to virtuous choices and predict how one will respond when they are acted on by the world. The reason that the disciples are promised leadership roles at the renewal is because in Jesus' view, the current leaders have failed to show mercy and shepherd God's lost people. The Jewish leaders have taught well, but the manner of their service is inadequate, so the beatitudes are the starting point to cultivating leaders who embrace compassion as their principal response to the brokenness saturating their world. These new leaders replace the old ones as agents of the kingdom of heaven.

These two pathways—that of the failed leaders and that of the ideal disciples—are presented before the crowds as competing forms of discipleship. The same continues to be the presentation to Matthew's readers today. The beatitudes have something profound to contribute to the modern world, where faith communities major on teaching and sound doctrine but often neglect the "weightier matters" of mercy and care for the broken and forgiveness for the wayward. The Jewish leaders knew the law and they taught it well—it was their manner of service that Jesus criticized. It seems to me that many of our faith communities have the same problem. Jesus envisions beauty in meekness, in mourning over the ruptured state of the world, in depending on God for one's hope. When ideal disciples are pure in heart and they strive for righteousness, they extend mercy and work for peace, even in the face of various trials. This urgent mission is rewarded at some indeterminate time, but because the disciples trust the authority of Jesus, they rest securely in their hope for comfort, their fellowship with God, and in their share of the coming consummated kingdom.

It seems to me that the best way to conclude this study is to present reworded summaries of the findings for each beatitude. The beatitudes are dispositions that prepare disciples for the urgent task of leading God's people, and living out these dispositions results in abundant, kingdom-oriented rewards.

5:3: Flourishing are those who rely on God—who forsake the need for power and instead give themselves over to Jesus as king. They receive the right to participate in God's kingdom, a kingdom in which the ways of heaven are lived and proclaimed upon the earth by Jesus and his ideal disciples. At the renewal of all things, Jesus' disciples will live upon the renewed earth as citizens of God's heavenly kingdom.

5:4: Flourishing are those who mourn all that which Jesus mourns. They mourn because God's will is not yet done on earth as it is in heaven, but when the eschatological reversal takes place, they will be comforted.

5:5: Flourishing are those who are humble, and place the needs of God's kingdom above their own earthly desires. They will inherit a grander future than they could have imagined.

5:6: Flourishing are those who desire to live according to God's will. At the eschatological renewal of all things, they will experience the victory of God's kingdom.

5:7: Flourishing are those who show mercy to those who appear undeserving, extending forgiveness and hope. They will receive these things from God.

5:8: Flourishing are those who pursue God with the right motives. They will have fellowship with God.

5:9: Flourishing are those who actively love everyone, even their enemies. In this, they behave like God, showing themselves to be his children.

5:10–12: Disciples of Jesus will face persecution. Flourishing are those who respond to it well. Their reward will surpass the sorrow of their trials.

BIBLIOGRAPHY

Adams, Samuel L. *Social and Economic Life in Second Temple Judea*. Louisville: Westminster John Knox, 2014.

———. *Wisdom in Transition: Act and Consequence in Second Temple Instructions*. SJSJ 125. Leiden: Brill, 2008.

Alfeyev, Metropolitan Hilarion. *Jesus Christ, His Life and Teaching*. Vol. 2: *The Sermon on the Mount*. Yonkers, N.Y.: St. Vladimir's Seminary Press, 2019.

Allen, Leslie C. *Psalms 101–150*. WBC 21. Grand Rapids: Thomas Nelson, 2002.

Allison, Dale C., Jr. "The Embodiment of God's Will: Jesus in Matthew." In *Seeking the Identity of Jesus: A Pilgrimage*, edited by Beverly Roberts Gaventa and Richard B. Hays, 117–32. Grand Rapids: Eerdmans, 2008.

———. *The Historical Christ and the Theological Jesus*. Grand Rapids: Eerdmans, 2009.

———. *The New Moses: A Matthean Typology*. Eugene, Ore.: Wipf & Stock, 1993.

———. *The Sermon on the Mount: Inspiring the Moral Imagination*. New York: Crossroad, 1999.

———. *Studies in Matthew: Interpretation Past and Present*. Grand Rapids: Baker Academic, 2005.

Aristotle. *Aristotle's Nicomachean Ethics*. Translated by Robert C. Bartlett and Susan D. Collins. Chicago: University of Chicago Press, 2011.

Augustine, St. *The Lord's Sermon on the Mount*. ACW 5. New York: Paulist, 1948.

Barr, James. "'Abbā Isn't 'Daddy.'" *JTS* 39 (1988): 28–47.

Bauckham, Richard. "For Whom Were the Gospels Written?" In *The Gospels for All Christians: Rethinking the Gospel Audiences*, edited by Richard Bauckham, 9–48. Edinburgh: T&T Clark, 1998.

Betz, Hans Dieter. *Essays on the Sermon on the Mount*. Translated by L. L. Welborn. 1985. Repr., Minneapolis: Fortress, 2009.

Bird, Michael F. *The Gospel of the Lord: How the Early Church Wrote the Story of Jesus*. Grand Rapids: Eerdmans, 2014.

———. *Jesus Is the Christ: The Messianic Testimony of the Gospels*. Downers Grove, Ill.: Intervarsity Press, 2012.

Black, Max. *Models and Metaphors: Studies in Language and Philosophy*. Ithaca: Cornell University Press, 1962.

Blenkinsopp, Joseph. *Isaiah 55–66*. AB 19B. New York: Doubleday, 2003.

Blomberg, Craig L. *Jesus the Purifier: John's Gospel and the Fourth Quest for the Historical Jesus*. Grand Rapids: Baker Academic, 2023.

———. *Matthew*. NAC 22. Nashville: B&H Publishing, 1992.

Bock, Darrell L. *A Theology of Luke and Acts*. Grand Rapids: Zondervan, 2012.

Bonhoeffer, Dietrich. *The Cost of Discipleship*. New York: Touchstone, 2018.

Booth, Wayne C. "Metaphor as Rhetoric: The Problem of Evaluation." In *On Metaphor*, edited by Sheldon Sacks, 47–70. Chicago: University of Chicago Press, 1979.

Bornkamm, Günther. *Jesus of Nazareth*. London: Hodder & Stoughton, 1960.

Bornkamm, Günther, Gerhard Barth, and Heinz Joachim Held. *Tradition and Interpretation in Matthew*. Philadelphia: Westminster, 1963.

Boxall, Ian. *Matthew through the Centuries*. WBBC. Hoboken: Wiley Blackwell, 2019.

Brown, Jeannine K. *The Disciples in Narrative Perspective: The Portrayal and Function of the Matthean Disciples*. AB 9. Atlanta: SBL, 2002.

Bruner, Frederick Dale. *Matthew: A Commentary*. Vol. 1: *The Christbook, Matthew 1–12*. Grand Rapids: Eerdmans, 2004.

Buechner, Frederick. *The Alphabet of Grace*. San Francisco: HarperCollins, 1989.

Bultmann, Rudolf. *Theology of the New Testament*. Waco, Tex.: Baylor University Press, 2007.

Calvin, John. *Sermons on the Beatitudes*. Translated by Robert White. Edinburgh: First Banner of Truth, 2006.

Carter, Warren. "Narrative/Literary Approaches to Matthean Theology: The 'Reign of the Heavens' as an Example (Mt 4:17–5:12)." *JSNT* 67 (1997): 3–27.

Chan, Yiu Sing Lúcás. *The Ten Commandments and the Beatitudes: Biblical Studies and Ethics for Real Life*. Lanham, Md.: Rowman & Littlefield, 2012.

Charlesworth, James H., ed. *The Dead Sea Scrolls: Hebrew, Aramaic, and Greek Texts with English Translations*. Vol. 6B: *Pesharim, Other Commentaries, and Related Documents*. Tübingen: Mohr Siebeck, 2002.

Colijn, Brenda B. *Images of Salvation in the New Testament*. Downers Grove, Ill.: IVP Academic, 2010.

Collins, Adela Yarbro. "Polemic against the Pharisees in Matthew 23." In *The Pharisees*, edited by Joseph Sievers and Amy-Jill Levine, 148–69. Grand Rapids: Eerdmans, 2021.

Cooper, John M. *Reason and Human Good in Aristotle*. Cambridge, Mass.: Harvard University Press, 1975.

Cotter, Wendy J. *The Christ of the Miracle Stories: Portrait through Encounter*. Grand Rapids: Baker Academic, 2010.

Crump, David. *Encountering Jesus, Encountering Scripture: Reading the Bible Critically in Faith*. Grand Rapids: Eerdmans, 2013.

Daley, Daniel. *God's Will and Testament: Inheritance in the Gospel of Matthew and Jewish Tradition*. Waco, Tex.: Baylor University Press, 2021.

Davies, W. D., and D. C. Allison. *Matthew 1–7*. ICC. London: T&T Clark, 1988.

deClaissé-Walford, Nancy, Rolf A. Jacobson, and Beth LaNeel Tanner. *The Book of Psalms*. NICOT. Grand Rapids: Eerdmans, 2014.

Deines, Roland. "Not the Law but the Messiah: Law and Righteousness in the Gospel of Matthew—An Ongoing Debate." In *Built upon the Rock: Studies in the Gospel of Matthew*, edited by Daniel M. Gurtner and John Nolland, 53–84. Grand Rapids: Eerdmans, 2008.

deSilva, David A. *Introducing the Apocrypha: Message, Context, and Significance*. Grand Rapids: Baker Academic, 2018.

Deutsch, Celia. "Wisdom in Matthew: Transformation of a Symbol." *NovT* 32 (1990): 13–47.

Dodd, C. H. *More New Testament Studies*. Manchester: Manchester University Press, 1968.

Dunn, James D. G. "How Did Matthew Go about Composing His Gospel?" In *Jesus, Matthew's Gospel and Early Christianity: Studies in Memory of Graham N. Stanton*, edited by Daniel M. Gurtner, Joel Willitts, and Richard A. Burridge, 39–58. LNTS 435. London: T&T Clark, 2011.

Dupont, Jacques. *Les béatitudes*. Vol. 2: *La bonne nouvelle*. Paris: Gabalda, 1969.

Eklund, Rebekah. *The Beatitudes through the Ages*. Grand Rapids: Eerdmans, 2021.

Eubank, Nathan. *Wages of Cross-Bearing and Debt of Sin: The Economy of Heaven in Matthew's Gospel*. BZNW. Berlin: De Gruyter, 2013.

Evans, Craig A. "Fulfilling the Law and Seeking Righteousness in Matthew and in the Dead Sea Scrolls." In *Jesus, Matthew's Gospel and Early Christianity: Studies in Memory of Graham N. Stanton*, edited by Daniel M. Gurtner, Joel Willitts, and Richard A. Burridge, 102–14. LNTS 435. London: Bloomsbury T&T Clark, 2013.

———. *Matthew*. NCBC. Cambridge: Cambridge University Press, 2012.

———. "Sorting out the Synoptic Problem: Why an Old Approach Is Still Best." In *Reading the Gospels Today*, edited by Stanley E. Porter, 1–26. Grand Rapids: Eerdmans, 2004.

Farmer, Ron. "The Kingdom of God in the Gospel of Matthew." In *The Kingdom of God in 20th-Century Interpretation*, edited by Wendell Willis, 119–30. Peabody, Mass.: Hendrickson, 1987.

Foster, Paul. "The Text of the New Testament in the Apostolic Fathers." In *The Early Text of the New Testament*, edited by Charles E. Hill and Michael J. Kruger, 282–301. Oxford: Oxford University Press, 2012.

France, R. T. *The Gospel of Matthew*. NICNT. Grand Rapids: Eerdmans, 2007.

Garland, David E. *The Intention of Matthew 23*. Leiden: Brill, 1979.

———. *Reading Matthew: A Literary and Theological Commentary on the First Gospel.* New York: Crossroad, 1993.

Gnilka, Joachim. *Das Matthäus-Evangelium* I. HTK I/1. Freiburg: Herder, 1986.

Goff, Matthew J. *4QInstruction.* Atlanta: SBL, 2013.

———. "Discerning Trajectories: 4QInstruction and the Sapiential Background of the Sayings Source Q." *JBL* 124 (2005): 657–73.

———. "The Mystery of Creation in 4QInstruction." *DSD* 10 (2003): 163–86.

———. *The Worldly and Heavenly Wisdom of 4QInstruction.* Leiden: Brill, 2003.

Goldingay, John. *Hosea-Micah.* Grand Rapids: Baker Academic, 2021.

Good, Deirdre J. *Jesus the Meek King.* Harrisburg, Pa.: Trinity Press International, 1999.

Goodacre, Mark. *The Case against Q: Studies in Markan Priority and the Synoptic Problem.* Harrisburg, Pa.: Trinity Press International, 2002.

Goppelt, Leonhard. *The Theology of the New Testament.* Vol. 1. Grand Rapids: Eerdmans, 1981.

Green, H. Benedict. *Matthew: Poet of the Beatitudes.* Sheffield: Sheffield Academic, 2001.

Greenman, Jeffrey P., Timothy Larsen, and Stephen R. Spencer, eds. *The Sermon on the Mount through the Centuries: From the Early Church to John Paul II.* Grand Rapids: Brazos, 2007.

Gregory of Nyssa, St. *The Lord's Prayer, The Beatitudes.* ACW 18. New York: Paulist, 1954.

Guelich, Robert A. "The Matthean Beatitudes: 'Entrance Requirements' or Eschatological Blessings?" *JBL* 95 (1976): 415–34.

Gundry, Robert H. *Matthew: A Commentary on His Handbook for a Mixed Church under Persecution.* Grand Rapids: Eerdmans, 1994.

Gurtner, Daniel M. "Interpreting Apocalyptic Symbolism in the Gospel of Matthew." *BBR* 22 (2012): 525–45.

Haacker, Klaus. "What Must I Do to Inherit Eternal Life? Implicit Christology in Jesus' Sayings about Life and the Kingdom." In *Jesus Research: An International Perspective*, edited by James H. Charlesworth and Petr Pokorný, 140–53. Grand Rapids: Eerdmans, 2009.

Hagner, Donald. "Apocalyptic Motifs in the Gospel of Matthew: Continuity and Discontinuity." *HBT* 7 (1985): 53–82.

Hagner, Donald A. *Matthew 1–13.* WBC 33A. Dallas: Word, 1993.

———. "Matthew: Apostate, Reformer, Revolutionary?" *NTS* 49 (2003): 193–209.

Hanson, K. C. "How Honorable! How Shameful! A Cultural Analysis of Matthew's Makarisms and Reproaches." *Semeia* 68 (1994): 81–111.

Hare, Douglas R. A. *Matthew.* Louisville: John Knox, 1993.

Hays, Richard B. *Echoes of Scripture in the Gospels.* Waco, Tex.: Baylor University Press, 2016.

Heim, Erin M. *Adoption in Galatians and Romans: Contemporary Metaphor Theories and the Pauline Huiothesia Metaphors*. BIS 153. Leiden: Brill, 2017.

Holladay, Carl R. "The Beatitudes: Happiness and the Kingdom of God." In *The Bible and the Pursuit of Happiness*, edited by Brent A. Strawn, 141–68. Oxford: Oxford University Press, 2012.

Holmes, Michael W. *The Apostolic Fathers: Greek Texts and English Translations*. 3rd ed. Grand Rapids: Baker Academic, 2007.

Howell, Timothy D. *The Matthean Beatitudes in Their Jewish Setting: A Literary Speech Act Analysis*. SBL 144. New York: Peter Lang, 2011.

Hoyt, Thomas, Jr. "The Poor/Rich Theme in the Beatitudes." *JRT* 37 (1980): 31–41.

Hummel, Reinhart. *Die Auseinandersetzung zwischen Kirche und Judentum im Matthäusevangelium*. Munich: Kaiser, 1963.

Jacob, Haley Goranson. *Conformed to the Image of His Son: Reconsidering Paul's Theology of Glory in Romans*. Downers Grove, Ill.: IVP Academic, 2018.

Jipp, Joshua W. *Pauline Theology as a Way of Life: A Vision of Human Flourishing in Christ*. Grand Rapids: Baker Academic, 2023.

Jobes, Karen H., and Moisés Silva. *Invitation to the Septuagint*. Grand Rapids: Baker Academic, 2015.

Josephus, Flavius. *Antiquities of the Jews*.

Kampen, John. "Aspects of Wisdom in the Gospel of Matthew in Light of the New Qumran Evidence." In *Sapiential, Liturgical and Poetical Texts from Qumran*, edited by Daniel K. Falk, Florentino García Martínez, and Eileen Schuller, 227–39. Leiden: Brill, 2000.

———. *Matthew within Sectarian Judaism*. New Haven: Yale University Press, 2019.

———. *Wisdom Literature*. ECDSS. Grand Rapids: Eerdmans, 2011.

Keener, Craig S. *A Commentary on the Gospel of Matthew*. Grand Rapids: Eerdmans, 1999.

———. *The Gospel of Matthew: A Socio-rhetorical Commentary*. Grand Rapids: Eerdmans, 2009.

———. *The Historical Jesus of the Gospels*. Grand Rapids: Eerdmans, 2009.

King, Martin Luther, Jr. *Strength to Love*. Minneapolis: Fortress, 2010.

Kinney, Robert S. *Hellenistic Dimensions of the Gospel of Matthew*. Tübingen: Mohr Siebeck, 2016.

Koch, Klaus. *The Growth of the Biblical Tradition: The Form-Critical Method*. London: Adam & Charles Black, 1969.

Konradt, Matthias. *Christology, Torah, and Ethics in the Gospel of Matthew*. Waco, Tex.: Baylor University Press, 2022.

———. *The Gospel according to Matthew: A Commentary*. Translated by M. Eugene Boring. Waco, Tex.: Baylor University Press, 2020.

———. *Israel, Church, and the Gentiles in the Gospel of Matthew*. Translated by Kathleen Ess. Waco, Tex.: Baylor University Press, 2014.

Kümmel, W. G. *Promise and Fulfilment: The Eschatological Message of Jesus*. London: SCM Press, 1961.

Lakoff, George, and Mark Johnson. *Metaphors We Live By*. Chicago: University of Chicago Press, 1980.

Lapide, Cornelius a. *The Great Commentary*. 5 vols. Translated by Thomas W. Mossman. London: John Hodges, 1890.

Larsen, Matthew D. C. *Gospels before the Book*. Oxford: Oxford University Press, 2018.

Le Donne, Anthony. "The Jewish Leaders." In *Jesus among Friends and Enemies: A Historical and Literary Introduction to Jesus in the Gospels*, edited by Chris Keith and Larry W. Hurtado, 199–217. Grand Rapids: Baker Academic, 2011.

Levine, Amy-Jill. *Sermon on the Mount: A Beginner's Guide to the Kingdom of Heaven*. Nashville: Abingdon, 2020.

Limburg, James. *Hosea-Micah*. Atlanta: John Knox, 1988.

Linebaugh, Jonathan A. *The Word of the Cross: Reading Paul*. Grand Rapids: Eerdmans, 2022.

Liu Xiaobo. *June Fourth Elegies*. Translated by Jeffrey Yang. Minneapolis: Graywolf Press, 2012.

———. *No Enemies, No Hatred: Selected Essays and Poems*. Edited by Perry Link, Tienchi Martin-Liao, and Liu Xia. Cambridge, Mass.: Belknap, 2012.

Luther, Martin. *Luther's Works*. Vol. 21: *The Sermon on the Mount*. Edited by Jaroslav Pelikan. St. Louis, Mo.: Concordia, 1956.

Luz, Ulrich. "The Disciples in the Gospel according to Matthew." In *The Interpretation of Matthew*, edited by Graham Stanton, 115–48. Edinburgh: T&T Clark, 1995.

———. *Matthew 1–7*. Hermeneia. Minneapolis: Fortress, 2007.

———. *Matthew in History: Interpretation, Influence, and Effects*. Minneapolis: Fortress, 2007.

———. *Studies in Matthew*. Grand Rapids: Eerdmans, 2005.

Macaskill, Grant. *Revealed Wisdom and Inaugurated Eschatology in Ancient Judaism and Early Christianity*. SJSJ 115. Leiden: Brill, 2007.

Marguerat, Daniel. *Le jugement dans l'évangile de Matthieu*. Geneva: Labor et Fides, 1981.

Martínez, Florentino García, and Eibert J. C. Tigchelaar, eds. *The Dead Sea Scrolls: Study Edition*. Leiden: Brill, 1999.

Mason, Steve. *Flavius Josephus on the Pharisees: A Compositional-Critical Study*. Boston: Brill Academic, 2001.

Matthews, Victor H. *The Hebrew Prophets and Their Social World*. Grand Rapids: Baker Academic, 2012.

Mattison, William C., III. "The Beatitudes and Moral Theology: A Virtue-Ethics Approach." *Nova et Vetera* (English ed.) 11 (2013): 819–48.

———. *Introducing Moral Theology: True Happiness and the Virtues*. Grand Rapids: Brazos, 2008.

Mays, James Luther. *Hosea*. OTL. Philadelphia: Westminster, 1969.

McKenzie, John L. *Second Isaiah*. AB. Garden City, N.Y.: Doubleday, 1968.

McKnight, Scot. *Sermon on the Mount*. SGBC. Grand Rapids: Zondervan, 2013.

Meier, John P. *The Vision of Matthew: Christ, Church, and Morality in the First Gospel*. Eugene, Ore.: Wipf & Stock, 1991.

Merton, Thomas. *No Man Is an Island*. New York: Harcourt, 1955.

Metz, Johannes Baptist. *Poverty of Spirit*. Mahwah: Paulist, 1998.

Metzger, Bruce M. *A Textual Commentary on the Greek New Testament*. Stuttgart: UBS, 1994.

Mitch, Curtis, and Edward Sri. *The Gospel of Matthew*. CCSS. Grand Rapids: Baker Academic, 2010.

Morgan, Robert. *The Nature of New Testament Theology: The Contribution of William Wrede and Adolf Schlatter*. Eugene, Ore.: Wipf & Stock, 1973.

Mumford, Stephen. *Dispositions*. Oxford: Oxford University Press, 1998.

Murphy, C. M. *Wealth in the Dead Seas Scrolls and in the Qumran Literature*. STDJ 40. Leiden: Brill, 2001.

New International Dictionary of New Testament Theology and Exegesis. Edited by Moisés Silva. 5 vols. Grand Rapids: Zondervan, 2014.

New International Dictionary of Old Testament Theology and Exegesis. Edited by William A. VanGemeren. 5 vols. Grand Rapids: Zondervan, 1997.

Nickelsburg, George W. E. *1 Enoch 1*. Hermeneia. Minneapolis: Fortress, 2001.

Nolland, John. *The Gospel of Matthew: A Commentary on the Greek Text*. NIGTC. Grand Rapids: Eerdmans, 2005.

Nouwen, Henri. *Peacework: Prayer, Resistance, Community*. Maryknoll, N.Y.: Orbis, 2005.

Nouwen, Henri J. M. *The Return of the Prodigal Son: A Story of Homecoming*. London: Darton, Longman and Todd, 1992.

Olmstead, Wesley G. *Matthew 1–14: A Handbook on the Greek Text*. Waco, Tex.: Baylor University Press, 2019.

Overman, J. Andrew. *Matthew's Gospel and Formative Judaism: The Social World of the Matthean Community*. Minneapolis: Fortress, 1990.

Patte, Daniel. *Discipleship according to the Sermon on the Mount: Four Legitimate Readings, Four Plausible Views of Discipleship, and Their Relative Values*. Valley Forge, Pa.: Trinity Press International, 1996.

Pennington, Jonathan T. *Heaven and Earth in the Gospel of Matthew*. Grand Rapids: Baker Academic, 2009.

———. *Reading the Gospels Wisely: A Narrative and Theological Introduction*. Grand Rapids: Baker Academic, 2012.

———. *The Sermon on the Mount and Human Flourishing: A Theological Commentary*. Grand Rapids: Baker Academic, 2017.
Perrin, Nicholas. *Jesus the Priest*. Grand Rapids: Baker Academic, 2018.
Perrin, Norman. *The Kingdom of God in the Teaching of Jesus*. London: SCM Press, 1963.
Pickup, Martin. "Matthew's and Mark's Pharisees." In *In Quest of the Historical Pharisees*, edited by Jacob Neusner and Bruce D. Chilton, 67–112. Waco, Tex.: Baylor University Press, 2007.
Pinckaers, Servais. *The Pursuit of Happiness—God's Way: Living the Beatitudes*. Eugene, Ore.: Wipf & Stock, 1998.
Porter, Stanley E., and Bryan R. Dyer. *Origins of New Testament Christology: An Introduction to the Traditions and Titles Applied to Jesus*. Grand Rapids: Baker Academic, 2023.
Powell, Mark Allan. "Matthew's Beatitudes: Reversals and Rewards of the Kingdom." *CBQ* 58 (1996): 460–79.
Przybylski, Benno. *Righteousness in Matthew and His World of Thought*. SNTSMS 41. Cambridge: Cambridge University Press, 1980.
Quarles, Charles L. *Sermon on the Mount: Christ's Message to the Modern Church*. Nashville: B&H Publishing, 2011.
Reeve, C. D. C. "Beginning and Ending with *Eudaimonia*." In *The Cambridge Companion to Aristotle's "Nicomachean Ethics,"* edited by Ronald Polansky, 14–33. Cambridge: Cambridge University Press, 2014.
Reeves, Rodney. *Matthew*. SGBC. Grand Rapids: Zondervan, 2017.
Ricoeur, Paul. *Hermeneutics*. Translated by David Pellauer. Cambridge: Polity Press, 2013.
Rowland, Christopher. "Apocalyptic, the Poor, and the Gospel of Matthew." *JTS* 45 (1994): 504 18.
Saldarini, Anthony J. *Matthew's Christian-Jewish Community*. Chicago: University of Chicago Press, 1994.
———. *Pharisees, Scribes and Sadducees in Palestinian Society*. Grand Rapids: Eerdmans, 2001.
Schnackenburg, Rudolf. *The Gospel of Matthew*. Grand Rapids: Eerdmans, 2002.
Schröter, Jens. "How Close Were Jesus and the Pharisees?" In *The Pharisees*, edited by Joseph Sievers and Amy-Jill Levine, 220–39. Grand Rapids: Eerdmans, 2021.
Schweitzer, Albert. *The Mystery of the Kingdom of God: The Secret of Jesus' Messiahship and Passion*. Translated by Walter Lowrie. Amherst, N.Y.: Prometheus, 1985.
Schweizer, Eduard. "Formgeschichtliches zu den Seligpreisungen Jesu." *NTS* 19 (1973): 121–26.
———. *The Good News according to Matthew*. Atlanta: John Knox, 1975.
Scott, James M. *Paul and the Nations*. Tübingen: Mohr Siebeck, 1995.

Senior, Donald. "Between Two Worlds: Gentiles and Jewish Christians in Matthew's Gospel." *CBQ* 61 (1999): 1–23.

Sievers, Joseph, and Amy-Jill Levine, eds. *The Pharisees*. Grand Rapids: Eerdmans, 2021.

Sim, David C. *Apocalyptic Eschatology in the Gospel of Matthew*. Cambridge: Cambridge University Press, 1996.

———. *The Gospel of Matthew and Christian Judaism: The History and Social Setting of the Matthean Community*. Edinburgh: T&T Clark, 1998.

Snodgrass, Klyne R. *You Need a Better Gospel: Reclaiming the Good News of Participation with Christ*. Grand Rapids: Baker Academic, 2022.

Sockett, Hugh. "Dispositions as Virtues: The Complexity of the Construct." *JTE* 60 (2009): 291–303.

Soskice, Janet Martin. *Metaphor and Religious Language*. Oxford: Oxford University Press, 1985.

Stanton, Graham. *A Gospel for a New People: Studies in Matthew*. Edinburgh: T&T Clark, 1992.

Stephens, William O. *Stoic Ethics: Epictetus and Happiness as Freedom*. London: Bloomsbury, 2018.

Strecker, Georg. "Die Makarismen der Bergpredigt." *NTS* 17 (1970–71): 255–75.

———. *The Sermon on the Mount: An Exegetical Commentary*. Edinburgh: T&T Clark, 1988.

Strugnell, John, Daniel J. Harrington, and Torleif Elgvin. *Discoveries in the Judaean Desert XXXIV: Sapiential Texts Part 2, 4QInstruction*. Oxford: Clarendon, 1999.

Stuart, Douglas. *Hosea-Jonah*. WBC 31. Waco, Tex.: Word, 1987.

Stuckenbruck, Loren T. "4QInstruction and the Possible Influence of Early Enochic Traditions: An Evaluation." In *Wisdom Texts from Qumran and the Development of Sapiential Thought*, edited by Armin Lange, Charlotte Hempel, and Hermann Lichtenberger, 245–62. Leuven: Leuven University Press, 2002.

Suggs, M. Jack. *Wisdom, Christology and Law in Matthew's Gospel*. Cambridge, Mass.: Harvard University Press, 1970.

Talbert, Charles H. *Matthew*. Paideia. Grand Rapids: Baker Academic, 2010.

———. *Reading the Sermon on the Mount: Character Formation and Decision Making in Matthew 5–7*. Grand Rapids: Baker Academic, 2004.

Tcherikover, Victor. *Hellenistic Civilization and the Jews*. Grand Rapids: Baker Academic, 1999.

Thiessen, Matthew. *Jesus and the Forces of Death: The Gospels' Portrayal of Ritual Impurity within First-Century Judaism*. Grand Rapids: Baker Academic, 2020.

Thompson, Marianne Meye. *The Promise of the Father: Jesus and God in the New Testament*. Louisville: Westminster John Knox, 2000.

Tilborg, Sjef van. *The Jewish Leaders in Matthew*. Leiden: Brill, 1972.

Tuckett, Christopher M. “Synoptic Tradition in the Didache.” In *The Didache in Modern Research*, edited by Jonathan A. Draper, 92–128. Leiden: Brill, 1996.

Vanderkam, James C. “The Pharisees and the Dead Sea Scrolls.” In *In Quest of the Historical Pharisees*, edited by Jacob Neusner and Bruce D. Chilton, 225–36. Waco, Tex.: Baylor University Press, 2007.

Vermes, Géza. *The Complete Dead Sea Scrolls in English*. London: Penguin, 2011.

Viljoen, Francois P. “Righteousness and Identity Formation in the Sermon on the Mount.” *HTS* 69 (2013): 1–10.

Watts, John D. W. *Isaiah 34–66*. WBC 25. Nashville: Thomas Nelson, 2005.

Wellhausen, Julius. *Das Evangelium Matthaei: Übersetzt und Erklärt*. Berlin: Georg Reimer, 1904.

Wenham, Gordon J. *Psalms as Torah: Reading Biblical Song Ethically*. Grand Rapids: Baker Academic, 2012.

Weren, W. J. C. *Studies in Matthew's Gospel: Literary Design, Intertextuality, and Social Setting*. BIS 130. Leiden: Brill, 2013.

Westerholm, Stephen. *Understanding Matthew: The Early Christian Worldview of the First Gospel*. Grand Rapids: Baker Academic, 2006.

Westermann, Claus. *Isaiah 40–66*. OTL. Philadelphia: Westminster, 1969.

Wilkins, Michael J. *Discipleship in the Ancient World and Matthew's Gospel*. Eugene, Ore.: Wipf & Stock, 2015.

Willis, Wendell, ed. *The Kingdom of God in 20th-Century Interpretation*. Peabody, Mass.: Hendrickson, 1987.

Willitts, Joel. *Matthew's Messianic Shepherd-King: In Search of “The Lost Sheep of the House of Israel.”* Berlin: De Gruyter, 2007.

———. “The Twelve Disciples in Matthew.” In *Jesus, Matthew's Gospel and Early Christianity: Studies in Memory of Graham N. Stanton*, edited by Daniel M. Gurtner, Joel Willitts, and Richard A. Burridge, 166–79. LNTS 435. London: Bloomsbury, 2011.

Wilson, Walter T. *The Gospel of Matthew*. Vol. 1: *Matthew 1–13*. ECC. Grand Rapids: Eerdmans, 2022.

Windisch, Hans. *The Meaning of the Sermon on the Mount*. Philadelphia: Westminster, 1951.

Witherington, Ben, III. *Matthew*. Macon, Ga.: Smyth & Helwys, 2006.

Wold, Benjamin G. *4QInstruction: Divisions and Hierarchies*. STDJ 123. Leiden: Brill, 2018.

———. *Qumran Wisdom and the New Testament: Exploring Early Jewish and Christian Textual Cultures*. Cambridge: Cambridge University Press, 2023.

Wolff, Hans Walter. *Hosea*. Hermeneia. Philadelphia: Fortress, 1974.

Wright, William M., IV. *The Lord's Prayer: Matthew 6 and Luke 11 for the Life of the Church*. Grand Rapids: Baker Academic, 2023.

Yinger, Kent L. *The Pharisees: Their History, Character, and New Testament Portrait*. Eugene, Ore.: Cascade, 2022.

Zamfir, Korinna. "Who Are (the) Blessed? Reflections on the Relecture of the Beatitudes in the New Testament and the Apocrypha." *SS* 5 (2007): 75–100.

Ziegler, Joseph. *Sapientia Salomonis*. Septuaginta 12.1. Göttingen: Vandenhoeck & Ruprecht, 1980.